RESILIENT ECONOMICS

ABOUT THE AUTHOR

Dr Peter McManners is an author, consultant, and Visiting Fellow of Henley Business School. His expertise in sustainability comes from a multidisciplinary stance including business, geography, engineering and economics. He works with stakeholders ranging from green campaigners and activists to business and government. This broad reach enables him to develop a unique perspective on issues at the nexus of environmental, economic and social policy. This book brings together his deep expertise in sustainability and real-world approach with a radical forward look at how economics should be reframed for the current era. He writes about economics for policy makers, avoiding economic jargon, to deliver a textbook of resilient economics.

RESILIENT ECONOMICS

FINANCE, SOCIETY
AND THE ENVIRONMENT

PETER McMANNERS

susta

SUSTA PRESS
12 Horseshoe Road, Pangbourne, Reading,
Berkshire RG8 7JQ, UK

Susta Limited is UK registered company
www.susta.co.uk

First published in Great Britain 2022
Copyright © Peter McManners, 2022

A catalogue record for this book is available from the British Library

ISBN: HB: 978-0-9557-3696-4; PB: 978-0-9557-3697-1;
EBOOK: 978-0-9557-3698-8

Copyedited by Jill Laidlaw
Proofread by Lauren MacGowan
Project managed by Alysoun Owen Consulting Ltd.
Typeset by Catherine Lutman Design

CONTENTS

List of Tables

List of Boxes

List of Abbreviations

ADB	Asian Development Bank
AI	Artificial Intelligence
AIIB	Asian Infrastructure Investment Bank
ATM	Automated Teller Machine
BAS	British Antarctic Survey
BRICS	Brazil, Russia, India, China and South Africa
CDO	Collateralized Debt Obligation
CHP	Combined Heat and Power
CIC	Community Interest Company
COVID-19	Coronavirus Disease 2019
EPA	Environmental Protection Agency
EU	European Union
FDI	Foreign Direct Investment
GATT	General Agreement on Tariffs and Trade
GDP	Gross Domestic Product
GNP	Gross National Product
IMF	International Monetary Fund

MNC	Multinational Corporation
NDB	New Development Bank
NGO	Non-Governmental Organization
OPEC	Organization of the Petroleum Exporting Countries
SDG	Sustainable Development Goals
SEE	Society Embedded Enterprise
UK	United Kingdom
UN	United Nations
UNEP	United Nations Environment Programme
US	United States
VAT	Value Added Tax
WTO	World Trade Organization
WW1	World War One
WW2	World War Two

PREFACE

Since the dawn of the new millennium the world has suffered twice from economic crisis on a global scale. The first of these, in 2008–9, was caused by problems within the financial system itself. The second economic crisis was a consequence of the COVID-19 pandemic causing the most severe economic contraction in modern history. In both cases, the consequences for society were significant. It became evident that conventional economic policy was struggling to cope. World leaders can take some credit for making policy on the fly to keep the economy afloat, but it would have been preferable if economic policy had been designed to be resilient by default.

The 21st century could be the best in human history. Intelligent automation could remove the drudgery of routine tasks, further advances in medicine could mean we live long healthy lives, and space flight could become routine, extending the reach of civilization to other planets. It is also possible that the century could take a different direction ushering in a new dark age. Environmental overload could cause irreparable damage to the ecosystem helping to initiate economic collapse, leading to society disintegrating into lawless dystopia. I am optimistic that the former vision will win out, but only if we take steps to make it so.

We have a tendency to carry on and hope for the best, but it should be evident to anyone who pauses and reflects that humanity has chosen a dangerous path. Putting economic growth before other considerations will eventually sink us. At the heart of our dilemma is an approach to economics which gives the economic analysis too high a priority, overriding

1

environmental limits and sidelining important social issues. Reforming economics is vital to ensure that the next phase of human history builds on past success, eliminates the negative attributes of current economic policy, and enables humanity to take its next step forward.

Resilient economics is a change of direction away from focusing on expansion and growth, towards focusing on security, stability, and sustainability. This framework for economic policy promotes security for society now and into the future. It provides a stable economic platform which is resilient in the face of crisis. Adoption of the resilient policy presented in this book may not have prevented recent crises, but it would certainly have limited their impact. Above all, it is a framework for a sustainable society living on a planet of finite resources.

From my research into sustainability over many years it became clear to me that apparent economic success was masking consequent problems, including rampant resource utilisation and environmental overload. These are serious concerns, yet the inference has been slow to emerge that core economic policy should change to alleviate them. Two global crises later, there is now clear evidence that the problems go deep. All is not well with the package of economics that world leaders have chosen to embrace, so a rethink is required.

In seeking to reboot economics, we face the problem of needing to challenge existing economic norms. It is deeply ingrained in the conduct of economics that theory should evolve on an incremental basis. It is expected that progress is made by adding to existing economic theory, but real progress is not possible without challenging established economic rules of thumb. Expanding the economic toolbox is not enough. Old concepts need to be cleared away and replaced with new perspectives more appropriate to our current circumstances.

In writing this book, I have not taken the academic approach of carefully reviewing current thinking before adding further insights. Instead, I have taken the bold approach of examining economics afresh. No doubt I will be criticized, but abject failure thus far means it is worth the risk to break out to a new approach. Rather than use the lens of what has gone before, I have peered through the lens of the challenges we will face in the future. This is important because the historic path tells us more about what is wrong with economic policy than what is right. Economic policy cannot be considered sound when it facilitates overexploitation of resources and undermines stewardship of our planet. Central to the problem is economic policy designed to boost the economy. We don't need more of the same but a change of approach.

Much good work has already been done to criticize current economic policy and to propose adjustments. The sad reality is that such criticism tends not to gain traction, and alternative approaches to economics are written off without proper debate. I apologise that I do not provide an echo box for the numerous other voices criticizing economics and calling for reform. I present my analysis to stand on its merits. I don't claim necessarily to present groundbreaking original new insights. I simply present logic backed up by a huge dose of common sense. Where others have had similar ideas that I do not acknowledge, that is my omission. I ask forbearance, as it matters little who claims ownership; what matters is that we fix economics before it sinks us.

By writing this book, I want to be instrumental in persuading people that the way economics is practised must change. I hope that this leads to people calling for change, but protesting on its own will not be enough. We need people at the heart of the system, people who are respected and have real clout, to change attitudes and orchestrate the required change of direction. I want to confront those who defend the current economic order to protect vested interests; and to reach out past radical activists who want to break the system. I want to engage with a wide range of people in many walks of life who want the economy to serve society into the long future. Everyone can take a lead within their own area of expertise to take decisions which add up to wholesale change. This is not without personal risk. The status quo could remain for longer than is sensible or safe, leaving early backers exposed. If change comes only slowly, and people insist on continuing down the current economic path, those who lead calls for change could be isolated. Policymakers, and the economists who support them, will have to decide whether to take the risk of joining the groundswell of support for a change of direction, or continue to believe in the current growth-based economic model.

This book outlines a framework for economics which puts society at the forefront and gives a high priority to resilience against potential shocks. The concept of economic resilience is different to what has become widely understood to be good economic policy. My exploration of this different approach is not perfect and there is plenty of room for improvement, but it provides a foundation from which to move economics forward. Adopting it will not maximize growth, nor make everyone richer, but it will enable societies across the world to adapt to their particular circumstances. A stable world economy is possible as a network of thriving national economies appropriate to each country's resources, climate, culture, and capabilities.

Resilient economics is important not only because change is sorely needed but because our future may depend on it. I present economic resilience as the basis of an approach to economic policy that can help the world to navigate the challenging decades ahead.

CHAPTER 1

LEARNING FROM CRISIS

Never let a good crisis go to waste.

The 21st century could be the best or worst of times. We have the potential to use our knowledge and technology to build the most advanced civilization in history. There is also the potential to lose it all if we do not update economics to support this next phase of human progress. We have been using pro-growth economic policy without thinking through the long-term consequences. In the short-term it seems to have served us well enough, but following recent crises the world economy is in a perilous state.

In the space of little more than a decade, the world economy has been hit by two major shocks, the financial crisis of 2008–9 and the COVID-19 pandemic. The narrow focus on growth, at the expense of resilience, has made the economy vulnerable. Whilst times were good, there was no appetite for changing economic policy which had seemed so successful. Now is the opportunity to implement changes which would not have been thought possible before.

Crisis response

In the face of recent crises, to keep the world economy afloat, politicians have used all their available economic firepower. At the time of writing, interest rates are effectively zero (or in some cases negative), governments have taken on huge debt and have turned to exotic economic tools such as quantitative easing. In desperation they have even embraced unusual concepts like 'helicopter money', where every person is given free cash by the government to get the economy moving.[1] As transient economic policy fixes get ever more extreme, they do little more than treat the symptoms of an ailing economic system. We need to accept that there are systemic problems within the economy which can no longer be ignored. Unless these problems are addressed, when the next crisis comes along, we may be unable to cope.

In responding to crisis, and struggling to defend the economy, governments have thrown out the conventional economic rulebook. Having embraced free markets and deregulation before the financial crisis, governments discovered that they could not stand back as the crisis unfolded. There was no alternative but to commit public money on a huge scale to bail out the financial system. This is not what governments foresaw as a consequence of free-market policy. The COVID-19 pandemic required the unconventional response of paying people not to work, as society was locked down to counter the spread of the Coronavirus. We should expect that another crisis is brewing even now. We may not be able to predict its specific nature, nor the timing, but there are many tensions and pressures in the current global economy so we should not have to wait long. Rather than be surprised again, we should brace to deal with the next crisis, applying economic policy which is resilient by design.

An important question is why people at the top of global finance were so blissfully unaware of approaching crisis? Leading into the financial crisis of 2008–9, there was a widely held view that the global economy had never been in better shape. From a UK perspective, the Chancellor of the Exchequer Gordon Brown declared repeatedly that the era of boom and bust was over (Lee

---

1   In the United States, there was bipartisan support for direct payments to citizens as part of Coronavirus relief measures. President Donald Trump agreed to legislation in December 2020 which included $600 direct cash payments. In March 2021, President Joe Biden signed off a $1.9 trillion Coronavirus relief package with direct payments of $1,400 to most Americans.

2009). Most commentators before the crisis did not challenge this claim and saw nothing odd in it. To me, this seemed very odd indeed. In a book I completed in 2007, and published in February 2008 before the crisis unfolded, I suggested that the global economy was a house of cards ready to collapse (McManners 2008). Whilst the crisis played out, people were dumbfounded, and scrambling to understand how it could have happened. To me it was confirmation that my analysis of the nature of the global economy was correct. The massively interconnected globalized financial system was inherently unstable. My analysis indicated that any number of triggers could have initiated the collapse. Her Majesty the Queen asked the obvious question on many people's minds: 'Why did nobody see it coming?'[2] The wider question is why were people at the top of global finance so wilfully unaware of the true state of the global economy? Did they have a vested interest in maintaining the pretence that all was well, or were they so blinkered that they did not see it coming?

In the midst of the financial crisis, there was no time for a fundamental review of economic policy. Governments had to do whatever was needed to keep the financial system afloat. Governments took unprecedented measures to stop the economy from crashing. They pumped in cash, nationalizing the banks most at risk, and took on huge government debt to bail out parts of the financial system judged to be 'too big to fail'. These were indeed unprecedented measures, way beyond what might be regarded in normal times as prudent economic management. But these were not normal times. This was a financial crisis with potentially severe consequences. There was concern that this could have led to an economic depression as deep as that of the 1930s.

---

2   The Queen asked this question whilst attending an event at the London School of Economics in November 2008.

Post-financial-crisis review

Following the financial crisis, there was time for a more considered analysis. In the UK, two commissions were set up: The Independent Commission on Banking chaired by Sir John Vickers and The Parliamentary Commission on Banking Standards (Edmonds 2013). These bodies recommended detailed changes including ring-fencing retail (utility) banking to separate it from investment banking. It was also recommended that banks retain higher capital reserves. These measures were focused on strengthening the current system. In addition, it was recognized that some financial corporations had become so large, interconnected and complex, that their failure posed a serious threat to the financial system (HM Treasury 2011). There was little appetite to go to the next logical step and question whether the whole complex interconnected system of global finance might be flawed.

On the other side of the Atlantic, the US government set up The Financial Crisis Inquiry Commission to examine the causes. It concluded that there were widespread failures in financial regulation and supervision including failures of corporate governance and risk management. It also concluded that a combination of excessive borrowing, risky investments, and lack of transparency had put the financial system 'on a collision course with crisis'. The finger of blame for starting the crisis was pointed firmly towards sub-prime lending in the United States housing market:

We conclude collapsing mortgage-lending standards and the mortgage securitization pipeline lit and spread the flame of contagion and crisis.

The Financial Crisis Inquiry Commission 2011: xxiii

The commission concluded that the financial crisis was avoidable, and put the blame on those running the system:

The captains of finance and the public stewards of our financial system ignored warnings and failed to question, understand, and manage evolving risks within a system essential to the well-being of the American public.

The Financial Crisis Inquiry Commission 2011: xvii

Around the world governments took action to reinforce oversight with the intention of improving the stability of the financial system. The Bank of England concluded that there is the 'need for a fundamental overhaul of the regulatory safeguards used to mitigate systemic risk within the financial system' (Bank of England 2008: 52). The Financial Services (Banking Reform) Act 2013 tightened banking regulations in line with the post-crisis review recommendations. In the United States, tighter regulations were brought into law by the Dodd-Frank Act.[3] This included a wide range of provisions to tighten oversight, protect consumers and limit speculative activities by banks. These actions on both sides of the Atlantic did not change the economic system, only provided additional safeguards.

It was fascinating to watch, from my perspective, the slow deliberate reflection take place in the years that followed. The wilful disregard of economic and financial reality continued. Not only had the post-crisis reviews failed to expose the fundamental problems of globalized finance, but some members of the US Financial Crisis Inquiry Commission felt that the Dodd-Frank Act was an overreaction. Their dissenting view was published at the end of the final report, arguing that the crisis was

---

3   Dodd-Frank Wall Street Reform and Consumer Protection Act, United States federal law 21 July 2010.

solely caused by problems of lending in the real estate market and too much government involvement in the housing market. This alternative view argued that the Dodd-Frank Act went too far and would have economically adverse effects.

> *The stringent regulation that the Dodd-Frank Act imposes on the U.S. economy will almost certainly have a major adverse effect on economic growth and job creation in the United States during the balance of this decade.*
>
> The Financial Crisis Inquiry Commission 2011: 533

The true reason for the financial collapse, according to my analysis, was the dangerous extent of increasing global economic interdependence. This gives the impression that the world financial system is a robust self-regulating system, when in fact such a system is prone to occasional massive collapse. When financial systems are intertwined, and interconnected, the apparent resilience arises from huge flows of capital chasing the best returns. Countries and corporations can lean on the system to remain solvent until there is so much debt that the system itself is at risk of falling over. It was not so much the fault of the captains of finance – although they were guilty of failing to recognize the fundamental flaws within the system of which they were part – it was more about the fact that they were stewards of an unstable system. My analysis indicated that no amount of oversight and regulation can be sure of keeping an inherently unstable system up and running. The failure to recognize, let alone deal with, this problem at the core of globalized finance means that the same risk remains today.

The limited changes since the crisis have been enough to shore up the system and rebuild trust, but global finance has been propped up rather than reformed. The same old rule book of economics is being used again, when it should have been rewritten. It seems that we are not prepared to face the reality that a better more secure financial system has less scope to reap short-term profits. Resilience has a cost which is not welcome when markets are booming. The current system provides incentives for politicians and bankers to chase growth rather than be stewards of stability, as they focus on boosting short-term economic performance. This is reinforced by rewarding executives in our financial and industrial base through bonuses linked to annual performance, which incentivizes them to be wilfully blind to the needs of long-term stability. A sound economic system would not be like this. It should be designed and managed to be closely aligned with reality, and be resilient in the face of crisis.

Responding to the Coronavirus pandemic

A decade later in 2020, the world was again mired in crisis. This time it was a health crisis as the Coronavirus (SARS-COV-2) spread to every continent, and eventually to every country. In response to the pandemic, governments were forced to implement lock-downs in society to slow down the spread of the virus. These lock-downs to protect public health also closed down huge parts of the economy, putting people's livelihoods at risk. A headline on the front cover of *The Economist* summed up the challenge: 'A grim calculus: The stark choices between life, death and the economy' (The Economist 2020). Governments again took unprecedented measures to try and stop the economy from crashing.

In the UK, Rishi Sunak, who was appointed as Chancellor of the Exchequer just weeks before the crisis erupted, implemented a series of measures pumping billions of pounds into the economy. Businesses were given access to government-backed loans and were paid up to 80% of the salary of staff laid off but kept on the payroll. Another tranche of money was provided to the charitable sector to keep that afloat as their income dried up alongside increasing demand for their services. These commitments would over the space of just a few months ratchet up government debt faster than at any time since the Second World War. Rishi Sunak must have wished that the UK economy had been structured to be more resilient. The emergence of a new Coronavirus was unexpected, but this was not war. The pandemic was severe for those directly impacted, but history will perhaps record it as a relatively minor crisis. That such drastic action was required indicates the fragility of the current economic system.

The economic fallout from the two crises in the opening decades of the 21st century has been considerable. Each has required unprecedented measures to prevent the economy from crashing. The decade between was not long enough to return the economy to normal. We were therefore ill-prepared for the economic consequences when the pandemic hit, having used up economic policy firepower on the first crisis, thus limiting the choices available.

The post-Coronavirus world is under even greater economic stress, with even fewer options to mount an economic defence. When the next crisis comes along, what further unprecedented economic measures can be grabbed and implemented? Rather than ever more exotic economic policies, dreamed up under the pressure of crisis, we should return to the basic concept of stable and prudent economic policy. Adjectives like *steady* and *predictable* should regain legitimacy as we push back against the gamblers and risk takers. For something as important as the global economy it should look more like a staid old-fashioned bank than a casino. There will always be gamblers, but they should not be managing economic policy.

Building resilience

Building resilience into the economy is a task to do before crisis looms. Those sitting in the seats of power, in the government and central banks, should be admired for doing what was required. These were difficult times, and they faced difficult decisions. The crisis response was appropriate; the problems lay in management of the economy prior to the crisis. The focus on chasing growth delivered what was expected of such policy, and growth was attained. Encouraging business, including the banks, to focus on delivering shareholder value, delivered high corporate profits. The price of booking such 'success' was a pumped-up economy which lacked resilience. In good times, growth and profits are welcome, but in bad times we need resilience, and resilience cannot be spirited up overnight.

Dreaming up unprecedented measures as economic collapse seems imminent is not the way to craft good economic policy. The adoption of resilient economics should allow an economic system to evolve that is stable by default. The next crisis could be any number of issues, some very closely aligned with the economy and others related to health and environment, or something else. A truly resilient economy should be able to weather crisis and bounce back when the crisis abates.

Now is the opportunity to consider fundamental change to build resilience. When the economy was booming there was little appetite to look under the bonnet and check whether all was well. Now that the economy is misfiring, there is an opportunity to slow down and consider the economic situation and take measures which would not have been countenanced when the economy appeared to be strong. It is obvious that we should learn from crisis to understand why it happens and make changes to prevent similar repetitions. It is worth remembering that we also have history as our guide.

Learning from history

Two major crises of much greater scale than recent difficulties were the Great Depression of the 1930s and the Second World War. There are lessons here for what to do – and not to do.

LEARNING FROM THE GREAT DEPRESSION OF THE 1930S

Prior to the crisis, politicians were celebrating a booming economy. In 1928, Republican Presidential nominee, Herbert Hoover, said:

> *We in America today are nearer to the final triumph over poverty than ever before in the history of any land.*[4]

The overbearing confidence that existed in 1928 hid the extent to which the world of finance had become disconnected from reality. In 1930, finance was brought crashing down to Earth. Herbert Hoover said less than two years later as US President:

> *While the crash only took place six months ago, I am convinced we have now passed the worst and with continued unity of effort we shall rapidly recover.*[5]

The same political denial was at play again leading into the financial crisis of 2008–9.

In 2007, UK Chancellor of the Exchequer, Gordon Brown said:

---

4   11 August 1928.

5   1 May 1930.

We will never return to the old boom and bust.[6]

A little over a year later, in 2008 as UK Prime Minister, he said:

Had we not acted to stabilize the banking system, the effect on households and business would have been even more severe... the world is facing a severe global economic downturn... [7]

We have here two prime examples of political denial leading into severe financial crisis. We are destined for a third major financial crisis in the decades ahead unless, this time, we actually do learn from the past and make changes to our approach to economic policy.

LEARNING FROM WORLD WAR TWO

A crisis does not have to be financial at its core to have severe economic consequences. World War Two (WW2) is an example. Towards the end of the war, the basis of the current global economic order was created as a post-crisis response in order that it should not repeat. World leaders followed through on the mantra attributed to Winston Churchill: 'never let a good crisis go to waste'.

A meeting of forty-three countries was convened in Bretton Woods, New Hampshire, US, in July 1944. The institutions at the heart of our current global economy were set up, including the World Bank and the International Monetary Fund (IMF). There were also plans for an International Trade Organisation (ITO) but this would not be fully implemented until the World Trade Organisation (WTO) was created in 1995. The aim of the negotiators at the Bretton Woods conference was to rebuild the post-war economy in a way which promoted international economic

6   21 March 2007.

7   20 October 2008.

cooperation. The intention behind such a radical reordering of global economic affairs was to prevent the world from descending into yet another world war. It was thought that greater economic opportunities brought about by facilitating trade and opening economies would increase prosperity and cement the peace. The fact that there has not been a third world war, would suggest perhaps that these intentions have been fulfilled.

Those who crafted the new world economic order in the 1940s could not have envisaged the long-term consequences of their decisions extending into the 21st century. They made plans for the post-WW2 peace, and could not have been expected to see beyond a few decades at most. They could not have anticipated that, half a century later in the 1990s, a new generation of political leaders would turbocharge the post-WW2 economic order to drive an expansion way beyond anything that had gone before. I believe that our forebears who crafted the post-WW2 peace economy would find a narrow focus on chasing growth an alien concept. They designed an economic system which facilitated peace and stability. They would be horrified to find that the economic system they created was being used to drive growth at any cost, in a world dominated by global corporations, with social and environmental consequences pushed aside.

It is worth reflecting on the momentous changes agreed at Bretton Woods because there are interesting parallels with the circumstances faced today. The 20th century was dominated by the two world wars. After World War One (WW1) the Treaty of Versailles was signed, and the world tried to return to normal. The economy boomed through the roaring twenties, but this was not to last. The deep depression of the 1930s laid the foundations for the rise of Hitler and ultimately WW2. After WW2 it was recognized that simply returning to normal could mean the cycle repeating. Something much more radical was required.

The thinking behind the discussions at Bretton Woods has interesting parallels with our current situation. It was realized that the response to the Second World War needed to be much more ambitious than the aftermath of the First World War if crisis was not to repeat. The lesson for today is that the response to the financial crisis of 2008–9 was nowhere near radical enough, leaving us ill-prepared to deal with the economic consequences of the pandemic a decade later. This time we need bold action to embed resilience at the core of economic policy.

Reframe economics

In 2000, as celebrations for the new millennium marked the end of the booming 1990s, some of us were already thinking that the past decade of frothy economic excess could only ever be a short-run splurge. But such concerns did not grab attention whilst the economy was still motoring along. Questioning whether good times can last is never popular. Politicians in particular are reluctant to see reality, preferring to claim credit and let the party roll on. They had to experience the crisis of 2008–9 to start to break out of their complacency, and the pandemic of 2020 provides the circumstances to force a substantive response.

After two crises in close succession, we are forced to confront economic reality and have good reason to question economic orthodoxy. The current approach to economic policy is to measure success by the extent to which it delivers growth. Governments work on the assumption that to grow the economy is good for society. It is assumed that everyone benefits, implying better employment opportunities and a higher standard of living. This has become deeply ingrained in the conduct of economic policy and is seldom questioned, but question it we should (McManners 2014).

It is worth returning to the very start of measuring economic growth to see how it arose and to get a feel for how to regard it now. The concept of measuring Gross National Production (GNP) – now called Gross Domestic Product (GDP) – was developed in the 1930s by the economist Simon Kuznets. He proposed gathering data of economic activity from across the economy and adding it up to deliver a single number. He put this forward as one of the metrics for monitoring the economy, stating that: 'The welfare of a nation can scarcely be inferred from a measure of national income' (Kuznets 1934). This piece of advice, from the creator of GDP, seems to have been ignored.

Historically, when poor countries lift people out of extreme poverty, there is often a correlation between economic growth and improvement in people's lives. We are beginning to understand that this is not always the case. Research in developed countries has found that growing richer does not make people happier (Layard 2005). Economic growth has only ever been a metric which provides limited insight and it is not a good way to measure success. To continue with such a flawed approach is dangerous. Advancement measured in purely financial terms is no guarantee that people's lives get any better. If the costs of maintaining economic growth include negative social and environmental consequences, the reverse might be true. It is therefore imperative that resilient economics abandons the growth objective. Economies might continue to grow but that would be secondary to delivering security, stability, sustainability and quality of life.

It is worth examining the 1990s in hindsight, not as the booming decade, but as the decade when it all started to go wrong. The cause of the boom and the seeds of economic fragility came from the same source. This was the divergence between management of the economy and the management of society.

Focusing economic policy on the economy caused the economic boom (unsurprisingly). Allowing this to override social policy left society behind. A blooming economy and the hollowing out of society can be seen in hindsight as a recipe for disaster. But through the 1990s leaders were blinded by the assumption that growing the economy should be the prime objective. In 1987 Margaret Thatcher, one of the architects of the policy which would fuel the economic boom, expressed the view that 'there's no such thing as society'.[8] It was this view which shaped the economic policy of the 1990s, and which planted the seeds of crisis decades later.

The double whammy of financial crisis followed by pandemic exposed the dangers of incestuous economic policy. After the financial crisis, governments focused on kickstarting the economy, rather than building resilience through bringing the economy back in close alignment with society. They were still struggling with repairing the economy when the pandemic hit. For this second crisis, the prime objective was to protect public health, but measures were taken also to try to protect the economy. It was seen as a conflict between maintaining people's health and maintaining the health of the economy. Rather than the two objectives being in conflict, both should be working hand-in-hand. Reinforcing the close integration of the economy with society is how to prepare for the next crisis. This provides resilience, not only to deal with crisis, but to bounce out of it when the immediate danger has passed.

---

8   'They are casting their problems at society. And, you know, there's no such thing as society. There are individual men and women and there are families. And no government can do anything except through people, and people must look after themselves first...' Quoted in an interview for the magazine *Women's Own* in 1987, reported in the *Guardian*, 8 April 2013.

Conclusions

We need to learn from recent crises to put ourselves in a much stronger position. It would be dangerous to enter the next crisis with the economic armoury empty and a lack of firepower. We need to rebuild and rearm to have the economic wherewithal to deal with whatever challenges arise. This means being much more radical with reconfiguring the economy to ensure that the economic consequences of the next crisis do not spiral out of control.

There is a pressing need for resilient economic policy to help to navigate the next crisis. And there will be another crisis. Climate change could be the next crisis to hit the economy as prime agricultural areas become deserts, and the world's major port cities are threatened with sea level rise. At least climate change is something we know is happening and can predict, only the timing is uncertain. The next issue which explodes into crisis may be something quite different. We need an economic model closely aligned with society which will help us cope with whatever the next crisis might throw at us.

The current global economy is based on growth, weighed down with colossal debt, and managed using economic policy in which social and environmental impacts are regarded as inconvenient externalities. Rather than further measures to prop up the old economic paradigm, we need a new way to frame economics. The framework proposed is resilient economics. This has been carefully crafted to facilitate building a resilient economy which is stable by design, serving society, and enabling people to improve their lives and make the best of their circumstances.

CHAPTER 2

THE NEED FOR RESILIENT ECONOMIC POLICY

Resilient economics comprises a range of economic tools working in concert to build a strong and stable economy designed to support society over the long-term.

Economics has huge influence over how society is managed. Through economic choices it is decided how much people earn, how much things cost, how to fund public services, build and maintain infrastructure, and save for retirement. Everything which happens in the modern world seems to have a financial and economic basis. The importance of finance is hard to overstate, even though there may be little real substance, consisting only of numbers in computer systems. These numbers may not be real, but they are a vital lubricant to the management of human affairs, so how finance is managed is important to the success of society.

Framing economics to support people and society

How economics is framed and applied has huge significance for society and dictates the quality of life people enjoy. At a simplistic level, a strong economy makes it easier to build a strong society. A strong economy has the capacity and resources to provide people with a good quality of life including excellent services, education, healthcare, transportation and every other material need. There is also a common perception that a strong economy is a necessary prerequisite for a clean and protected environment. This is based on the argument that only an affluent society can afford to invest in environmental protection. It has become normal to accept the dominance of economic policy, accept the assumptions on which it is based, and not question too closely the advice of economists.

Economics is often regarded as a fixed set of principles and rules to be applied. The reality is not so simple. It is not a precise science, such as the Laws of Physics. Economics is not a set of fixed relationships but a set of assumptions and rules of thumb. It is correct that economics should evolve and change to suit changing circumstances. We tend to allow economists to select which assumptions to apply and to design the rules of thumb, with the rest of us accepting their judgment. We should not be so compliant. People outside the economics profession should get more involved. The problem is that in many cases current economic practice is no longer facilitating good policy and, in some cases, has become a block to finding solutions to the challenges we face.

The virtual construct termed 'the economy' is regarded as primary. To suggest that the economy needs to change in response to challenges in the real world is resisted. We are complicit in accepting significant environmental degradation and social upheaval as the price of optimising the economy. People who are primarily economists may not accept responsibility for such shortcomings, conveniently sidelining them as externalities. It will be for people outside the profession to expose such economic fundamentalism as delusional and lead the revival in economic thinking. There are many good economists who will rise to the challenge but only by engaging more widely. Economics owned by economists is an incestuous relationship of limited use. Framing economics to support people and society should rebuild trust and give economics a new lease of life.

Reining back economics to engage with the real world requires a reversal of the current approach. Turning the situation around starts with thinking through desirable outcomes for society, now and into the future. This method is not economy-centric but society-centric. Economic-centric thinking leads to the dangerous notion that there can be an ideal standard economy. Applying society-centric thinking, it soon becomes clear that there can be no such thing. The whole idea of a standard economic model misses the point entirely. No society is identical; no economy can be standard. All societies are different; every economy should be different. Taking this as the starting point for the economic analysis opens up a wealth of opportunities to rejuvenate economics. This means that the formulation of economic policy becomes more difficult, perhaps much more difficult. For this reason alone, the direction I champion may not be welcomed by the people who currently have responsibility for policy. We need people who see the challenge as an opportunity. The prize is a resilient economy aligned with people's needs and operating as the servant of society. Such a prize is worth fighting for. If that means those who teach and practise economics have to work harder to remain relevant, so be it.

The approach of focusing economic policy on the economy is relatively easy. To embrace the higher standard of setting economic policy to serve society is harder. The focus becomes desirable outcomes for society – as it should always have been. The short-cut of assessing economic policy with economic measures has distracted us from the real goal. This is like a football team whose training is focused on retaining possession of the ball. This is usually a good tactic but only if it is remembered that the prime aim is to get the ball in the goal. The execution of policy must conform to economic literacy (which could be regarded as retaining possession of the ball) but desirable outcomes for society (scoring goals) are the prime aim. Economic literacy means, in layman's terms, that the numbers should add up. So, although the focus of economic policy should be an uncompromising commitment to serve society, this should not be used as an excuse for profligacy or economic incompetence (if you cannot retain the ball you will never score). In the short-term, policymakers are likely to find this greater complexity exceptionally difficult.

The choices which need to be made to ensure stability and embed the economic model into each level of society may reduce the headline economic numbers. As the economy is re-engineered according to altered priorities, it should be expected that the economy could weaken according to current measures. Such seeming weakness might be used by critics of the resilient approach to argue that it is the wrong approach. Certainly, if politicians were to misuse these ideas to steer the economy into a wonderland, it would be counterproductive and undermine the approach.

There are examples of national leaders setting policy which pushes back against a conventional view of economics. North Korea under the Kim dynasty and Zimbabwe under Robert Mugabe are examples where this has been shown to fail, but there are also good examples such as Bhutan and Ecuador.

Alternative value frames

Bhutan pioneered the idea of national happiness as an objective of policy. Ecuador adopted the concept in 2008 setting the prime objective of policy as 'good living' (buen vivir), placing well-being and sustainability at the heart of Ecuador's development. There have been substantial positive transformations in both countries through switching to focus on such objectives.

An important factor, which resilient economics takes into account, is that we share a planet of finite resources as the ultimate non-negotiable constraint on the economy. This insight is behind the league table of countries called the Happy Planet

Index. This index includes measures that relate to human welfare such as life expectancy. It also measures the impact the country is having on the environment (ecological footprint) as this is vital to any realistic measure of the long-term sustained well-being of a society. The top ten countries for sustainable well-being according to the Happy Planet Index are (Jeffrey et al. 2016):

1. Costa Rica

2. Mexico

3. Colombia

4. Vanuatu

5. Vietnam

6. Panama

7. Nicaragua

8. Bangladesh

9. Thailand

10. Ecuador

These countries are succeeding in sustaining the welfare of their society in tune with ecological sustainability. To those of us who live in advanced developed economies, this list is surprising. It does not include any countries which would be regarded by conventional measures as rich, providing a fascinating insight into the divergence of the rich world from the fundamentals of true well-being. Ecuador entered the top ten in 2016 reflecting a substantial improvement in the country. The Ecuadorian government has shown that departure from the prioritization of economic growth, and a direct focus on policy which improves people's lives, delivers positive results.

A rival index is the World Happiness Report (Helliwell et al. 2017). This makes much more sense to those indoctrinated into the economy-first mindset. This list is biased by two crucial assumptions. First, it does not take into account ecological footprint, sidelining an important aspect of our long-term welfare. Second, GDP per capita is used as one of the main criteria. This is perpetuating the assumption that GDP is intrinsically good. This list is therefore a list of the happiest rich countries:

1. Norway

2. Denmark

3. Iceland

4. Switzerland

5. Finland

6. Netherlands

7. Canada

8. New Zealand

9. Australia

10. Sweden

This list is much more aligned with a western perspective of a well-run country. The fundamental flaw is that GDP is included as a specific measure of happiness, thus perpetuating the assumption that high GDP is needed to be happy. The measurement factors for happiness should include health, life expectancy, and well-being but there should be no reason to include GDP unless you deliberately want to skew the index. The divergence between the World Happiness Report and the Happy Planet Index shows the extent of the divide in policy between those who put the economy first as a proxy for human progress and those trying to measure directly the long-term welfare of human society.

Rather than fall into the lazy assumption that countries with low GDP are economic basket cases, it would be more interesting to examine the economic policy of those countries which focus on other value frames such as 'good living', with an open mind to borrow aspects that work. An economy which is weak by economic measures may simply be different, having evolved to suit the country and its people. It is not for outsiders to advise otherwise unless they engage closely with the country, its culture, geography and understand its historic path.

Economic self-determination

Countries should have the right to manage their own affairs, in their own way, according to their own values and priorities. This includes economic policy, but when leaders decide economic policy by political dogma, the results can be disastrous. Shifting away from a blinkered economic focus makes sense, throwing away economic competence does not. Hugo Chávez was elected President of Venezuela in 1998, selling a socialist ideal of giving power to the people and promising to end the corruption of the past. Once in power, he took control of all branches of power – the executive, legislative, judicial, and military – thus cementing his position to remain president until his death in 2013. He was profligate in spending and nationalized much of the private sector. His successor, President Nicolás Maduro (appointed by Chávez) continued with the same economic policy; poverty did not improve, corruption remained rampant and the local currency became worthless.[9] Such populist and incompetent administration gives bad press to the idea of economic self-determination.

There are examples of sound economic management by countries which are largely unheralded and often unremarkable. This is what you want from an economy; to serve society without drama. An example you do not read much about is the economy of Finland. I do not present Finland as an example of perfect economic policy, but of sound economic policy which works in support of society. This country situated in northern Europe is an example of low-key steady management of national affairs and a model from which other countries might learn. Finland has not had an easy economic history. During the Second World War the Finns fought both the Germans and Russians as they struggled to keep control of their country. At the end of WW2, they were on the 'wrong' side and were landed with a huge war retribution bill from Russia. Finland took another economic hit in 1990 as the result of an unsustainable housing boom. The country has navigated through these challenging times. They repaid their war debt of $300 million to the Soviet Union in full in 1952. After 1990 they brought their bank lending under tighter control. When the global crisis struck in 2008, Finland weathered the storm better than many economies. Finland has other challenges, having a tough climate and limited natural resources with no oil or gas. Despite all of this, Finland has one of the world's best run societies, placing top of league tables for education and environmental stewardship. This comes from sound fiscal discipline and an economy designed to support society.

The Nordic economic model, when compared with an Anglo-US economic model, seems to work better when judged by

---

9   http://theconversation.com/how-todays-crisis-in-venezuela-was-created-by-hugo-chavezs-revolutionary-plan-61474. [accessed 25 May 2021].

the delivery of outcomes for society. Critics complain that taxes are high, but this comes with high-quality services. The message is not that taxes should necessarily be high but the lesson from this part of northern Europe is that policymakers should not be afraid to use fiscal means such as taxation to ensure the economy supports society. This is careful housekeeping by centrist politicians to show how economic policy can be brought closer to society.

Economics as servant

It would be good if economic policy was almost invisible, quietly and diligently bringing order to our affairs. Like a good servant, not taking over, not getting in the way, but always there for us, keeping the administration of our lives in reasonable order. A servant who forgets their place and starts to think that they are the master needs to be brought back into line.

Conventional economics is not serving us well and not supporting society as it should. It has become an incestuous game where economic policy is focused on the economy. This game uses advanced technology to build a virtual world of finance. There are some similarities with top-selling computer games which get ever more advanced, encouraging people to immerse themselves within alternative realities where they can be whoever they want to be, and behave anyway they like. Such escape *from* the real world holds danger for how this might spill over into changing people's behaviour *in* the real world.

The same dangers lurk within the virtual world of economics when people start to believe that they can do whatever they like and behave as they wish without regard for the consequences. The virtual world of economics is a serious game with real-world purpose and real-world consequences. It is not a game to be played irresponsibly. In trying to reconnect economics with the real world, the speculators need to be reined in and restraint placed on those who put financial gain as their only priority. Those who seek to use economics to build a casino do not serve society, and when they call themselves economists, they give economics a bad name.

New impetus

The success of economic policy is measured, all too often, by the metric of economic outcomes – such as GDP. It is assumed that what is good for the economy is good for society. This eases the burden on policymakers and seemed to work well enough whilst resources were plentiful, and the environmental load was within safe limits. Now that we can foresee resource shortages and understand the potentially severe impact on the environment, continuing with this assumption is not just lazy, but incompetent.

Human society in the 21st century faces several challenges. It has always been thus throughout human history. Disease, famine and war have never been far away. Huge progress has been made in banishing some of the problems of the past, with advances in medicine and other technologies, but a situation has been allowed to evolve in which civilization is at risk (McManners 2009). Our newfound abilities mean we are capable of making our planet unfit for a healthy and thriving human society through over-exploitation and pollution.

The prime challenge of the current era is to bring our evolving capabilities under control to put progress on a safe trajectory. Society has never before faced such an existential challenge. This is truly a unique juncture in human affairs.

There are solutions to the bind we find ourselves in, sometimes obvious and easy solutions, but our blinkered approach to how economics is applied can prevent progress. Framing the economic analysis in a way which facilitates solutions can invigorate economics with fresh impetus.

Economics, when applied well, can help take us into a bright and sustainable future. Continuing with conventional economics framed by 20th-century attitudes may lead to self-destruction. Rather than wait and pick up the pieces in the decades ahead, we should learn a new way to frame economics and start to use it without delay.

The new framing presented in this book contains universal principles for managing human affairs. These may not be new but need to be reaffirmed, at this important point in history. We have become confused and human values have been sidelined by a myopic focus on a particular interpretation of economics. This book is more about policy and society than it is about economics. This is as it should be. Economics only has purpose and value in its ability to steer the financial system to delivering benefit to society. We need straightforward economics in support of good policy for a society living on a planet of finite resources. We do not need complex economic ideas (comprehensible only to economists) focused on delivering economic outcomes. This book aims to recalibrate economics to regain its place as a solid and respected discipline at the heart of policymaking.

How did economics lose its way?

The way economics has evolved, and the way it is applied, is leading us into a trap of our own making as we chase ever more growth and ever more consumption. It is a plain fact that this cannot continue indefinitely; but some people choose to ignore plain facts.

THE PERPETUAL GROWTH DELUSION

There is little doubt that economics has lost its way. The only uncertainty is whether this is a small deviation which is easy to fix or if it requires a major reappraisal of what is expected of economics. It would be helpful to spot where economics started to lose direction. Some robust questioning is called for. Was there a logical misstep at some point in the development of the discipline which we failed to spot? Perhaps there was some flaw which seemed of little consequence but which, over the years, has infected the discipline. If economics was a computer program, has a virus been sneaked into the code to be activated under certain circumstances? Has a malevolent hacker inserted a piece of rogue code called the 'growth paradigm' for the pleasure of watching the system collapse? Have vested interests been complicit in designing the virus, aiming to profit from the consequences? Could economics be a con? Perhaps we have an economic system which gives the appearance of helping society but will actually end up destroying it.

The paragraph above is attention grabbing and reads like a conspiracy theory, but could there be a grain of truth in such wild conjecture?

I do not believe there has been deliberate malice in the progression of economics. Adam Smith, credited as the father of economics, was not malicious in writing *An Inquiry into the Nature and Causes of the Wealth of Nations* (Smith 1776). This is the book which contains many of the concepts which still underpin economics today. If you read his earlier book, *The Theory of Moral Sentiments* (Smith 1759), it is clear that Adam Smith was a principled man with a strong sense of moral purpose. I am sure that if Adam Smith were alive today, he would be horrified at the way his economic ideas have evolved losing touch with many of the values of civilized society. My view is that we have not lost our values, but the modern approach is to allow them to be consumed in the furnace of 'good economic policy'. We should be much more aware of the human suffering and environmental damage caused by giving primacy to economic outcomes.

There are people, both inside and outside of the temple of economics, who do not see that a problem is looming. There are economists who argue that perpetual growth is possible, provided it is the right sort of growth. This is an example of hope over reason and slavish adherence to conventional economic thinking.

Simple common sense should be enough to make us at least pause for thought. At some point in the development of economic theory it became wedded to growth as a necessary and fundamental requirement of a good economy. This assumption is forcing the economy on a path which eventually cannot support society, as resources are depleted, and environmental damage starts to undermine the ecosystem services on which we rely (Victor 2010).

THE PROBLEM OF EXTERNALITIES

Currently, inconvenient consequences of economic policy are pushed outside the economic model by calling them externalities. This is both lazy and irresponsible. We should be much more willing to challenge modern economics when it uses this escape clause to avoid facing up to reality.

A common approach to such externalities is to seek to address them outside the frame of economics with social and environmental policy. It is not surprising that progress is limited. The more effective approach is to accept that economic policy should not be divorced in this way, acknowledging that in some cases inappropriate economic policy can be the cause of social or environmental problems. The time is long overdue to move beyond the easy cop-out of referring to problems arising from economic policy as externalities.

A way is required to frame economic analysis so that the consequences can be properly addressed. If this means solutions which are less than the perfect economic solution, so be it. It seems odd to have to write this, when of course effective solutions need to cover a broad set of factors. When economics has been put back in its place as the servant of good policy, there will be no need for such statements of the obvious. For now, the idea that economics should conform to higher policy seems to be a difficult constraint for some policymakers to accept.

REMAINING ON THE ROAD TO PERDITION

The flaw in modern economics is not a single misplaced equation or false assumption. Economics has reached its nadir through a series of logical steps which taken in isolation seem to make perfect sense. Simple analysis indicated that economic growth correlated with improvement in society, so growth was adopted as an objective. It was found that free trade could provide cheaper goods, so borders opened and tariffs were removed. Privatizing public sector companies provided an initial improvement in efficiency, so privatization became the norm. Allowing the free movement of capital increased investment opportunities and made access to capital easier. It is only when each element comes together as the package of conventional economic policy, that the danger can be fully appreciated.

Growth, free trade, privatization, and unrestricted flows of capital have their attractions when considered in specific situations to achieve a specific outcome. When they are deployed together as the foundation of economic policy, important social and environmental issues can get pushed aside. Retaining the full package of conventional economics will keep us on the road to perdition, with potentially ruinous consequences.

LACK OF COURAGE TO INTERVENE

There are other examples in history which fit this model of small steps of little apparent significance building into a calamitous episode. Looking back, it is possible to examine what happened and understand why, but at the time people were doing their best, making decisions in good faith, without foreseeing the consequences.

Whilst writing this book, I happened to watch a documentary on the rise of Adolf Hitler. I realized that this is a good example of a disaster building which could have been stopped much earlier. This is perhaps a controversial example to use in this context, but I make no apology because the consequences of failing to reframe economics could be as dangerous as failing to stop the rise of Hitler. The Second World War could look tame compared with the future we are entering by ignoring the obvious dangers of environmental overload and resource limits. Insights from the rise of Hitler are useful and should persuade us to make tough choices sooner rather than later.

It is deeply troubling that a great nation like Germany could have been hoodwinked into the role of oppressor of continental Europe and responsible for horrendous crimes such as the Holocaust. Each stage in the rise of Hitler and Nazi Germany was a small step. When did it first go wrong? Was it in 1933 when the Nazi Party took control of the German Reichstag? Was it in 1935 when Hitler pushed back against the provisions of the Treaty of Versailles (which constrained Germany following the First World War) and started to rebuild its military capability? Was it in 1936 when Hitler moved his troops into the Rhineland (which had been declared a demilitarized zone)? His commanders had orders to retreat if the French army tried to stop them, but the German army was not resisted. Was it in 1938 when British Prime Minister Neville Chamberlain returned from Munich with a paper signed by Hitler and declared 'peace in our time'? This series of events culminated in the start of the Second World War when Nazi Germany invaded Poland in 1939. Could the carnage of World War Two have been prevented by intervening at an earlier point in the rise of Hitler?

Each step in the rise of Hitler is small but taken together the journey was disastrous. People at the time were thinking short-term to avoid conflict and did not have the courage to act. We are at the same place now with economics. We know it is not working as it should for the benefit of society, but we are scared to make fundamental changes because of the short-term risks of economic downturn. The longer the delay in reframing economics, the more severe will be the consequences. We should find the courage to make changes before it reaches a crisis point which forces the abandonment of current economic policy.

Getting Back on Track

To put economics back on a safe trajectory requires some short-term pain. We will have to forego some of the apparent wealth which the current system provides, to recover to a point where economics is brought back under control in support of society. Instead of allowing the concepts of economics to override human moral values, we should insist that the way economic theory is applied must change. Perhaps I should not have used the rise of Hitler as an analogy, as we are not being hoodwinked by a megalomaniac and a bunch of cronies. Anti-capitalist protesters might use rather colourful language when describing bankers as vampires, but my observation is that the people at the centre of economics are clever people who mean well. There are no evil people to accuse. If there were, there would then be a clear enemy who might be confronted. We are all complicit in misguided thinking, which has evolved without being challenged, so we are all responsible.

It is hard for policymakers to grasp the nettle that there might be fundamental problems with the financial system. This will require intervention; people outside the financial system should insist on change and people inside the financial system work to deliver it. It is likely to have short-term negative consequences, but that should not interrupt our resolve. A relatively small kerfuffle now is preferable to major calamity later.

Earlier in this chapter, I likened economics to a computer program illustrating rather well the nature of the bind we find ourselves in. Computer code is not fixed but can, and should be, rewritten when it fails to deliver what we want from it. As economics was being developed two centuries ago, it was in the same era that Isaac Newton discovered the Laws of Physics. Newton's equations explained how the physical world works; and these equations continue to rule the physical world around us. The Laws of Physics are fixed rules which are integral to our universe and are not in our power to change. Newton did not invent the Laws of Physics; he discovered and explained them. Since Newton, we have added deeper insights and more detail to our scientific understanding with theories such as Einstein's Special Theory of Relativity. This is solid science and remains the bedrock of how engineers design safe structures. As Newton was developing this real science it seemed to make sense for economics to take a similar direction using equations and rules. Perhaps this is where the seeds of economic discord were sown. The equations and rules of economics are not precise science but are as transitory as lines of code in a computer program. The 'Laws of Economics' are not fixed scientific relationships but capture a set of choices we have decided to adopt. There are more rules of thumb than precise cause-and-effect relationships. This is why economics is referred to as the 'dismal' science because it is not really a science at all. Economics is code which economists apply for as long as it seems to be fit for purpose; but if circumstances change the code can, and should, be changed.

Adam Smith's ideas fitted the economic challenges of the 18th century. They encouraged greater efficiency within the economy to be better able to support society. Continuing to apply the same theoretical concepts today, to complex modern economies facing different challenges, is not necessarily a good idea. We need to rewrite the code of economics to suit our current challenges. Instead, there seems to be a tendency towards regarding economic theory as scientific fact. This is dangerous for two prime reasons. First, economics has pushed forward an agenda of growth and increasing consumption which cannot continue indefinitely. Second, adherence to conventional economic theory starts to change people's behaviour.

Economic modelling requires assumptions about people's behaviour – they are built on the assumption that people act rationally out of self-interest and the desire for wealth. The term '*Homo economicus*' has been coined to describe such behaviour.[10] The current economic models rely on people behaving like *Homo economicus*. This is why economic models so often break down.

---

10 Much of economic theory is based on the assumption that people make rational choices behaving like '*Homo economicus*'. The 19th-century economist John Stuart Mill described this theoretical person as one 'who inevitably does that by which he may obtain the greatest amount of necessaries, conveniences, and luxuries, with the smallest quantity of labour and physical self-denial with which they can be obtained' (Mill 1844: 144). Other economists, such as the influential 20th-century economist John Maynard Keynes, observed that this is not the case and that humans behave irrationally. This is problematic because the fundamental basis of much conventional economic theory, and the logic which underpins economic models, is that people will act rationally out of self-interest and the desire for wealth.

People generally do not behave in this way, seeking only to maximize their personal circumstances. Humans have a rich heritage of moral and cultural values. This is what makes us human and is important to the smooth running of society. We do not want people to abandon such values to adopt instead rational economic behaviour; that would be the end of society. Economic theory is not fixed; it can and must change to suit the current era. One important change is to abandon using *Homo economicus* as a role model for people to aspire to.

Very human personal choices, such as who to marry, can be presented as economic choices. How sad to think that *Homo economicus*, instead of allowing that elusive emotion of love to drive their marital decisions, may use economics to choose their mate. This is not likely to be the basis of a happy marriage. Such economic-centric thinking sinks deeper and deeper into our psyche. I hate the job, but it pays well. I know my car is polluting, but it is cheap to run. As an extreme example, it is only a degree of scale to decide to rent out your child to a paedophile for a few hours because it would generate an income. *Homo economicus* might analyse such a transaction by discussing the net return after considering the cost of counselling and support that the child would need afterwards. If this cost was greater than the income, then it would not make economic sense. In this case it is obvious that such action would be plainly morally wrong. It does not need an economic analysis at all. We should not rent a child to a paedophile; decision made.

Conclusions

Economics has a central role in the management of society, often presented as the prime basis of decisionmaking. We have accepted this as a convenient way to navigate the complexities of the modern world. The problem is that the economic toolbox has evolved to become domineering, with huge power and influence. It needs to be reviewed, adjusted and brought back into line as the servant of policy.

In setting the scene, an issue which exposes the overbearing nature of the current approach to economic policy is what to do about fossil fuel. We know we must stop burning fossil fuel within a time frame that prevents dangerous climate change. It should not matter what short-term economic pain is inflicted; this is something we must do. Our adherence to economics – as currently framed – means we override such irrefutable logic, delay, and procrastinate to protect the economy. Why is the economy so much more important than the climate of our planet? How can we sell our children's future for financial gain today? The questions I pose imply pessimism, but that is not how I feel. We can be optimistic, because there is no need to accept economics as it is currently coded. We need to take on the difficult task of rewriting a complex program. Adjusting a line or two here or there will not do it. This book starts anew with looking at economics as it should be framed for the challenges of today.

PART 1

FRAMING ECONOMIC RESILIENCE

The way economic analysis is framed is important. If the analysis is focused on growth, then it will generate policy proposals which deliver growth. If it is focused on increasing quantities of trade, it will generate policy proposals which increase trade. Adopting such targets works on the assumption that what is good for the economy is also good for society. This is how policymakers navigated macroeconomic analysis in the 20th century. Entering the third decade of the 21st century it has become clear that increasing growth and increasing trade is not a universal recipe for good economic policy. Not only are these not necessarily the best policies, but when you get into deep analysis without preconceptions, these policies start to look dangerous and undermine our ability to cope with the unexpected.

There will always be challenges and crises. It is our ability to meet them and bounce back which matters. How the economy is structured during good times has a huge influence on how resilient the economy will be in times of crisis.

Not only the economy is at risk, society and the planet on which we live are coming under increasing pressure. Over exploitation of resources and the hollowing out of society are very real, whereas the economy is only an abstract concept. It soon becomes clear that economic resilience cannot be achieved over the long-term by considering only the economy. Thinking must be framed by the need for a resilient society and respect for environmental limits. Resilience needs a sustainable balance between social, environmental, and economic factors. Although this book focuses on resilient economics, social-ecological resilience (Folke et al. 2016) will always be a prime consideration which should influence how economics is moulded.

The old established idea of economics focused on growing the economy should be supplanted by a direct relationship between economic policy and desirable outcomes for society. Rather than being a groundbreaking new insight, I suggest this is a statement of the obvious. There are moments in the evolution of thought when a return to basics pays huge dividends, not because of expanding and deepening the theory but to strip away outdated ideas. This is what is needed now to allow the concept of resilience to flourish.

This part of the book sets the frame for economic analysis to be able to deliver a resilient and sustainable economy. It consists of three chapters: reconnecting the economy with society (Chapter 3); examining trust as the bedrock of any financial system (Chapter 4); and considering how to hold economics to account by society (Chapter 5).

RECONNECTING THE ECONOMY WITH SOCIETY

The disconnection between the economy
and society indicates that the world
is coming apart at the seams.

Over recent decades, the economy has become decoupled from society with potentially dangerous consequences. The first priority of a resilient economic model is therefore to realign economics with the needs of society. This is the fundamental reframing which underpins the resilient approach to economics. This chapter examines the issues at the interface between the economy and society starting with considering how economic policy aligns with reality.

Alignment with Reality

Finance and the economy are concepts which help us to manage our affairs. Sitting alongside this virtual world is the real world of people and places; factories and schools; cities and farms. What happens in this real world matters a lot. We use the world of finance to help to manage the real world, so what happens in finance also matters a lot. This is where we buy and sell; save and invest; borrow and spend. It is important to remember that whatever we do within the virtual world of finance and the economy only has real value when it impacts on the real world. The conceptual economy should remain aligned with the needs of society and the challenges it faces.

Current economic policy is focused on the virtual world of finance and has become increasingly separated from the real world. The dangers were not apparent as we continued to believe in the assumption that what is good for the economy must be good for society. As we realise that this is no longer a safe assumption, we have to be clear about what we expect of economic policy. For it to have value for society, economic policy should orchestrate a financial system that is robust, stable and secure such that it delivers successful outcomes in the real world.

Politicians have been focusing on the economy and papering over the cracks in the current financial system. The world of finance continues to expand leaving the real world behind and laying the foundations for long-term difficulties. Reform of our approach to economics is required to reconnect the economy with society. Because the virtual world of finance has no real substance, it can be designed in any manner we wish. Changing a virtual world can be done without the delay that projects in the real world are subject to. We have total freedom to think clearly about the concept of the economy to ensure that policymakers make decisions with a positive impact on people's lives and livelihoods. First, let us consider the elements of the supporting financial system.

The Supporting Financial System

The financial system consists of a number of elements. These include currencies, bank deposits, loans and bonds. These are simple to describe and the role they play is transparent. Another element is the financial markets; here the mechanism might be straightforward but what happens inside the market can be hard to predict. The oddest market is that for equities where the divergence between the virtual world of finance and its relationship with the real world can be considerable. There are also esoteric financial instruments which can be opaque and have great complexity where the real purpose is obscure. Each of these categories is described briefly below.

CURRENCIES

The lifeblood of world finance is the world's currencies. These are used to denominate what we spend, save and borrow, and put a number to the value we give to everything from land and property to patents and brands. The importance of currencies and how they are managed is covered in Chapter 9.

BANK DEPOSITS

It is reassuring to think of bank deposits as equivalent to bags of gold coins in a secure vault ready to withdraw when needed. In reality this is not the case. An efficient bank will have deposits matched by loans and an almost empty vault. The bank will only have enough liquid cash available to pay a normal level of expected transactions. The number on the bank statement is nothing more than a promise to provide that amount of money when requested. If everyone tried to take their deposits out of the bank, it would collapse. Fortunately, people pay in and withdraw money in rough balance, so all is well, provided trust in the bank is maintained.

LOANS

Governments borrow money; corporations borrow money; we all borrow money, building up piles of debt. The oddity here is the freedom banks have to generate new loans. Bank staff can key in numbers to make new money to lend to borrowers. This new money is plucked out of thin air which in the virtual world of finance is perfectly fine. There are limits and controls on what is allowable but in modern banking huge amounts of debt can be generated. It has never been easier to borrow and the sum total of global public debt now exceeds $58 trillion.[11] The United States has debts of $16 trillion, and Greece has debts of $231 billion which is an unsustainable 150% of annual GDP. It is hard to see how such debts could ever be paid off, but in the virtual world of finance it hardly matters. These debts are not real and can be wiped out through default or bankruptcy. A loan is a promise to pay back at some point in the future, and promises can be broken.

BONDS

Another place to park money is in bonds. Governments, companies or public bodies can sell bonds with an interest rate which would usually be greater than the interest available from a bank account. The entity which issues the bonds gets the money to pay for infrastructure, equipment or other expenditure. With bonds, it is the issuer of the bond who promises to pay back the money at some point in the future. Unlike money in a bank account, the funds used to buy bonds are tied up for the period of the bond. This provides some certainty and stability. The interest the bondholder receives depends on the level of risk. A reliable and well-run organization can sell bonds with a low interest rate. More risky ventures need to offer a higher return. The investor uses judgment to balance risk and return. In simple terms, if the bond seller's business does well it will be in a position to pay back the bond as promised; if the business flounders the bondholder can lose their stake. I use gambling terms to describe them, but bonds are a sensible and useful part of the financial system, provided everyone involved behaves responsibly and with integrity.

---

11   http://www.economist.com/content/global_debt_clock [accessed 18 March 2021].

MARKETS

There are numerous markets operating within the economy to trade almost anything. These can be very efficient tools but need careful design and close oversight to ensure they perform as intended. The detail of the role of markets is covered in Chapter 7.

EQUITIES

Equities are firmly entrenched as one of the most important forms of investment. When you consider how they operate, they are also one of the strangest parts of the financial system. These allow people to own shares in a business and to buy and sell them in the equity markets. A business with a good story can go from being worth nothing to over $1 billion in just a few years (WhatsApp was founded in 2009 and valued at $1.5 billion four years later). Such companies need not be making a profit, and may actually be losing money, but investors believe that the future for the company may be bright so bid up the value of its shares. Conventional investment advice is that long-term savings such as pension funds should be held in equities because over the long-term they have tended to outperform holding cash on deposit or owning bonds. Again, we can observe that in the world of finance, equity markets are just a chimera. The value of shares on equity markets only remain high because of the quantity of money flowing into the market. The prices are set by the small number of transactions of those people entering and leaving the market. If everyone tried to sell up, without any buyers, the shares could be worthless.

OTHER FINANCIAL INSTRUMENTS

The financial world has many financial instruments such as derivatives and a particularly ignominious financial instrument called the Collateralized Debt Obligation (CDO) applied to mortgage lending. These consist of mortgages packaged into bundles and sold as safe investments secured against property. These 'safe' investments have been traded widely and held by banks as assets.

In traditional banking, a bank manager will consider a mortgage application and if he or she considers that the applicant can service the mortgage over the lifetime of the loan then it will be granted. The bank which made the loan retains oversight and it is in that bank's interest to ensure that the loan is secure. Mortgages are particularly safe because they are secured against the property. If the mortgage holder defaults, the property can be repossessed and sold to pay back the loan.

The game (perhaps scam is the more accurate term) that was being played with creating the CDOs was somewhat different. Brokers were selling mortgages to people without a steady income who were therefore unable to pay back the loan. These mortgages were euphemistically called 'sub-prime'. They got around the limitation that these sub-prime borrowers would not be able to pay back the loan by lending more than the property cost to give the mortgage holder the funds to make the initial payments. The final nail in the coffin being constructed by the financial gamesters was that the property was worth less than the mortgage. Whilst property prices were rising it was argued that the increasing value of the property would overtake the liability of the mortgage. The 'clever' part of the plan was to package together sub-prime mortgages into CDOs. Further complexity was added by selling the CDOs in a number of tranches. Senior tranches had first priority on the collateral in the event of default so were safer than junior tranches. The ratings agencies gave CDOs triple-A ratings, as they were ostensibly secured against property. Leading up to the financial crisis of 2008, sales of such CDOs reached over $200 billion annually.

If mortgage lending was left to banks that retained the loan for the entire term of the agreement, they would not make such sub-prime loans because it would be blatantly obvious that it could go bad. If these were prime mortgages – that is loans to people who could afford them and where the scale of the loan is at a discount to the value of the property (ideally 20% or better) – these would indeed be safe debt secured against property.

Why does the financial system need CDOs? What purpose could they possibly have? The brokers, intermediaries and traders all take their cut, so there was profit in it for those running the system, but you have to spin a good yarn to explain why such complex financial instruments need to exist. There are reasons, but they can be convoluted and not apparent to a layperson. Rather than be browbeaten by people who claim greater expertise, it should be perfectly correct for anyone to query the real-world purpose of any financial instrument. If there is not a clear purpose, which can be expressed in plain English without resort to obscuration using economic terms, then it should be treated with caution and is not likely to be useful.

A stable and useful financial system should have straightforward elements where it is transparent where the risk lies. The financial system should be useful for society and not act as an aim in itself. Like a good servant, it should provide honest and reliable service. We might want parts of society and parts of the business world to be vibrant, innovative and highly imaginative, but not the financial system. This should be stable, transparent and managed by reliable and risk-averse competent managers. Banking used to be dull; it can be again.

Financial Introspection

Managing the financial system is a potentially difficult and complex task. It is understandable that those who do so look for ways to simplify their work. The financial system is therefore managed according to financial measures and the wider economy is managed according to economic metrics. The number for GDP is used to assess the health of the economy. Businesses are judged on the profit they generate for their shareholders. Such measures have consequences, as those in charge strive to deliver against them. Instead of focusing on real-world outcomes, their behaviour is driven to deliver economic and financial results. But these are not real outcomes. Real outcomes are what happens at the touch points between the financial system and the real world.

Ideally, the financial system would be managed by real-world measures. So instead of GDP, a country could measure the performance of economic policy by outcomes such as health, quality of life or that elusive factor, happiness. Instead of judging a company on its profit it could be judged on its impact on society and the benefit it delivers to all its stakeholders. The difficulty of defining real measures, and from a financial viewpoint the lack of precision of such measures, makes it too problematic to bother. When Simon Kuznets proposed using GNP (Gross National Product), the precursor to GDP he wrote:

> *The welfare of a nation can scarcely be inferred from a measure of national income.*

> Kuznets 1934: 7

These words of advice have been ignored throughout the 20th century leading to a level of introspection within finance which is quite astounding. Measuring progress/success with financial measures is the easy way to manage the financial system, but that does not make it right. The real world is enormously complex and to avoid that complexity, because it is too difficult, is lazy policymaking.

Speculation

If introspection is the dullard of financial management, speculation is its dynamic cousin. Speculators exist because it is possible to game the financial system for financial reward. An ideal financial system would be designed to limit or even prevent speculation. That is unlikely to be possible. We could try relying on expecting high standards of behaviour to make speculators feel ashamed but in the real world that would seem to have little chance of success. When is a transaction speculation and when is it a sensible investment? Lawyers could run up huge fees arguing this way or that. What we can do is to recognize that pure speculation, divorced from investment for real-world purposes, is a drain on the system. Rather than praising the speculators for making good financial returns, and hoping that successful speculators are managing our pension fund, we should try to design a system less at risk from exploitative speculation.

From the speculator's viewpoint, they are looking for an imbalance or opportunity to trade a financial investment to make a profit. There is a positive role in bringing liquidity to the financial markets, and helping the market to adjust, but each time a speculator closes a trade which makes a profit, value is extracted from the system. There may not be an identified loser, but everyone who relies on the financial system loses. When speculative flows of capital are ten times greater than required by the real economy, the financial system looks more like a gaming machine than a stable financial system.

From the perspective of the Occupy movement[12] or other radical opponents of big finance, the speculators are vampires that

---

12 The Occupy movement started in 2011 with Occupy Wall Street in New York (http://occupywallst.org) and quickly spread to other cities (http://occupy-london.org.uk).

are sucking the lifeblood out of the system. Big finance should be serving society not paying exorbitant salaries to people playing the City of London like a slot machine. Such a colourful description of city professionals is not warranted, but action is needed to prove this to be a wrong characterization. If the financial community cannot find a fix, people outside the community (perhaps government officials) would need to regulate to improve the system. All of us should recognize speculation as a negative term instead of regarding it as good provided we hold a winning hand. Investing is useful; gambling is not.

The Interface Between the Economy and Society

At each place where the virtual world of finance touches the real world there are consequences. This might be a person buying a house, the government building infrastructure, or a business delivering a product or service. This is the true purpose of finance and why it has value for society. Where we observe games being played with complex financial derivatives without a real-world purpose, we should be highly critical and if it does not survive examination, or is simply too complex for an ordinary person to understand, it should be resisted. I want, and we should all want, a financial system which serves society, not those who manage the system.

To ensure that the financial system is useful to society, and relevant to society's challenges, it needs to be wedded to the real world. We should back off from pure financial analysis, to embrace analysis of issues in a real-world context as the primary decision frame. The economic analysis should mesh neatly with wider policy objectives. Most economists would accept this as a sensible and reasonable statement, but it is not always complied with. Some economists can become overconfident and overbearing, supported by policymakers who ask more of their economists than their methods can deliver.

The relative hierarchy between the economy and society is that the economy exists to serve society. The touchpoints at the interface are what really matters. Aligning the conceptual framework of economic policy with the needs of society can ensure that its influence on decision making is positive.

Conclusions

The financial system provides vital lubrication for transactions in the real world, to buy and sell, to save and to invest. How it is managed can have a huge impact. Sound economic policy is needed so that we can spend and borrow with confidence, save for the future, and have reason to trust the financial system. Above all it should be designed so that its workings align closely with society.

In reconnecting the economy and society, it is important to note that introspection and speculation are weaknesses to address. Financial systems will always be judged by financial measures, and there will always be speculators, but these should not be allowed to become dominant forces.

Where the financial system interacts with the real world, we should seek positive outcomes. This does not mean a nirvana where nothing bad happens but outcomes should be appropriate and proportionate. A badly-run business should not be kept afloat by financial engineering; a well-run business should not be brought down by asset strippers. It should be easy to buy a home which you can afford and hard to buy a house which is beyond your means. Governments should be able to raise funds for sensible long-term investment; corrupt leaders should find it hard to increase national debt for their personal use. Ultimately, the financial system is little more than a complex system of IOUs which only works because there is trust between the parties. It is the fundamental issue of trust to which I turn next to really get inside how finance works.

CHAPTER 4

IT IS ALL ABOUT TRUST

Trust is the only true currency.

The modern world of finance has no real substance, consisting of numbers within computer systems, but it is important because these numbers support decisions which impact on people's lives. When there are problems in the virtual world of finance there can be very real impacts on society, so we need our finances to be secure. The glue which connects the real and virtual worlds is trust. When there is trust in finance, policymakers can navigate real world challenges with confidence, leaning on economic tools to deliver appropriate outcomes. Trust is important throughout the economic system, particularly with regard to markets. Allowing the invisible hand of financial markets to manage the economy can work better than attempting to micromanage the complex web of transactions which make up the economy. The mantra of 'leave it to the market' might seem hollow in the warped financial system we have now; but establishing an effective market, and allowing participants in the market to find the way forward has merit – provided the market can be trusted.

Knowing who or what organization is responsible, allows a judgment to be made about whether they can be trusted. If you lend money to a particular individual, you can assess the likelihood that they will pay you back. If you borrow money from a particular person, you can judge whether they are a respectable lender or a loan shark likely to rip you off with exorbitant charges. The modern financial system has become so complex and inter-dependent that we can no longer be sure where responsibility lies and therefore who to trust. These interconnections bring advantages, allowing elements of the system to lean on each other. So, weakness can be bolstered by drawing on the larger system. Banks do not generally collapse when people withdraw more funds than they have as liquid reserves, because banks can draw on cash from elsewhere in the system to cover their liabilities. So, connected finance provides the impression of stability but none of this is real.

Leading up to the financial crisis of 2008, world finance had never before been so interdependent and interconnected. The trust which had been vested in each bank was now vested in the entire system. It was no longer each bank at risk of failure but the whole system at risk. If everyone across the globe decided to withdraw their funds the entire banking system would collapse. If every shareholder decided to sell up, shares would be worthless. The world had changed from stand-alone banks and separate national economies to look more like a single super financial system. Whilst trust is maintained such a system can be more efficient with easier access to capital and plenty of investment opportunities. Both borrowers and investors benefit, earning more on their investment or paying less for their capital. People who understand banking and finance should have known that this was a house of cards, but they kept quiet or closed their minds.

Before the financial crisis, I wrote that the world financial system might be a house of cards waiting to collapse (McManners 2008). In 2007, well before the crisis erupted, I shared a draft of the book with a business school colleague. He was dismissive of my analysis. He thought that this was not a message anyone wanted to hear. People were pleased that the global economy was booming and the idea that we might be on the cusp of a crisis would not be welcome. It was clear to me that a crisis was looming; it was only the precise timing which was in doubt. It was as if no one wanted to admit that a crisis might be brewing for fear that it would be self-fulfilling. This attitude is perhaps not surprising and it comes from banking. A prime role of bankers is to reassure the markets that all is well because loss of trust is all it takes to break a bank; and when all banks connect, loss of trust could break the financial system. Central bankers are best placed to see potential problems but a central banker is never going to suggest there is a problem with the system because simply making the suggestion is enough to cause problems. So, everyone carries on regardless. That was the situation leading into the financial crisis of 2008.

This chapter examines the vital role that trust plays in the financial system, to work out the implications for resilient economic policy. First, it is useful to examine the nature of trust.

Trust Within the Family

To explore the nature of trust I will start with trust within the family. Here trust is, or should be, absolute. There should be no need to use finance to grease the wheels of family life. Family members do what needs to be done without expecting payment and can rely on family members to provide help and support. There might be an informal unwritten ledger of who owes what, with the occasional argument fuelled by accusations that someone is not pulling their weight. The family finds an accommodation and way of operating which works for the benefit of all. The use of money or IOUs is not needed, except for transactions which go outside the immediate family. Some families might be closer and the bonds of trust stronger than other weaker families, but each person knows the others intimately so the lines of trust are clear and well understood. If you are let down you know exactly who to blame. If you make a huge investment in time or effort it is a choice you make for all sorts of reasons. Within the family you find the gold standard of trust and little need for operating a financial model to regulate who does what for whom. As the family interacts with others in the community it becomes necessary to have a financial system, as pure trust is no longer sufficient.

Trust Within the Community

Within small tight communities, people know each other and trust each other – or more accurately know who they can trust. The give and take of distributing labour are more complex and there is less willingness to give without expecting a benefit in return.

The activities required to operate the community are diverse. Taking a simple model, a community needs a doctor, a dentist, a farmer, a shopkeeper, a builder, a lawyer, and of course a banker. The community needs a means of exchange so everyone's efforts can be mobilized to the benefit of all. Communities therefore use currencies to enable dividing up of labour. The doctor can focus on treating patients; the farmer grows food; the building worker repairs buildings; and the bank manager holds people's savings and makes loans. The modern world has much more complexity but the simple model works for explaining the concept (as well as having attractive attributes which we might want to rediscover).

At the community scale, people know who to trust. The most trusted people are the doctor and the bank manager. To one you entrust your health; to the other your wealth. The needs of the local economy go beyond everyday transactions to transactions which reach forward in time. A young family needs a mortgage to buy their first house; the farmer needs capital to purchase machinery; and everyone has savings they want to keep safe for their retirement or a rainy day. Before modern finance went through a step-change in scale and complexity, the local bank or building society facilitated these transactions between generations. The bank manager was a named individual who made judgments as to who to trust when lending money. Trust within communities used to be a local matter – and could be again.

When you live within the same community and personally know the people with whom you have financial transactions, security and stability comes from trust. Of course, in a real sense the bank has an empty vault but it is transparent what is going on with safe local loans balanced against local saving deposits. Such a simple transparent system can be self-regulating, in that local banks can observe the behaviour of each other. If a well-managed bank needs capital, because withdrawals over a particular period exceed the capital held by the bank, other bankers will lend cash to them (requiring the payment of interest of course). A bank suspected of being dodgy will not be supported to the same extent. As mentioned before, any bank can be subject to a negative rumour which causes a run on the bank. In a simple system of local banks, whether a bank folds or survives depends on the natural interplay of trust. In the current banking system, self-regulation has a bad name, but independent local banks really can be self-regulating.

The local economy does not sit alone but nestles inside a national economy. It makes sense for the national level to add formal oversight and regulation in exchange for limited guarantees on deposits held in banks. This is additional to the natural self-regulation which comes with independent local banks. It is unfortunate that community banking has largely been destroyed in the name of greater economic efficiency. The idea to reinvigorate local banks seems almost quaint within modern banking. Rediscovering the value of such apparently antiquated ideas within a modern context is a theme explored in Chapter 9.

Trust Within a National Economy

Lifting the viewpoint to the national level, trust becomes less personal and more institutional. The national financial system facilitates transactions between people, communities and organizations who probably know little about each other. Trust is vested in the national financial system. The ultimate arbiter of trust is the government and the country's leadership. In addition to all the current transactions required to run the country day-to-day, there are investment decisions and financial obligations of long-term scale. For example, major infrastructure projects need capital in order to be built to deliver benefit back to society over many decades. Another example is pensions so people can save for a secure retirement. A national financial system will have a central bank, overseeing a national currency, together with the government which sets economic policy. This works because we trust the government and trust our leaders to run the country's financial affairs in a prudent and careful manner.

When voting in elections, a prime consideration is whether you trust the candidates. Trust goes deeper than this, in that national institutions, over time, build up a reservoir of trust. Citizens of a well-run country have every reason to trust the financial system. The people who run it are held to account by the elected politicians and constrained by institutional rules and regulations. A country has (or should have) close control over its finances and its economy. This can be the case provided it has not opened up to global finance to the extent that trust has been transferred from the national system to reliance on international finance.

Trust Within the Global Financial System

When banks come together to facilitate a global financial market, there is increased liquidity, more investment options, and more sources of capital. While the system is working it seems to be advantageous but we return again to the fundamental foundation of banking – trust. The system works whilst it is trusted. If trust evaporates, for whatever reason – a real weakness or a believable rumour of weakness – the system stops working. This is the fundamental nature of banking. To reap safely the efficiencies of interconnected global finance, a way would have to be found to preserve and retain trust at the global level – if indeed this is possible at all. If that is not possible, we need to reassess support for global financial integration. A system which is efficient according to economic theory but relies on a level of trust which does not exist, is not a workable system.

Let us consider some candidates for where to place trust in global finance, starting with the International Monetary Fund (IMF).

THE INTERNATIONAL MONETARY FUND

Created in 1945, the International Monetary Fund (IMF) is an organization working to foster global monetary cooperation, secure financial stability, facilitate international trade, promote high employment and sustainable economic growth, and reduce poverty around the world.

IMF 2020

To examine whether the IMF can be trusted, let us consider who owns the IMF and who it answers to. The IMF is owned by its near-global membership of 189 countries. Financial contributions are set according to the size of member countries' economies. On the Executive Board, eight countries have their own Executive Director: United States, Japan, China, Germany, France, the United Kingdom, Russia, and Saudi Arabia. In addition, there are sixteen other directors representing constituencies consisting of four to twenty-two countries. Voting power is proportional to financial contributions, so the country with the most votes is the United States, followed by Japan, China, Germany, France and the United Kingdom. These six countries together hold 42% of the votes. Whether you trust the IMF depends on whether you trust these countries and in particular the United States which has more than twice the number of votes of any other country. The overall situation is that the rich developed countries control the IMF but tend not to borrow; whilst the poorer developing countries contribute little capital but hold the bulk of the borrowing. This leads to tensions between the priorities of the lender and the borrower.

The head of the IMF is by tradition a European. This arises from an informal arrangement which ensures that the head of the World Bank is an American.

THE WORLD BANK

The World Bank is another component of the post-WW2 economic order. It was established in 1944 to help rebuild countries devastated by the war. It now places emphasis on the poorest countries, with the eradication of poverty and the promotion of shared prosperity its primary goals. It has 193 member governments who together own the bank. The President of the World Bank is nominated by the President of the United States. The United States has 16.4% of total votes, Japan 7.9%, Germany 4.5%, the United Kingdom 4.3%, and France 4.3%. Changes to the Bank's Charter require an 85% super-majority, so the US can block any change to the Bank's governing structure. So, whether you trust the World Bank boils down to whether you trust the United States and other Western powers. I gained an insight into how the World Bank operates in 2007 (see Box 4.1).

Box 4.1 World Bank – overbearing advice

In 2007 I was invited to attend a conference on policy for cities in the developing world.[13] I presented a paper titled 'Cities for People: Removing Cars from Urban Life'. This started with the premise that Western cities had been developed around the car and were dominated by infrastructure for the car. I argued that on reflection this can be seen as a mistake, which would require considerable investment to reverse. Rather than repeat this mistake, developing countries should bounce forward to cities designed for people rather than cars. I was nervous that representatives of developing countries would resist my idea, thinking I was denying them the cars which were ubiquitous in the developed world. I should not have been concerned on this front. I received a warm reception from developing countries but a very frosty reaction from a senior World Bank official. The World Bank message was that investment in road infrastructure is preferred because the return on investment is better than other transport options.

The presentation which followed mine was given by a city official responsible for rubbish collection. He proposed a fleet of locally produced handcarts for the narrow streets of densely populated areas. In discussion afterwards, he shared with me his frustration that the World Bank had insisted on a fleet of compactor trucks which required bulldozing access roads through the communities. These trucks now stood idle as the local community had neither the skills nor money to keep the trucks running.

The experience of this conference showed me the problem of overbearing, well-intentioned advice from the World Bank being at variance with local needs and local capabilities.

---

13 Beyond the Tipping Point: Development in an Urban World, London School of Economics, 19–20 October 2007.

This limited insight into the ethos and values of the World Bank should not be taken as a comprehensive analysis of the organization. What is clear is that the United States and Western interests have huge influence over the work of the World Bank. I like to assume that the United States has good intentions but it seems to me that the de facto aim is to steer progress in the developing world to reflect the American world viewpoint. The problem is (and Americans might not like me for writing this) America does not have the culture and economic model appropriate to many other countries with different circumstances. To be really useful to more countries, the World Bank would have to be culturally neutral and more nuanced in its advice.

TRUSTING GLOBAL FINANCIAL INSTITUTIONS

There is growing distrust of both the IMF and the World Bank, which has led to the establishment of other development banks such as the Asian Development Bank (ADB) and the New Development Bank (NDB), established by the BRICS (Brazil, Russia, India, China and South Africa), and the Asian Infrastructure Investment Bank (AIIB). The latter is a Chinese initiative to give the country more say over investment infrastructure in poorer parts of Asia reflecting its exasperation with the continued dominance by the United States and Japan in the region.

This brief overview of global financial institutions shows a fragmented collection of international organizations controlled by a small number of countries reflecting the post-Second-World-War power structure. For smaller countries in particular, it can be difficult to know who to trust. The United States has had huge influence over the last seventy years and looking to the future it appears that China will have growing influence. Are they to be trusted? The simple answer is yes; these are powerful countries who understand the need for international stability. However, it cannot be ignored that these countries have their own agendas; they do not hide the fact that they steer policy to suit their national interests. The United States seeks to impose its view of human rights and democratic government as well as ensure its corporations are free to operate internationally. China is less interested in improving the probity of other countries with a focus on getting access to resources, whether it be commodities out of Africa; or technology through buying companies on the world's stock markets; or infrastructure such as ports to facilitate continued expansion of Chinese exports.[14] It seems that global financial institutions cannot be trusted to be neutral agents. I wonder if the very idea that there is global financial system on which we can rely is perhaps misplaced.

There is a category of agent within the global financial system that has not yet been considered – the major international banks.

INTERNATIONAL BANKS

The major international banks have huge influence over global finance so it is worth considering the extent to which they can be trusted.

The structure of world banking has changed considerably since the financial crisis. In 2007, there were no Chinese banks in the top ten; in 2020 the world's four largest banks are Chinese. These ten banks are at the heart of global finance. They facilitate cross-border flows of capital and investment between countries. The Chinese banks in the list are all state-owned commercial banks, responsible to the Chinese state and by definition instruments of the Chinese state. The others are listed corporations

---

14 In 2016, the Chinese shipping group COSCO, a state-owned company, bought Greece's largest port of Piraeus as a gateway to Asia, Eastern Europe and North Africa.

responsible to their shareholders. So, can we trust the global banks? Are they governed by an ethos of supporting global society, or are they out to generate profits for their shareholders? The latter is of course the reality; even the banks themselves would not pretend otherwise. The assumption made is that despite the profit-earning motives of international banks they provide an efficient and liquid global financial system.

Table 4.1 World's largest banks[15]

World's Largest Banks		
Rank	2007	2020
1	Royal Bank of Scotland	Industrial & Commercial Bank of China
2	Deutsche Bank	China Construction Bank
3	BNP Paribas	Agricultural Bank of China
4	Barclays	Bank of China
5	Credit Agricole	Mitsubishi UFJ Financial Group
6	UBS	HSBC Holdings
7	Societe Generale	JPMorgan Chase
8	ABN AMRO	Bank of America
9	ING Bank	BNP Paribas
10	The Bank of Tokyo-Mitsubishi UFJ	Crédit Agricole Group

The network of connected international banks is important so governments should consider taking more control. International banks have a headquarters location, which implies that the host country has regulatory control. However, the large global banks have balance sheets bigger than many countries so,

---

15   Sources: BanksDaily (2020) and S&P Global Market Intelligence (Ali 2020).

unsurprisingly, governments are wary about setting regulations and even more careful with how they are enforced. Governments are concerned, and right to be concerned, that if an international bank is brought to book, it may shift its operations to another country. If the interests of shareholders would be best served by shifting to the jurisdiction of a country with less onerous regulations, or shifting the funds they control to support other economies, that is what corporate banks will do. This is the consequence of having a system of listed corporations controlling international banking. It is wrong to blame these banks; they are behaving exactly as you would expect them to behave.

International banks do provide liquidity and efficiency defined in a narrow financial sense, but they are not going to change the way they operate to support the circumstances of a particular country if this conflicts with delivering return to their shareholders. A logical appraisal of international banking shows therefore that the current model, in which listed banking corporations run the show, is the wrong model from the viewpoint that banking should support global society. Instead of putting trust in a model where shareholders are first and foremost, we need to find a way to manage global finance which puts society first and foremost. The emergence of Chinese state-owned banks at the top of global banking is equally concerning as there is no pretence that their role is anything other than to serve China's interests.

EXERTING CONTROL OVER GLOBAL FINANCE

Having examined the agents of global finance, I conclude that it is actually at the country level where real power and responsibility should reside. National governments of course have a huge interest in ensuring stability. For the United States and countries with significant voting rights in the IMF, have considerable power. China has marked out its role to influence and control global finance through its gigantic state-owned banks. Other countries need to consider how they can regain greater control. Perhaps the reality is that countries should take more financial control at the national level to ensure that global finance plays a lesser supporting role. This should not be controversial, but simply reaffirmation of the responsibility of national governments to ensure financial stability.

Rebuilding Trust

The virtual world of finance is based entirely on trust. It is the nature of finance and not something we can choose to alter. An IOU is an IOU. The paper on which it is written is worthless. So, the item you can hold and safeguard is not the IOU but the trust you have in the person who issued it. In fact, you could set alight an IOU written by a trusted person without changing the situation. When you know and trust the person who issued it, you could expect them to honour the debt even if the IOU itself had gone up in smoke. On the other hand, an IOU signed by Bernard Madoff (or any of the world's crooked financiers) would be worthless no matter how expensive the paper on which it was written.[16]

I keep banging on about trust because once we accept that trust is the only true currency in the financial system, it becomes easier to see through the smoke and mirrors to design a financial system that works for society. The key to sound stable finances is to clarify lines of responsibility. Knowing who to trust, and who can be trusted, brings transparency. Instead of the financial system running out of control, with even those in the driving seat not really understanding where risk lies, clear lines of trust can

---

16 In 2009, Bernard Madoff was convicted of fraud in a federal court in Manhattan for setting up a Ponzi scheme which defrauded investors of an estimated $64.8 billion.

deliver a system which works. That does not mean it would be a perfect system, and certainly it will mean forgoing potential efficiencies. The greater prize is stability, and improved predictability which comes with nailing responsibility, and therefore having a tight handle on trust. This is the sort of financial system we need. Less innovative, less ambitious, less volatile, less risky; these are the attributes of a sound financial system. We need boring bank managers, not financial wizards.

My analysis of trust began with the small and personal. Rebuilding trust also starts at the lowest levels. We need to invigorate local banking closely aligned with the needs of local communities. Personal relationships and natural oversight can regulate such a system. Ideally these local institutions would be owned by the community as mutual or cooperative banks.

Moving up a level, the state is the most powerful actor in world affairs. The state is responsible for the national financial system, national currency, and financial policy which suit the culture and the circumstances of the country. We would hope to live in countries with good fiscal discipline and be able to use the ballot box to decide who to trust. There will be differences in how individual countries manage their financial affairs but when countries have more autonomy it will be clear who is responsible. It is inevitable that some countries, at some point in their history, will suffer financial weakness and potential economic collapse. Human affairs will never be perfectly organized; and there will never be a perfect economy. It is therefore sensible to have global institutions which can provide advice and financial support when required. This is where the IMF and World Bank have potentially valuable roles, but only if they operate to an ethos of independence and neutrality.

Currently the IMF and World Bank have been captured by those who champion neoliberalism. Those who believe fervently in the free market may be genuine in their belief that it is the best system for all countries. However, entering a country seeking changes which conflict with the basis of the indigenous society is not how to build trust. Global financial institutions can rebuild trust by respecting that countries are sovereign and have their own priorities influenced by culture and geography.

My analysis returns again to the idea of a global financial system. It is the idea itself which is so dangerous and corrosive to the stability of global finance. Finance is all about trust. We can know and trust our local bank manager; we should be able to trust our government and its institutions; we do not have grounds to trust the global financial system. This is because there is no formal system, no clear responsibilities, and no clear lines of trust.

A perfect global financial system would be dominated by strong national financial systems; each operating according to local culture, geography, resources and circumstances. There would be limited and tightly controlled connections between economies. The system would not be dominated by free flows of capital chasing the highest return, but flows of capital would be restricted to funding real-world cross-border transactions. To return to such a trusted system will be seen by proponents of economic globalization as retrograde. These are the same people who did not see the impending crisis of 2008 and continue to deny the fundamental weakness of an open and interconnected global economy. I understand that those people most committed to conventional economic thinking will resist my analysis. As the reader, you may not yet be convinced. All I ask for now, is that you read on and discover how these ideas play out in a real-world context to deliver pragmatic and resilient economic policy.

At the risk of sounding like a scratched record, the financial system is all about trust. So, ensuring clear lines of responsibility is important to securing a robust and stable financial system. It is fundamental to the stability of the financial system that it can be trusted, and fundamental to its usefulness that it supports society. We have to be able to hold finance and economics to account, so this is where I turn next.

CHAPTER 5

HOLDING ECONOMICS TO ACCOUNT

The importance of economic policy is not so much the effect it has on the economy but the impact it has on the real world of people and places.

The current approach when considering economic policy is to put the economy first. The economic numbers, such as GDP, are monitored and policy adjusted to boost growth, boost sales, and boost investment. It is assumed that improving these numbers will be beneficial to society. This simplification becomes dangerous when it is accepted without questioning whether it continues to reflect the complexity of current real-world challenges.

When a simplification crafted for a different era is retained as the basis for decision making, it may be an inappropriate approximation leading to misdirected policy. This is the case with the assumptions which lie at the core of 20th-century conventional economic theory based on chasing growth. This has simplified the difficult task of crafting economic policy but is based on the aspirations and mindset of the 20th century.

The Need to Think Differently

We are now in the 21st century and there is a need to retreat from the misconception of economic policy based on growth. The challenges the world now faces require a different approach. Many politicians, government advisors and some economists have retained a 20th-century mindset and find it difficult to make the transition to thinking differently to match the challenges of the 21st century. Even amongst people who are committed to solving the world's environmental and social challenges, some of the current thinking misses the mark. An example is the UN Sustainable Development Goals (SDG). These are certainly well intended, containing a comprehensive set of ideal outcomes for global society (UN 2015).

The SDG have come out of discussion amongst experts and academics seemingly without applying a reality filter. It is a wish-list of aspirations for global society. The list of seventeen SDGs includes desirable outcomes for almost every problem and perceived injustice, ranging from the elimination of poverty and hunger to climate action and affordable clean energy. The fact that it would be impossible to achieve the SDGs without solving inherent dilemmas is conveniently ignored. It makes for feel-good reports and justifies a number of international aid initiatives. In terms of making policy real, the SDG are as useful as the outdated economic policy which continues to be peddled by the IMF and World Bank. A better starting point than the false promise of the SDG would be to bring policy down to Earth and make it real. Not only would that expose more clearly the difficulties, but it would open the way to solving them.

The world does not need solutions driven by 20th-century economic ideas and values promoted by Western societies. Most of us who live in stable well-managed Western societies believe it works well enough. That does not mean that the universal adoption of Western aspirations is sensible, or even possible. That would be a route to destroying the planet. Liberal-minded people in the West think that it is their duty to promote Western economic norms as a fair and equitable solution ignoring completely the impossibility of doing so.

There is also a particularly invidious idea termed 'contraction and convergence'. This requires that developed countries cut back severely allowing less-developed countries to increase consumption to converge on a world where every person has the same 'equitable share' of the world's resources. Such delusional ideas are often presented by people without the slightest intention that their share will be any less than it is now. They can present themselves as reasonable people occupying the moral high ground when they are nothing of the sort. They know that policymakers would never embrace such policy. There is more than a whiff of hypocrisy when people put themselves in a place of moral superiority in full knowledge that they can rely on pragmatic realists to defend the society and community in which they live.

Thinking differently requires facing reality in the search for resilient policy.

Resilient Sustainability

The thinking which underpins this book is all about real-world challenges and real-world solutions. In looking for solutions which have a real chance of success, I lean on an idea I developed of 'resilient sustainability' (McManners 2017). It is quite different to the mindset which dominated the 20th century and a radical departure from what has become business-as-usual. Having developed the concept, and researched in depth its consequences, on reflection all I have done is to capture common sense. All I seek is to put society back on the path which it should never have left. In this section, I explain briefly the core concept of resilient sustainability, starting with the underlying concept of sustainability.

'Sustainability' is the idea that the successful management of human affairs should strike a balance between the economy, society and the environment. This is now widely employed in government and in business, using a checklist to assess the impact of a policy or a decision on these three areas. Such 'weak sustainability' is proving to be largely ineffective leading to marginal change rather than transformation. When applying weak sustainability, environmental damage is acceptable provided it is balanced with benefits for society or the economy which have greater value than the damage.

Weak sustainability may lead to adjustment to policy but will not halt environmental decline.

An improvement is to embrace the concept of 'strong sustainability'. This requires acceptance that some constraints are immovable and not to be traded away. At the highest level, the fundamental constraint is the capacity of the planet. This is a fixed constraint which economic policy has to respect. Currently, strong sustainability is not widely understood and has limited support.

My concept of 'resilient sustainability' is a level yet further up the hierarchy of sustainability and has not so far had wide exposure. In my opinion this should be the gold standard to which policy should conform. The idea here is that people, communities and countries are empowered to work within the constraints of strong sustainability and are empowered to proactively manage their affairs, not only to put society on a safe path but to engage society (and the economy) in reversing the negative consequences of past policy.

Resilient sustainability can be summarized with a walking analogy. Sustainability is about walking safely without falling over; strong sustainability is about stepping carefully not to crush nature under our industrial boots; resilient sustainability is about taking a new direction which allows previously trampled ground to recover. The concept of resilient sustainability leads to considering transformative change.

Reverse Thinking

To implement resilient sustainability, we need to open our minds by considering a reversal of thinking.

The argument central to this book is that economics should be subservient to higher-order policy – this argument may not seem intuitive at first, because our thought processes have been captured by an economic view which distorts our perception. If you find it hard to accept initially, keep an open mind. I can see clearly now the way ahead but I remember how over a decade ago I blindly accepted the pre-eminence of economic analysis without realizing I was being hoodwinked into conformance. These might seem strong words but the grip that economic fundamentalism has over policymaking is a distortion which must be corrected.

The easiest way to start to understand this new approach to economics is to think about it as a reversal of the current policy-making process. The process with which most people are familiar starts with an economic analysis. The proposed project, policy, or whatever is being examined, is fully costed, sources of finance identified and payback periods calculated in order to construct a detailed business case. This is then tested with environmental and social impact analysis. This way of thinking is well established and seems to make sense. The reverse approach requires a shift in mindset. It starts with thinking about society and the real-world context. What are the challenges, risks and opportunities? What sort of outcomes would we like to achieve? What are the priorities? Are there any vital non-negotiable factors which constrain or direct policy? These questions lead into an analysis of pragmatic balanced policy which achieves a sustainable solution. This sets the frame for the formulation of economic policy or business case that can deliver the desired outcome.

Pausing to reflect, it becomes obvious that this is how economics should always have been handled. Two centuries ago, Adam Smith's ideas brought greater efficiency to the operation of society which at the time proved useful. When he was formulating the principles of economics, the long-term sustainability of how society interacts with the environment was not at risk. Also, he was not to foresee the threat to social cohesion of overzealous economic efficiency. There was no need for Adam Smith to think through how such ideas could play out over the centuries. It would be reasonable for him to assume that future generations would keep the theories of economics under review and alter them as circumstances changed. I believe Adam Smith would be horrified to see his name associated with contemporary economic thinking which has perverted the intentions behind his original work, and put the economy before society.

This way of thinking, where society and the environment come first, is not new but a reversion to how it should always have been. The late-20th-century approach to economics was the deviation from good policymaking. We cannot revert to the situation of the 18th and 19th centuries (nor would we want to) but we can leap forward into the 21st century by throwing 20th-century economic textbooks into the incinerator (keeping one copy for the museum). The challenges of the 21st century require forward thinking to design an economy appropriate to society living on a planet of finite resources. Economics in the 21st century should be, and has to be, different.

The Resilient Approach

The resilient approach to developing economic policy is to begin with a broad examination of the real-world context. This puts the analyst in a strong position to understand the circumstances, priorities, and importantly the constraints, which inform economic policy. These come together as thoughts on what would be desirable outcomes, tempered by a pragmatic realism of what might be possible. It is important right at the beginning, before anything specific is drafted, that the notion of standard economic solutions is rejected. So, for example, presenting what is known as the 'Washington Consensus' economic policy package to a country, without thinking carefully about the circumstances, is exactly the distorted thinking which needs to be avoided.[17] Theoretical economic policy frameworks can be presented in textbooks; resilient economic policy frameworks arise out of society, place and circumstances. Standard templates fit standard situations; but no country is 'standard', so standard economic templates have limited value. All countries have their own circumstances, so all countries need their own economic policy. It is not until this central idea of economic self-determination is accepted that the transformative power of resilient economic policy can really be appreciated.

Getting into the detail of the resilient approach, policymakers need to keep the real-world context uppermost in their minds. The aim is to develop economic policy for the real circumstances of a particular place and a particular society with all its limitations and constraints. This seems initially like holding back economic policy. The reality is seeking to build on strengths, capabilities and opportunities with pragmatic real-world policy. It is not about hitting economic targets; it is about building a resilient and sustainable economy which supports a resilient and sustainable society.

Before embarking on an economic evaluation, the resilient

---

17 The economist John Williamson coined the term Washington Consensus in 1989. It refers to a set of free-market economic policies promoted by prominent financial institutions such as the IMF and the World Bank.

approach examines place and society to frame the detailed analysis. This framing is vital to capturing the real-world context of geography and culture within which the economy operates. The geography of a society is a broad term which covers the complexity of how society and its supporting economy operate in relation to its place on the planet. The geography of a country which straddles the Arctic Circle is very different to one located at the equator. The former is a very tough place for human society requiring close cooperation, pre-planning and discipline to survive a long hard winter. The latter is more suited to humans with a benign climate and easy access to food. The different geographies lead to different cultures.

THE SIGNIFICANCE OF CULTURE

Culture is fundamental to who we are, how we behave, what we value, and our priorities. It is not a random process in which cultural elements are dealt out like a hand of playing cards. Culture evolves over decades, or centuries, in response to the challenges and opportunities a society faces. For example, the culture of the United States has its roots in the circumstances prevailing when it was founded in 1776.

In the area which is now the United States, the indigenous population had a deep respect for nature, and a culture that considered the impacts of decisions on the next seven generations (Booth 2008; Vecsey 1994). This was a culture in which sustainability was deeply ingrained, before the modern notion of sustainability had been formed. For a Native American, it was the right and proper way to behave. We cannot know how such a culture had evolved, or what incidents framed its development, but we can look at the culture and see its evident merits – and wish it had been retained. Perhaps we would not be facing the current challenges of resource shortages and environmental damage if the modern culture of the United States had not been so economically successful and become a beacon for the aspirations of so many people across the planet.

The culture of the modern United States has roots in settlers from Europe arriving on a continent of apparently limitless resources. This provided the incubator within which the culture of extravagant consumption was born. When there is abundance, prices are depressed. In a place of abundant resource availability it makes economic sense (although not common sense) to have policy to deliberately drive up consumption. We can understand through the lens of conventional economics why the culture of the modern United States is as it is. It is only relatively recently that the dangers have become apparent of a culture based on the assumption of limitless resources. Whether the United States changes its culture in the 21st century is for the United States to decide. What is certain is that its culture is not a culture which should be exported to other places on the planet where circumstances are different.

Some cultural artefacts no longer have a purpose, but the general principle is that culture is integral to a particular society and remains intact for good reasons. When circumstances change, culture will need to evolve but there is a time lag providing stability and consistency. Europe is an example of cultural diversity arising from circumstance. Northern Europeans face a tough climate steering society towards a culture of good organization to be able to survive the long winter. Southern Europeans have a more forgiving climate allowing a rather more laissez-faire culture to develop.

Beyond Europe, Bangladesh is a highly populous country teeming with people so a culture of frugality is normal. This enables a large population to live on the limited resources available. Each society has a culture which endures because it works.

People brought up in one culture should not seek to impose their cultural norms on another nation with different circumstances. It would be wrong to plant the idea that a Bangladeshi can live a high-consumption lifestyle modelled on a European or North American lifestyle. It would be equally wrong to argue that a North American should survive on next to nothing. The two countries are very different: different circumstances, different resources, and different cultures. That is the real world. It is a wonderful checkerboard of different cultures and societies to be retained and enhanced, not subjugated by economic conformity.

Conclusions

Holding economics to account is important to ensuring that the selection of economic tools brought to bear on policy is appropriate to time and place. Economic analysis should be undertaken framed by the issues, opportunities and constraints of the real world. The resilient approach knocks economics off its pedestal, and brings it down to Earth such that economic sense coincides with common sense. Economics is rejuvenated when used to implement higher-order strategic decisions respecting the needs and priorities of society and accepting the constraints of geography. This sets the context to consider what should be adopted as the core tools of resilient economics.

PART 2

CORE ECONOMICS

Economics is not a precise science ruled by fixed relationships such as the Laws of Physics. Economics contains a wide range of concepts, theories, and rules of thumb. At any given time, some are in their ascendancy and others drop out of vogue. These are choices we make. Rejuvenating economics for a new era requires that we review priorities, confirm the principles to apply, and decide the levers to use for implementation.

Agreeing and implementing a new version of core economics could ripple through economic policy changing the basis of decision making. What not to include can be just as important as what is selected for inclusion. For example, there is a long-standing rule of thumb that to boost employment you need to boost the economy. This comes from an era when tasks were carried out by people. In the age of increasing automation this policy mechanism no longer operates as intended. Boosting the economy can increase consumption but will not necessarily generate more jobs. This is an example of an economic rule which is therefore obsolete. The clean-up which fresh thinking allows will sweep through all areas of economics from markets and trade to currencies and taxation. Many tools of economics will survive but with a different approach to how they are applied.

An important aspect of the proposed revitalized economics is that the measures outlined in the following chapters should apply in a coherent manner. Resilient economics should be applied as a coordinated set of actions rather than the applications of individual economic tools. A limitation of the book format is that the measures need to be explained one at a time in the chapters which follow. However, it is only when the measures are applied in a coordinated manner that the effectiveness of the approach becomes fully apparent. The reader is encouraged to read and digest the full toolbox of resilient economics before reflecting on the opportunities which arise. Further clarity will come in Part 3 where the resilient approach is applied across a range of sectors.

Considering the toolbox of resilient economics, it should be borne in mind that the intention is to realign economics to the needs of society. This means that to develop the detail of resilient economics will require input from people outside economics. Left to their own devices, economists are likely to focus on the tools they like using, and make economic policy along lines with which they are familiar. Of course, in a well-run system, functionaries such as economists work to the strategy and objectives set by senior management. Likening the economy to a product, once the senior management team have decided what they want from the product, the design team can focus on utility, practicality and ergonomics. The resulting blueprint is handed over to the technicians to work out how to make it. Technicians consider how the product can be made most efficiently. They may suggest alterations to the design parameters so that it is easier to craft but the technician is not in control of the overall process. The same should be so for the relationship between economists and policymakers. Once senior leaders have decided what they want from policy, including social and environmental outcomes, policymakers supported by economists can focus on utility, practicality and fitting the economy to human society. Economists can suggest efficient mechanisms but they should not dictate the outcomes.

There are a huge range of economic theories and models which have been developed over two-and-a-half centuries of economics. It is interesting to glance at the list of winners of the Nobel Prize in Economics since the prize was first awarded in 1969. These range from Simon Kuznets' work on the interpretation of economic growth (awarded 1971) to Angus Deaton's analysis of consumption, poverty, and welfare (awarded 2015).

These are examples of great economists whose ideas have importance beyond the confines of economics, and can be understood by people outside economics. Other Nobel Prizes were awarded for less accessible economic concepts, such as the clarification of the probability theory foundations of econometrics[18] and a new method to determine the value of derivatives[19]. I admire the expertise displayed but it can be a struggle to understand exactly what their work means in terms of impact on everyday lives. The mathematics and logic employed is solid, and makes sense to other economists, but that is the point – economics for economists is a closed game.

Advanced esoteric economic models are developed, discussed and argued over within the ivory towers of academia. Such discourse may have limited value outside the bubble of economics. Some of these analytical tools are used within the financial system to help speculators to build models which predict the movement of markets. The investment community is free to use such algorithms in order to profit from their insight but real economics needs to be grounded in real-world outcomes. Governments may also need the output of complex economic analysis, but policymakers need to be wary of analysis that is intelligible only to economists. To be useful, the output of economic analysis should pass through the filter of pragmatism and transparency before being employed more widely.

The following chapters outline a toolbox of economic principles and methods which pass the test of pragmatism and transparency. This is not core economics according to economists. There is no mention of Pareto optimality, demand elasticity, or competitive equilibria. These are familiar terms

---

18 Trygve Haavelmo, awarded 1989.

19 Robert Merton and Myron Scholes, awarded 1997.

within economics but the following chapters avoid economic jargon. This is definitely not a textbook of economics for economists. It has the potential to become a textbook of resilient economics for policymakers who strive for a sound, stable and sustainable economy.

Part Two has six chapters. Chapters 6 to 8 outline three core principles: subsidiarity, resilient markets and real trade. Chapters 9 to 11 explain three implementation levers: money, tax and universal basic income.

CHAPTER 6

PRINCIPLE 1: SUBSIDIARITY

The principle of economic subsidiarity
is that economic decisions should be
taken at the lowest, most local level,
unless there are clear benefits to society
for the decision to be taken at a higher level.

The principle of subsidiarity has a long heritage in the effective management of human affairs. It holds that social and political issues should be dealt with at the lowest level that is consistent with their resolution. When decisions are taken at the lowest possible level in the hierarchy of society, such decisions maximize the buy-in from those involved and lead to outcomes most closely aligned with people's needs. This principle should apply also to economic policy, but too often the high-level economic case is given priority. This can mean that the needs of parts of society are obscured in what is seen as the 'greater economic good'. To rebalance economics, the first tool in the resilient economics toolbox is therefore economic subsidiarity. This is required to re-engage economics with the needs of society at every level.

In developing the concept of economic subsidiarity, my aim is to ensure that there is deliberate and careful examination of economic policy such that people, communities and, at a global level, countries, are empowered to run their economic affairs. This chapter explores what economic subsidiarity looks like as a fundamental principle of resilient economics.

Subsidiarity

The *Oxford English Dictionary* defines subsidiarity as:

> *The principle that a central authority should have a subsidiary function, performing only those tasks which cannot be performed at a more local level.*

It is a principle of social organization that has been widely adopted. It is on the UN's list of the five principles which are 'critical to guiding the reforms of global governance' (UN 2014: 14). The UN defines subsidiarity as:

> *Subsidiarity: Issues ought to be addressed at the lowest level capable of addressing them.*

Subsidiarity is part of the Treaty on European Union where it states (European Union 2007):

> *To ensure that decisions are taken as closely as possible to the citizens of the Union.*

Although the principle of subsidiarity is firmly established in political and social policy, its place in economic policy is less secure. There are even examples of economic policy being championed that is diametrically opposed to subsidiarity. For example, neoliberal ideology has been allowed to drive current macroeconomic policy even though it tends to limit the economic policy options available to national governments to decide what is best for the particular needs of the society they serve. It has become necessary to be explicit about bringing economic policy back under control and in support of society by enforcing the principle of economic subsidiarity. This might be hard for proponents of neoliberalism to accept but this principle is right for the current age.

Subsidiarity does not require that all decisions are delegated. Decisions can be taken at higher levels when there is a common benefit or advantage from doing so. Such decisions are an imposition on the lower level so may not be welcome. An appropriate balance needs to be struck between the power of higher-level authority and the self-determination of lower levels.

At the higher level, there will always be the temptation to control lower levels and interfere in local decision making; and the higher level would usually have the power to do so. Therefore, there needs to be restraint in the use of power, to only impose from above when there is a sound reason to do so. The principle of subsidiarity empowers people and communities making them more responsible for their affairs. When higher levels of authority become dictatorial, communities lose power, lose the sense of self-determination, and lose a sense of responsibility. Communities can descend into badly managed dysfunctional places where higher authority is blamed for their woes. When higher authority shows restraint and backs off, this gives communities freedom such that they have only themselves to blame and civic responsibility has the chance to bloom. Providing such fertile ground does not mean that all communities will thrive equally well, but what is certain is that the barren ground provided by excessive top-down control does not support the building of community cohesion and resilience.

Subsidiarity allows and expects that the mechanisms of government make decisions at the appropriate level. This is as low in the hierarchy of society as possible, only shifting the decision to a higher level for three reasons. First, that there might be common benefits which accrue to all communities when there is a coordinated approach. Second, a common resource is at risk and needs to be managed sustainably. Third, if the stability of the greater region is put at risk though failing to coordinate key aspects of society and the economy. Otherwise, decisions should be delegated. At all levels, economic policy needs to fit with the needs of society, hence the concept of ergonomic economic analysis.

Ergonomic Economic Analysis

> The aim of ergonomic economic analysis is to shape the economic analysis to fit with the needs, capabilities and expectations of a particular society.

Ergonomic economic analysis arises from a fusion of the soft skills of ergonomics with the hard logic of economic analysis.

Ergonomics is the study of how usable something is in terms of how people engage with it. It would apply to how the controls of a car are laid out so that it is easy to operate. The layout should be intuitive and allow safe operation of the vehicle. A simpler example would be the design of the shape of the handle of a knife. It should fit neatly and naturally into the hand so that it feels right, and the hand cannot slide along to be cut by the blade. The most ergonomic designs have a beauty and simplicity which means that the operator and the machine are in perfect harmony. The basic design could focus on making the car work, or the blade cut. To make a design ergonomic requires looking closely at people and how they work, and how they like to work. Controls and handles should be shaped to the human hand and the way they operate should suit human capabilities and expectations.

This concept of ergonomics can be applied to economics. The economy needs to operate according to sound economic principles of course (this is its basic function) but also where it engages with people it should fit with the capabilities and expectations of society. In the same way that a car which is perfect in almost every way but has poorly laid out controls could be a death trap, a perfect economy which is not designed to fit the needs of human society could crash spectacularly.

When designing economic systems, it is to be expected that economists will seek to design systems which conform to idealized economic models. This is like engineers using their hard skills to design cars for speed and fuel efficiency. This might be sufficient to achieve a basic capability, but the engineer needs to incorporate the soft skill of ergonomics for a car that works well. Economics should be employed with the same mix of hard economic choices coupled with the soft skill of ergonomics. It is perhaps early days in the development of a methodology of ergonomic economic analysis, but the potential is plain to see. I can offer only a hazy outline of ergonomic economic analysis based on the foundation of subsidiarity. Greater clarity should not be expected. Continuing with the analogy of car design, a great design will function well and be intuitive to drive. Although some standardization of the controls has emerged so that you can step into a hire car and be driving almost straightaway, the detail evolves to give each model its own characteristics. As ergonomic economic analysis evolves, good ideas will be widely copied and adopted but there is no need for rigid rules and top-down control.

Ergonomic economic analysis and economic subsidiarity are closely related concepts which lift economics to a higher level. This is where some policymakers may start to feel uneasy because hard economic logic is subverted in order to align more closely with society's needs. According to resilient economics, this is exactly as it should be.

Framing Economic Efficiency

A commonly used definition of economics is that it is about the efficient allocation of scarce resources.[20] So, it should come as no surprise that much of current economic policy focuses on the efficient allocation of scarce resources. There is more to real policy of course than maximizing the efficiency with which resources are utilized. Resources need to be carefully husbanded and care taken not to exceed the sustainable exploitation of them. Dealing with resources using raw economic efficiency will undermine conservation and could undermine our future on a planet of finite resources. Where resources are allocated, it makes sense to do it efficiently, but importantly this should take place within a frame of responsible stewardship. This is one aspect where the concept of economic subsidiarity is important to securing a sustainable future.

The importance of being prepared to retreat from economic efficiency, when circumstances require it, may not be apparent immediately. Food supply is a good example to draw upon to illustrate the point. Raw economic efficiency can lead to industrial practices in farming, long supply chains and dominance by large supermarkets. A focus on efficiency first and foremost leads to the development of such food supply systems. In Chapter 14 I will explore that these are only efficient within a narrowly defined context. If a wide-angle examination is made of all the factors including energy, biodiversity, animal health and,

---

20　A definition of economics is the 'study of how societies use scarce resources to produce valuable commodities and distribute them among different people' (Samuelson 1948). Paul Samuelson was considered to be the foremost academic economist of the 20th century (Weinstein 2009). His textbook was the most successful economics textbook of the 20th century, running to over nineteen editions.

of course, human health, it looks very different. Food supply is an area where economic efficiency is only one issue amongst a range of factors. The point I want to drive home is that there are clearly higher-order priorities than simple economic efficiency. Applying economic subsidiarity, people might choose to grow their own food (on an allotment perhaps), buy local produce, and support the local butcher who in turn sources meat from local farmers. These may fail the test of raw economic efficiency, but it is evident that the picture I draw is of secure, safe and healthy food supply arrangements, under the oversight of the community. There should be no reason why policymakers at higher levels would implement economic policy which undermines such local arrangements. This applies to communities, regions, and countries; each entity needs to ensure safe sources of food and continuation of supply. Economic efficiency is a factor but, particularly with regard to food, it is a secondary factor.

Economic efficiency is important but should not be allowed to overrule the needs of society, now and in the future. When the principle of economic subsidiarity is adopted, people at all levels in society are empowered to decide, weighing all the factors to strike an appropriate balance. The argument that there are other factors more important than economic efficiency is clearly correct, but it may be more difficult to craft policy with this more nuanced approach.

Economic Subsidiarity and Markets

Markets are a fundamental tool of economics (covered in more detail in the next chapter). There has been a strong drive to make more use of markets in almost every area, hoping that the invisible hand will bring improvement. For this to work, it is important that the market operates within a suitable framework. This is where economic subsidiary can be valuable to bring clarity to market design and confidence that a market is sound. Through the lens of economic subsidiary, it becomes clear that a market is only useful when it has been designed to support the needs of society at the most appropriate level. This requires pushback against those who champion 'market fundamentalism' as a basis for policy. Unfettered markets are by default markets which are out of control. 'Unfettered' might have a positive feel but 'out of control' is clearly a pejorative term. When is a market unfettered, and doing its job well; and when is it out of control, and in need of reining back in? Let us start by accepting the principle of economic subsidiarity and see where it takes this brief overview of markets. This means accepting the superiority of the needs of society in setting policy, and the importance of delegating decisions to be taken close to the people. It follows that markets should be controlled by people as low down the hierarchy of society as possible.

A local market operates in a local area or region. In small local markets, the participants know each other, and know who to trust, and who to avoid. Larger local markets operate between people who do not know each other but being local, there are communal networks and community knowledge so self-regulation has a good chance of success. In local markets, a supplier cannot afford to deliver shoddy products. Local producers cannot afford to provide unsafe food. There are all sorts of informal routes to share information. So, a local market can be unfettered by regulation because the community has de facto control.

A national market can no longer rely on self-regulation. The opportunity and temptation to game the market, to the detriment of some remote person who is outside the local trust network, is too great. Therefore, a national market needs legislation, rules and systems of inspection. The government can choose the extent of the controls which are appropriate. Such systems of regulation evolve over time. If there is a culture of good honest practice, then a minimum of formal regulation should suffice. If the culture is for traders to squeeze maximum profit by any means, then regulations will need to be extensive and detailed. National cultural differences dictate how markets are regulated with the government having a clear line of authority.

Global markets are more difficult. There is an argument for increased use of global markets because of the theoretical efficiencies. There are global markets for food, commodities, and goods and services. There is also discussion of new markets, such as a global market for carbon to help respond to the challenges of climate change. Support for such globalization was in the ascendancy in the 20th century, but in the 21st century the tide is turning towards protectionism. Within economics, protection-ism has become a negative term, and something to avoid, arguing that 'beggar-thy-neighbour' policies have more downside than upside. We need to turn away from such blinkered thinking. The problem with global markets is that there is little effective regulation (leaving aside for now the limited role of the World Trade Organization (WTO)) and no strong linkages between the global market and society. Such markets operate outside the control of society. When examined through the lens of economic subsidiarity we should be very wary of trusting global markets. There are goods and commodities which will be traded globally but 'leave it to the market' is a dangerous concept to apply at global level.

The most important insight which emerges from this exami-nation of economic subsidiarity is the need to pull back from reli-ance on global markets. They can be effective when resources are plentiful and it seems reasonable to allow global corporations to orchestrate them. As the world approaches resource limits, there is uncertainty about the extent to which global corporations can be trusted by national governments. This is not intended to be a corporation-bashing comment but a statement of the plain fact that the current ownership model for listed corporations is not aligned with governmental needs. What is clear from this brief examination of markets is that the time has come to change direction to ensure that markets work in support of society. This is different to the narrow perspective, which has been allowed to take hold, of markets supporting the economy. This may seem a nuanced point, as currently we assume that a strong economy is aligned with a strong society. The problem identified is that setting up markets to deliver on economic metrics is one step removed from outcomes for society. Closer oversight by society, of how markets operate, provides the closer relationship required.

Economic Subsidiarity in Practice

Economic subsidiarity is just one tool of resilient economics. Until you understand the full range of tools in the toolbox it is hard to appreciate the full value of applying the principle. Let us explore the application of economic subsidiarity to get a better feel for the concept, starting at the lowest and most basic level.

ECONOMIC SUBSIDIARITY AND THE FAMILY

The lowest unit of structure in society is the family. This is where the roots of subsidiarity are buried. The family should be able to run its own affairs free from outside interference by others. The economics of the family is a simple model of income and expenditure with perhaps a house as the main capital investment. Most people would agree families should be free to run their finances however they choose. Some will take a risk and live a big lifestyle built on debt which requires holding down well-paid jobs.

Others may choose a more frugal lifestyle with little debt and savings kept for uncertain times. In my family, we choose to live well within our means so as not to need to worry about money, and not to feel trapped in our jobs. I recommend such prudent financial management but I accept this is a choice people are free to make. We should note that it is very difficult for people at the lowest end of the income scale to make prudent decisions when living hand-to-mouth within the current economic model. (This will be addressed in Chapter 11 as one of the benefits of a universal basic income.)

The best place to consider the impact of economic subsidiarity on the family is to look at problematic families whose economic circumstances are weak. Such a family is in trouble and higher-level authority has a responsibility to help – at least that is the case in rich countries with advanced welfare systems. There will be public money available for unemployment benefit, housing benefit, and other specific financial help. Of course, the higher authority has a limited budget so has to try to keep welfare expenditure under control. Typically, savings are taken into account when payments are made, so there is an incentive to spend any savings or financial windfall without delay to maintain levels of welfare payments. If people are extravagant or feckless, spending every pound or dollar they have, the welfare system will step in with additional help, particularly where children are at risk. Such well-intentioned paternal intervention has a downside. First, this conflicts with economic subsidiarity. Second, people care more about their rights than their responsibilities. Third, being stuck on welfare handouts would be soul destroying for anyone. It should be no surprise that when people are caught up in welfare dependency many behave badly and become architects of their own descent into living hand-to-mouth taking what they can from the state.

Having painted a picture of a dysfunctional family micro-economy, let us see what happens with the application of the principle of economic subsidiarity. We need to begin by bringing another economic tool into play. We will find again and again that complex problems have complex solutions so the application of a single tool will not suffice. In terms of communicating complex solutions, I need to adopt a linear explanation – I therefore ask you to accept, for now, as I bring in another tool, which is the concept of a universal basic income (explained in Chapter 11).

Universal basic income is a fixed amount paid by the state to every citizen whatever their circumstances. I first came across this in 2004 at a conference I attended in Lancaster in Northern England on the Philosophy of Green Economics. At first, I was not convinced as it seemed like green mumbo jumbo. After reflection, and careful analysis over many years, I now appreciate that it can work. With such a policy, each adult is entitled to a universal basic income (also referred to as citizen's income). It is set at a basic level, decided by government, to provide the minimum required for a secure simple lifestyle. It is important that political interference does not push the universal basic income to higher levels. Basic should mean basic. If it is to deliver on its promise, it should retain its purest form as the only direct cash payment available from the state – with few exceptions.

Economic subsidiarity applied to the dysfunctional family in the example above plays out like this. The family becomes responsible for the choices they make. They are free to live a simple frugal lifestyle without suffering the stigma of being scroungers. Such a lifestyle choice with low consumption and low impact is to be admired not looked down on. There will be people who want to step off the treadmill of conventional work and consumerist lifestyles seeking to live sustainably, perhaps growing their own food and living a simple life by choice. There will be others who struggle to cope. For these people the state and other organizations can step in with innovative support models using the principle of establishing communities where every person works to the best of their ability, blurring lines between the carers and the cared for. The citizen's wage underpins an economic model for social care which allows this (see Chapter 13).

It is likely that most people will want more than a basic minimum. If they work to bring their income to a higher level, that is fine; and does not affect their basic income from the state. Economic subsidiarity provides this opportunity and freedom. This works in both directions by placing responsibility with people. If they choose to live a lifestyle which is beyond their means they are free to become bankrupt. The situation, which is corrosive to the health of society, of people expecting the state to provide for a decent standard of living, without playing a positive role in the community or prudence in their own affairs, need not occur.

The state retains an interest of course in ensuring that people, and particularly children, are safe. There needs to be a safety net of basic hostel accommodation and care facilities for the vulnerable. The state should also be interested in ensuring that there are jobs in the wider economy, so people who want to work have the opportunity to do so. Economic subsidiarity at the lowest levels of society is not about cutting people adrift, but is about ensuring people who are less able to manage their affairs have opportunities within their capabilities to contribute to society and be part of society. Adopting economic subsidiarity with regard to the family, works well looked at from both ends of the political spectrum. A left-wing view might welcome that everyone has a basic income by right. A right-wing view might welcome the way that the government's responsibilities are capped. It becomes worthwhile for families to get economic control of their affairs with those who cannot (or will not) ending up in safety-net facilities provided by the state. There is much more that can be done to achieve systemic improvements, but the core principle of economic subsidiarity is the right place to start.

Families are the basic building blocks of society. The highest level is the country within which we live. For a level in-between let us consider the city.

SUBSIDIARITY AND THE CITY

Economic subsidiarity can be instrumental in helping cities to thrive. Most cities have a long heritage stretching back centuries as they have evolved to suit the geography and circumstances of their location. They operate inside a sovereign country subject to the rules and regulations of that country. Where circumstances remain constant, or change only slowly, the city can evolve as a gentle progression. It is human nature for people to want a better life and for leaders to emerge who can deliver on people's aspirations.

Cities will always face problems and challenges. The problem could be as simple as the city management becoming complacent and lazy leading to decline, or perhaps central government is being dictatorial about policy for their cities without taking into account the individual circumstances of a particular city. It could be the closure of a major industrial facility upon which the city economy relies. For coastal cities it could be the economic challenge of how to afford defences against rising sea levels – an issue which will have increasing importance through this century. Navigating the future will require cities to be resilient to whatever might arise. I will explore how the principle of economic subsidiarity is important to securing the vitality and resilience of cities.

Cities work best when allowed to run their own affairs with people taking responsibility for *their* city. The principle of subsidiarity applies to cities, and economic subsidary applies to the city's economy. Some cities are well-run; others are a dysfunctional mess. There are many different ways to run a city economy; the only common factor being able to balance the books. It is interesting to examine a dysfunctional city to tease out why economic subsidary is so important. A city which does not have what is recognizable as its own economy, and which has not been given autonomy, is at risk of failing. When it does fail, the government will be blamed. This would be correct; governments which do not give their cities high levels of autonomy are responsible for how well (or how badly) they operate.

There are examples of old industrial cities becoming ghost towns, such as the rust belt cities in central America and some cities in the northern industrial heartlands of the United Kingdom. There is huge resentment in such cities against the central government. A common response is top-down assistance with cash injections and support. All too often this leads to people reliant on welfare payments with a lack of pride in their community and little hope for their future. The weak economy, reliant on government handouts, lacks the resources to maintain infrastructure. The city environment crumbles with the only successful entrepreneurs being the drug dealers and criminals exploiting people's vulnerability and the weakness of the city's institutions.

Let us examine such a problematic city to explore what the application of economic subsidiarity can do. Again, it needs a range of tools to be able to apply the principle of economic subsidiarity. Such a city might be short on jobs, short on income, and short on the wherewithal to deliver services and maintain infrastructure. The people are generally poor and reliant on welfare payments so are unable to afford to keep their houses in a good state of repair, or in some cases cannot afford even to pay the mortgage. The housing stock falls into disrepair or is repossessed by the banks, or both. This could be Detroit in the US, or Sheffield in the north of England as heavy industry retreated. These cities are rich in people with a capacity to work and rich in opportunities to make the city better and return it to health. The national government cannot afford to give the city huge handouts but the city can afford to repair itself. What is needed is an economic mechanism to connect the capacity of people to work with the jobs that need to be done. This is where I need to reach into the economic toolbox for other tools. The first of these is a local currency (more on this in Chapter 9).

There is growing interest in the potential of local currencies to grease the wheels of a local economy. Freed from reliance on the national economy the city can work its way back and rise again. I will make this seem simple and straightforward when of course it is actually complex and difficult. Printing a new currency can be a threat to the established system of taxation so national governments are wary of allowing local currencies to mature and deliver on their full potential. From this perspective, higher authority can either kill off local currencies or keep them curtailed to be only an attraction to tourists. Such a high-handed approach conflicts with economic subsidiarity. National governments should learn to understand the potential of local currencies, give them space to grow and perhaps even encourage their formation. It would be good to see local currencies as a normal component of city economies.

Cities in the 21st century have the potential to thrive if economic subsidiarity is applied and governments can resist the temptation to interfere, except in exceptional circumstances. Some cities will do exceedingly well and be examples to follow; others may descend into failed cities. The common factor should be that people are empowered and responsible. Elected mayors will be judged at the ballot box on how well the city works. I have great faith in the power of people to improve their circumstances when they are empowered to do so. For a failing city we can think about supporting the city to regain control of its affairs. Cash injections for temporary life support should be avoided. Where funds can be made available these should be for investment for the longer term such as infrastructure. Where advisors are sent in by government, they need to be versed in the resilient approach, and hold back from recommending standard templates. A city where the economy fits people's circumstances and the people are engaged in the economy is a 'good economy' by the only measure which really matters, that it supports the people, and has the support of its people.

NATIONAL ECONOMIC SUBSIDIARITY

It is the sovereign right of a country to run its affairs as it chooses. This should apply just as much to the economy as to any other policy area. The benefits of economic subsidiarity reinforce this point but over recent decades countries have been losing control as the perceived benefits of economic globalization have been promoted by global institutions and influential Western countries such as the US and UK. This rush to reap the advantages of globalization (it is advantageous to a number of players and theoretically advantageous to all countries) means that the principle of economic subsidiarity is sidelined. The theory in support of economic globalization is robust but the principle of economic subsidiarity is superior, so where there is a choice to be made the national interest should come first.

Interference in a country's economic affairs can come from many directions. Let us consider three. First, multinational corporations (MNCs) which have an interest in entering a country to pursue commercial opportunities. Second, global financial institutions such as the IMF or World Bank seeking to help the country to sort out its finances. Third, another country getting involved with motives ranging from a desire to assist to an intention to exploit.

In the first case, an MNC is managed to deliver benefits to its shareholders so countries need to be aware of that. Although working with an MNC can be mutually beneficial, the MNC will only do that which is good for its bottom line. I have no intention of bashing big business but MNCs are not to be trusted with anything other than delivering what they are contracted to deliver. Altruism is not in their DNA and when MNCs are accused of behaving badly it is usually because policymakers have misunderstood that international listed corporations are not beholden to national governments.

In the second case, the IMF and World Bank have particular ideas of what constitutes an appropriate model of economic development. Their advice is well-intentioned but over recent decades these institutions have promoted a neoliberal economic agenda. It takes a confident and strong government to face down such advice. This is what countries will have to do until global institutions embrace economic subsidiarity and show the restraint required to allow resilient national economies the space to establish strong enduring foundations.

In the third case, relationships with other countries are a complex mesh of conflicting and overlapping agendas, with a strong preponderance to put national interest to the fore. The strongest countries are most able to get what they want out of the relationship.

For economic subsidiarity to deliver on its potential, the powerful agents mentioned above have to show restraint. MNCs have to learn to respect and accept local policy decisions. World institutions have to observe and listen rather than dictate policy. Countries have to interfere less in the internal affairs of other counties; this applies particularly to powerful countries which need to adopt a responsible approach to how they use their power. If such restraint is lacking at world level, countries will have to be much more assertive in insisting that they remain in control.

Countries have a wide diversity of economies to suit geography, culture and circumstances. This is as it should be. Attempting to impose a one-size-fits-all economic policy is doomed to fail. Some economies will attract admiration (and perhaps envy), others will provide examples of policy to avoid. An example of the former is Norway which has the advantage of ample reserves of oil and gas together with a prudent economic policy giving the country a strong, rich and resilient economy. An example of the latter is Zimbabwe under Robert Mugabe, whose politics squandered the potential of a country with some of the best agricultural land in Africa. These counties have very different circumstances, culture and politics. To illustrate the power of economic subsidiarity let us consider a country in difficult economic circumstances.

The example I turn to for a country in difficult economic circumstances is Bhutan. This is a remote landlocked country nestled between Tibet and India. Its economy is based mainly on agriculture, forestry, tourism and the sale of hydroelectric power to India. Agriculture provides the main livelihood for the population consisting largely of subsistence farming and animal husbandry. Bhutan is a constitutional monarchy with an elected government. In 1972, the king was interviewed by the Financial Times in which he said:

Gross National Happiness is more important than Gross Domestic Product.

King Jigme Singye Wangchuck

From a conventional economic perspective, Bhutan is a poor and backward country in need of development. The current king acceded to the throne in 2008 at the age of twenty-eight.[21] He was educated in the United States and the UK. It might be expected that he would have implemented conventional development advice. He has had the foresight and courage to reflect on what is best for his country, its people, culture and geography. He has retained a focus on national well-being in its broadest sense and has resisted conventional economic advice. His plan is all about Bhutan. This is as it should be. A leader should do what is right for their country, not do what is required to be incorporated into the global economic order.

Bhutan continues to be a poor country (by financial measures) and it is at risk of being 'rescued' by champions of conventional economic policy. Outside agents like the IMF and World Bank would like to see what in their view are 'improvements' to be able to grow a larger economy (IMF 2016). Not every country will have a leader with the vision and the confidence to resist such advice from powerful external agents. Bhutan shows how economic subsidiarity can lead to national success as measured by the positive impact on its people. There could be no better measure.

Subsidiarity Applied to Development Projects

Economic subsidiarity brings benefits when applied to individual development projects. The principle of subsidiarity requires that project decisions and responsibility are delegated down to those people directly involved, except where there is a clear benefit

---

21   King Jigme Khesar Namgyel Wangchuck

from elevating the decision to a higher level. For this to work, restraint is required from higher authority. Examination of the implications of complying with economic subsidiarity supports the case for making this the normal way to manage projects.

The most obvious insight is the way that conventional economic analysis can be strengthened by adopting subsidiarity. The vesting of control and responsibility with those most directly involved can prevent, or make much less likely, the cost overruns or failure to deliver which are common with many large projects. However, in any project, the high-level players have the power. This could be the government or a corporation. This higher entity may not want to cede control, having motives and objectives to deliver benefit for the whole country (in the case of the government) or for the benefit of shareholders (in the case of a corporation). They will want to use their power to ensure they meet their objectives, requiring lower levels to conform. They might feel the need to take action to force compliance, with opposition from lower levels prevented from derailing a project with good economic outcomes – for the country (or the corporation). Such overbearing control can be counterproductive.

The benefits of adopting the principle of economic subsidiarity can be more profound, countering one of the flaws in conventional economics. Conventional economics is set up in such a way as to exploit the planet's resources starting with those which are easier (cheaper) to access but eventually working through to depletion. Although not widely understood or accepted by many mainstream economists, the conventional economic model leads inexorably to trashing the planet. The alternative to such inevitability is to adopt economic subsidiarity and defend it resolutely as the first principle of resilient economics. This would allow parts of the planet to remain free of industrial exploitation where local communities give environmental stewardship a high priority and exert control to enforce it. It could be argued that it is sufficient that governments defend the natural environment. They have an important role of course in establishing national legislation such as green belts and national parks. For other areas, there are powerful forces within the current economic model seeking to increase the value of land, through using it for intense agriculture or urban development. The adoption of economic subsidiarity can counterbalance such pressure.

Conforming to economic subsidiarity is likely to put a brake on some projects. The high-level power brokers might see this as evidence that economic subsidiarity is not the best policy. The converse is true; the broad examination of the wider context by those most directly affected leads to better decisions (even though those with power might resent it when decisions do not go their way).

Economic subsidiarity should be welcomed by everyone who wants to put society onto a sustainable path. Resilient economic analysis leads to quite different ways to plan and manage projects. Currently, project-by-project application of conventional economics seeks to maximize economic benefit (as perceived by the powerful players) with little real regard for degrading natural capital. Solid commitment to subsidiarity is not a guarantee that further environmental damage can be avoided, but I suggest that local residents are best placed to be the guardians of local environments – when empowered to do so. All too often, big corporations make deals with high-level officials and local views are drowned out. In conventional economics this is fine provided they are paid appropriate compensation. The principle of giving local people power and responsibility changes the parameters and steers the economic analysis towards value judgements rather than a blinkered examination of the raw numbers.

To illustrate how economic subsidiarity can improve the management of development projects I will use two examples.

The first is a proposed copper mine and the second a nuclear waste storage site.

EXAMPLE: COPPER MINE

Resources such as copper ore are located on the planet according to the vagaries of geology, with little regard for how the ground above is being utilized. As the easy-to-exploit high-grade deposits are mined out, the global mining companies are searching for new sources of supply. When a new site is identified, analysis is carried out on the purity of the ore and the cost of extraction to write a business case to invest in opening a new mine. The conventional economic analysis is based on: cost of extraction, cost of processing, and cost of transportation to market. There will also need to be a budget for additional measures to persuade the authorities to authorize the project. This type of economic analysis is bread and butter to the mining companies. This is what governments have come to expect, and whenever a new mine is proposed it is this top-down economic analysis which drives the decision making. The concerns of local communities are often a distraction at the margins, only entering the conventional economic analysis as a number for the compensation which will need to be paid.

Applying economic subsidiarity means that the local communities where the mine is proposed are allowed to have control and responsibility. The local community has to be persuaded of the benefits and be reassured about any impact on the local environment, in addition to compliance with national environmental regulations. The methods to be employed are those which the community will accept. It could be that the local community have an agrarian economy and a pristine environment which they wish to retain. They might interpret their responsibilities as protecting it, and use their control to insist only on methods which allow this. Economic subsidiarity requires that the corporation and the government show restraint by respecting such views. If this makes the project uneconomic from the corporation's perspective then so be it. It is not a question of assuming the project will proceed with discussion of compensation, but a genuine stakeholder dialogue which only moves forward when all parties agree that the project is viable – in a broader context than the financial analysis.

In advanced democracies, local people already have considerable influence over decisions. It is in the poorer countries where the danger is most acute. Instead of international bodies promoting conventional economic models, there needs to be strong commitment to economic subsidiarity with the idea of defending the economic empowerment of communities. International corporations and corrupt governments may not welcome such a rethink but it is clearly the way to handle sustainable economic policy. The challenge is to push back against the full weight of conventional economic thinking about development and the role of foreign direct investment (FDI).

How to carry out resilient economics for a new copper mine is a challenge faced by many developing countries because this is where virgin areas to prospect are located and where official oversight is least. A challenge more appropriate to the developed countries is how and where to store waste from nuclear power stations.

EXAMPLE: NUCLEAR WASTE SITE

Conventional nuclear power generation produces radioactive waste as an inevitable by-product. This can remain dangerous for thousands, or tens of thousands, of years. There is a question about the wisdom of embracing such a source of power when the long-term liabilities are so great. The argument in favour is based on nuclear power being low-carbon, so that through the lens of concern about climate change it is attractive. Rather than enter into that debate, I will examine here the sole issue of long-term storage of nuclear waste.

The requirement is to find a place which will remain undisturbed for tens of thousands of years without polluting water supplies or other ill effects. This is a tall order but there are places with stable geology which fit this requirement. Examples are the granite rock in remote parts of Finland and Yucca Mountain in the United States.

Applying economic subsidiarity is helpful in this case but the benefit is not immediately apparent. A conventional top-down analysis would be to identify a sparsely populated area with stable geology. No community is going to embrace willingly a radioactive waste storage facility but a nation which has decided to use nuclear power has to find a place to store the waste. Therefore, the decision is likely to be top-down. There will be the direct costs of designing and building a safe and secure depository which will survive for ten thousand years. There will of course be compensation to be paid to the local residents and investment to relocate people and/or improve local services and infrastructure to pacify local opposition. Let us consider allowing subsidiarity to frame this decision.

Economic subsidiarity means giving local communities control over decisions. In Finland, in order to decide where to site their nuclear waste repository each community under consideration as a repository location was consulted and promised veto power over the decision (Fountain 2017). It was up to local communities to make a balanced decision between the benefits of the jobs which the construction and operation of the nuclear waste repository would bring and the risks associated with hosting potentially dangerous material. It was the communities who had to be convinced that the plans were safe. The result is that the construction of the world's first permanent disposal site for commercial reactor fuel is progressing smoothly in the municipality of Eurajoki, on the west coast of Finland.

The UK has been less successful. This is a densely populated country with only a few places with the appropriate stable geology. There have been decades of studies and numerous proposals without agreement. The UK's radioactive waste stockpile continues to grow, stored safely for now and monitored in storage facilities adjacent to the power stations. The issue has been parked; the UK does not have a robust plan for nuclear waste to be stored safely and monitored ten thousand years into the future. There needs to be a dialogue with local authorities to decide who would be willing to provide a site. Engaging economic subsidiarity could lead to a solution – or not. If there are no local authorities in the UK who, despite the prospect of jobs and offers of government expenditure on local provision, are willing to host a site then that is an important conclusion. It would mean that for the UK to continue with nuclear power would mean the risk of maintaining above-ground stockpiles almost indefinitely. This would be an important factor to consider when planning the country's future energy generation capacity. A conventional approach leaves policy stuck in a stalemate where it is assumed safe storage can be built because there is an allocated budget, when the reality might be that it may never be built.

Finland's approach to its radioactive waste site is a good application of economic subsidiarity; although the Finns involved may not recognise the term. They would think that their approach is sensible and obvious. Using examples shows that economic subsidiarity is not novel or unusual but solid common sense. That is what we need from economics; a sensible policy frame with society central and bounded by the environment. The economy is a virtual construct which is only useful if it supports society and accepts environmental constraints. At each stage in planning economic policy and making investment decisions, we should not be blinkered by the economic arguments but see through to the true underlying facts.

The conventional economic analysis of nuclear power, in the context of concern about carbon dioxide emissions, leads to proposals to continue with expansion of the industry. Although people do not want nuclear power stations in their back yard, and particularly do not want radioactive waste, the government will find a way. The numbers add up so it must be possible. The government could, in theory, push through building a site against local wishes but few democratic governments would survive such a heavy-handed approach. Even so, the idea that it should be possible continues to allow nuclear generation to continue. Analysis through the lens of economic subsidiarity brings clarity, showing that the UK does not have a solution to radioactive waste and it looks unlikely that one will be found. If this means thinking again about policy for nuclear power, that would be the correct logical outcome rather than showing any weakness in the concept of economic subsidiarity.

Conclusions

Subsidiarity has a strong and solid heritage as a fundamental principle for the good management of human affairs. There is always the temptation for people with authority and power to break the principle. This could be because they know better (or believe they know better). It could be in order to exploit the situation for selfish reasons. There could be no malice involved but behaviour deriving from overbearing paternalism. The same is so for economic subsidiarity. It should be the fundamental principle of economic policy. There is the danger that people in authority may ignore it, because they know better or for selfish reasons. This is particularly the case at the international level with regard to those who champion the neoliberal economic agenda. There is suspicion that they further the interests of their home country rather than offering advice in the best interests of the country being 'helped'. More likely it is just an overbearing paternal view, based on Western cultural norms, which is offered with the best of intentions. It is argued here that policymaking needs to embrace economic subsidiarity with few exceptions. It does allow for economic policy decisions to be elevated to a higher level when there is compelling reason to do so. This might include when macro-economic stability is at risk or misguided economic policy is putting the commons (such as the atmosphere and oceans) under threat. In summary, the principle of economic subsidiarity means decisions taken at the most appropriate level for their successful resolution.

CHAPTER 7

PRINCIPLE 2: RESILIENT MARKETS

Resilient markets should operate at an appropriate scale, and be controlled to ensure desirable and sustainable outcomes.

Markets are important to delivering economically efficient outcomes, but over-reliance on markets can be problematic. It is important to strike an appropriate balance so that the market is free to operate but also subject to appropriate controls.

According to market theory, markets work best when they are open, free and transparent. The theory assumes participants make rational choices which align with their own best interests. It is also assumed that the ideal market would be perfectly competitive.[22] Such a perfect market can be expected to behave according to market theory, allowing predictions of how the market might react to any given situation.

No market is perfect, so a theory which assumes perfection can only ever be an approximation of markets in the real world. People do not behave as selfish rational machines but can make complex choices assimilating all sorts of inputs. This is what makes us human and allows society to navigate successfully into the future. It might be convenient to the economic analysis if markets were brought closer to perfection but is that really what we want or need? Neoclassical economists might argue

---

22 In a perfect market, it is assumed that prices are kept low by competitive pressure, the product traded is homogeneous, there is freedom of entry and exit, and perfect information is available to all participants.

that perfect markets are not only an analytical convenience but perfect competition is likely to produce the best outcomes for consumers, and society. This can be a dangerous belief if striving for economic perfection strips away the safeguards of established social and ethical norms undermining the ability of the market to serve society. Imperfection (in an economic sense) should be accepted as the reality of resilient markets.

The positive case for markets is that allowing market forces to play out can deliver efficient outcomes even in complex and difficult circumstances. The invisible hand (as Adam Smith described market forces) can find an accommodation between suppliers and customers through a myriad of micro decisions by the market participants. At the high level, it may not be possible to make accurate predictions of customer needs, or engage in capacity planning, but the market can find equilibrium. This almost magical power of the market can be hugely more effective than top-down planning, such as that attempted by the Soviet Union or China under Chairman Mao. Care is required not to be fooled by the magician and lose touch with reality in a confusion of smoke and mirrors. We cannot know precisely what is going on within the market, but we need confidence that the outcomes are likely to be beneficial to society. Markets are a useful tool if care is taken that they work in support of policy rather than bypass it.

When financial markets facilitate free flows of capital across borders, equity markets trade internationally, and bond markets deal with debt like any other global commodity; we need to know what the consequences could be, and have certainty that such trading results in benefit to society. The key insight, which is both obvious and easily forgotten when markets are booming, is that the markets are only as good as the rules and regulations which hold them to account. Without such controls, there is no certainty that markets will work as intended and provide net benefit to society.

In terms of managing markets, it is possible to imagine a market which is so transparent, and the ethos of market participants so honest, that light-touch regulations will suffice. At the other extreme, when the market is complex and opaque, and the participants are out to gain what they can by any means, there needs to be tight regulation and effective enforcement. In this chapter, the design of markets will be discussed together with focusing on three particular markets. These are markets which will see considerable change this century; markets for pollution, labour, and equity markets. First, let us review some old ideas about markets.

20th-Century Market Ideas

Through the second half of the 20th century there was strong support for market fundamentalism. The idea took hold that delegating control to the market could replace policy choices and planning activity by setting up a market; then leave it to the market. On the positive side, this provided short- and medium-term gains as freedom from regulations freed up capital, made markets more responsive and more liquid. It would only be a matter of time before these unfettered markets became dangerously out of control. The sub-prime mortgage market in the United States before 2008 is a good example of a complex and opaque market running out of policymakers' control. No one knew where the real risk resided – except perhaps the people who designed the complex financial instruments involved, but they adopted the approach of 'buyer beware'. They were complicit in allowing the impression to take hold that these were safe investments secured against property. We should learn from this experience that it is not sound policy to set up a market, set it free and wait to see what happens, hoping the outcome will be beneficial.

Another 20th-century idea is to construct false markets in the hope that the invisible hand can be brought into play to manage situations where there is no natural market. An example is the pseudo markets designed to support privatization of public utilities such as water and electricity. These are natural monopolies of course. A house has one electricity supply and one water supply. What policymakers have attempted to do is to construct a market by separating generation from supply networks and allowing a number of companies to operate as retail sellers. A regulator is appointed to represent the public interest. This false market sets up a situation where companies push against the regulator to maximize their profits. When the false market replaces a publicity-owned (and perhaps inefficient) utility, in the early years the commercial companies will drive profits from efficiency savings. When these have been harvested, the pressure increases to raise prices. This new situation has a huge amount of bureaucratic waste to run the complex market system. Initially, the false market gives the impression of improvement, but over the longer-term the inefficiency which often comes with public ownership is replaced by commercial gaming. The outcome for consumers could be so much better through accepting the monopoly and taking measures to ensure efficient management. Later in this chapter in discussing equity markets, I will explore how embracing different ownership models, which work directly to deliver value to society, could be a better way forward than privatization within a false market.

The 20th century has bequeathed us a legacy of excessive expectation of the power of markets. The idea took root that it is good economic policy to set up a market, and then leave it to the market. In the 21st century, we should backtrack away from free-market economics and instead work with the notion that real markets should be transparent, well-defined, well-regulated and tightly controlled to support the aims and objectives of society.

Design of Markets

A well-designed market should find a natural equilibrium delivering better outcomes than top-down planning, remembering that markets do not automatically deliver favourable outcomes. They need to be well-designed with a clear purpose and a defined extent. Once established, markets are free in so much as participants are free to make their choice, as that is how the market works. To ensure this freedom is used well, there needs to be total clarity about the market mechanisms, market rules, and the reach of the market. Without such safeguards, the positive attributes of markets can soon be lost.

THE PURPOSE OF THE MARKET

The first stage in designing a market, or examining an existing market, is to define the purpose of the market. What is to be traded; between which parties, and why. It should be remembered that markets exist to benefit participants not for the benefit of those who manage the market. The market managers are functionaries charged with making the market work. If a market becomes principally a vehicle for speculation, and a means of generating fees for the market makers, it has lost touch with its core purpose and is of little real value to society.

A prime example of a market which seems to have lost touch with its core purpose is the world's money markets. People and organizations need to be able to trade currencies in order to pay for international trade and other international transactions. The purpose is to connect one person's need for currency with another market participant who has currency to sell. Exchange rates should adjust according to supply and demand (except where governments decide to peg the value of their currency). In addition to these transactions for real users, there are traders looking for imbalances and trying to make money from predicting currency movements. The positive role of such activity is to provide liquidity and help the market to adjust. However, speculative flows in the world's money markets are now an order of magnitude greater than the real transactions. The world's money markets have become gambling dens. Real currency trades still flow through the market but the market looks like a moneymaking game out of touch with its core purpose (this issue will be covered in greater detail in the examination of money in Chapter 9).

THE EXTENT OF THE MARKET

The other important design parameter, in addition to purpose, is the extent of the market. For example, a market could be local, national, or international. The extent might be intrinsic to the purpose of the market following the logic of common sense; or the extent defined by those who manage the market. For example, markets for fresh food would tend to be local, and markets for commodities such as metals tend to be global. The food market can be international, if we so choose, using refrigerated transport to make it feasible. We could also decide that metal markets should be local in order to implement emerging concepts such as circular resource flows and cradle-to-cradle manufacturing. These are choices to make. The extent of the market should be defined according to clear reasoning.

A potentially dangerous perspective on markets is the view that the bigger the better. Market fundamentalists might seek to connect markets on their understanding that this is good in principle. In the grounded economic analysis championed in this book, markets should only be connected or enlarged for a reason which is clearly defined and easily understood. If the purpose of the market is best served by being local; keep it local. If the purpose of the market is best served by being national; keep it national. If the purpose of the market is best served by being global; make it global.

The extent is not a fixed parameter of the market but can evolve as circumstances change. For example, as the environmental impacts of global markets are better understood there are reasons to draw back to greater reliance on national and local markets. There might be trade-offs between raw economic efficiency and sound environmental policy. It is correct that such dilemmas enter the policy debate, and should not be filtered out by those who regard market efficiency as supreme.

CONTROL OF THE MARKET

Having defined the purpose of the market, and decided on an appropriate extent, there are details to work out. First, who is responsible for managing the market? Second, how will it operate? Third, are there ways the market can be gamed which will require safeguards against market abuse? This connects closely with the prime requirement of a successful market, which is trust. Where the market participants largely trust each other, and those who manage the market are trusted, the formal regulation can be minimal. Self-regulating markets are ideal, but only where participants demonstrate they can be trusted.

Often the market will be dominated by certain players who have the power to control how the market operates. It is in their long-term interests to consider all stakeholders and act responsibly, as participants have the choice to leave one market and set up or join another. Where a market is national, the government will of course be watching to make sure that the market is serving its purpose, and be on the lookout for abuse. Where a market is global, and therefore outside national oversight, regulation will always be problematic meaning global markets should be approached with caution.

Scale

The scale of a market is important. There is no ideal scale – only a scale which is appropriate to the purpose of the market. In general terms a market of large scale, with wide extent and many participants, will be more efficient in terms of economic outcomes. A wide potential customer base is good for suppliers, and having many sources of supply is good for buyers. Manufacturing or production will concentrate where costs are least, and products or resources flow to people and organizations most able to pay. Big markets therefore tend to be efficient. On the other hand, a market of small scale, limited extent, and with participants who know each other, can be closely entwined with community and society. A balance needs to be struck between efficiency and serving society. Let us consider one example to illustrate the dilemma, using a market familiar to everyone, milk.

Milk can be produced almost anywhere where cows can be kept and grazed or fed. In a local milk market, local farms supply local communities. A stable balance will emerge of a number of dairy farms to match the demand from the community. If demand increases, the price of milk increases. The existing farms might increase the size of their herds. Over the longer term if the price remains high it might attract other farmers to move into dairy farming. Demand for milk tends not to fluctuate greatly and dairy farms cannot be started or closed quickly. It can be envisaged that such a local milk market would tend to be stable and predictable. Such a market would have the natural oversight which is an attribute of local markets where any farmer operating dubious practices is likely to be found out. A perceived problem with a localized milk market is that milk may not be as cheap as it could be if the market were enlarged.

Milk could be cheaper if the market is allowed to operate at national scale. Milk production would tend to concentrate in places where the climate is most suitable for dairy farming. It would also support much larger farms bringing economies of scale. National supermarket chains will be able to negotiate prices and drive less efficient dairy farmers out of the industry. This more efficient market gives the consumer cheaper milk and ensures the milk industry is lean and efficient.

It is for society to decide the balance between a local market, where people know who produces their milk, and a national market which can deliver cheaper prices. In making this decision the increased need for transportation might be a factor. The direct cost of transportation will be factored into the market but additional effects on road congestion and air pollution may not. It would be sensible to examine all the relevant factors when deciding the scale of the milk market which would be most suitable. This example shows that deciding the appropriate scale of a market has more to it than a simple conventional economic analysis.

Continuing with the milk example, the market could be made international (as it is within the EU). Such a market allows countries or regions to dominate supply if they have an advantage. This might be a climate which supports grazing outdoors on fresh grass throughout much of the year. It could also be lax regulations so that farmers' costs are lower. Such international milk markets are dominated by supermarket chains with an international footprint driving prices yet lower. In Europe there are juggernauts crisscrossing the continent bringing German yoghurt to the UK and British dairy products to Germany. This is how brands compete in open international markets and we think nothing of it.

A particular problem arose in 2014, when Russia banned dairy imports from the EU in response to EU sanctions applied to Russia for its actions in Ukraine. This was a crisis for the EU milk market with reports that prices paid to farmers dropped by 25% over the following year (Stevens 2015). Allowing the milk market to operate internationally, made it vulnerable to circumstances outside national control. Again, as a society we need to decide whether we want an international market for milk based on raw efficiency or a stable and sustainable market under national or local control.

I present this discussion of the milk market because it illustrates the dilemma between the attractions of economic efficiencies which come with large scale compared with the connection with society which is an attribute of smaller scale markets. In the words I have used, I have not hidden my personal preference for reducing the scale of the milk market. I would prefer to rely on a stable local market where farmers are treated fairly and customers can trust the quality of the milk. That is a preference, rather than a watertight argument. Economists also have to accept that their analysis of the most economically efficient market is not a watertight solution but a contribution to the analysis. It might be entirely sensible to choose a less efficient market (defined by the narrow parameter of price to the consumer) in favour of confidence in quality, reduction in transportation requirements, greater stability, and fair treatment for farmers. The cost to consumers of safe and sustainable milk supplies could be a small percentage increase on a relatively cheap food item. I would argue that it is a price worth paying. The point of this example is that the analysis should be done completely and properly instead of leaping to the conclusion that the most economic and efficient outcome is the best solution.

In reality, a stable local milk supply system might have similar end-consumer prices, as local shops negotiate long-term agreements with local farmers without the national supermarket chains acting as middle men and taking their cut. It is for officials on behalf of society to decide what sort of milk supply system is wanted and design the market accordingly.

Markets for Pollution

A particular type of market is the special case of markets designed to reduce pollution. There is growing interest in such markets, and much is expected of them, but it is not certain that they can deliver. The concept is that markets can be more cost-effective in controlling pollution than specific regulation. Again, setting up the market is not sufficient; it has to have a clearly defined purpose and extent, together with robust mechanisms in order to deliver the desired outcome.

A SUCCESSFUL POLLUTION MARKET – US SULPHUR DIOXIDE EMISSION REDUCTIONS

A widely used example of effective pollution reduction using a market mechanism is sulphur dioxide emission reductions in the United States from 1990. The US Environmental Protection Agency's (EPA) Acid Rain Program was an initiative to reduce overall atmospheric levels of sulphur dioxide targeting coal-burning power plants. The market allowed these plants to buy and sell sulphur dioxide emission permits. Statistics show that sulphur dioxide emissions dropped by 40%, reaching the programme's long-term goal ahead of the 2010 statutory deadline. The purpose of the market was to steer investment in sulphur dioxide reduction measures and to hit targets set by government, at the least cost to the industry. The EPA estimates that using the market mechanism reduced the cost of complying from $1–2 billion a year, to a quarter of what was originally predicted (Schmalensee and Stavins 2017). The extent of the market was mainland United States therefore under tight national control. This was a well-defined market which worked well to support the flow of investment in the short-term to where it would deliver most pollution reduction.

WHERE REGULATION HAS BEEN MORE EFFECTIVE – THE OZONE HOLE

An example where regulation achieved a better outcome than using a market is the way the world dealt with the problem of the hole in the ozone layer identified by the British Antarctic Survey (BAS) in 1985. The scientists acted quickly to explain the urgency, and the politicians responded just two years later with the Montreal Protocol (1987). This international treaty controls the production and use of CFCs and other ozone-depleting chemicals.

The agreement amongst nations to ban the offending chemicals over a relatively short time frame showed decisive effective action. The BAS reports:

> *We are now seeing a slow recovery of the ozone layer over Antarctica. Nevertheless, the original compounds are so stable and long-lived that an ozone hole will exist each Antarctic spring for at least another 50 years.*

> BAS 2020

This is a crisis averted but it was a close call. Dealing with the problem of ozone-depleting chemicals focused on regulations to solve the problem without being distracted by attempting to establish a market.

WHERE MARKET INTENTIONS FAIL – CARBON DIOXIDE EMISSIONS

An example where a market is inappropriate, is the ongoing discussion about establishing markets for carbon dioxide emissions. Carbon dioxide is not a pollutant, but a normal component of the ecosystem so it is not surprising that pollution markets are not the model to follow. Even so, policymakers have explored whether a market could help.

The problem with carbon markets is a lack of clarity about the purpose, and confusion about defining the extent, thus failing fundamental market design criteria. They can have a useful role but only if there is clear purpose and defined extent. Hazy thinking is less than helpful as it can give the impression that action to deal with CO_2 emissions is in hand, when plainly it is not.

I was in discussion with a leading economist at an international conference in the mid noughties about carbon markets. The context of the conference, which set the frame for our discussion, was how to respond to climate change. Carbon markets came up as one part of the solution. I found it interesting that in the mind of this economist, all that was required was to set up the market and the market would deliver. This was the first time I had been on the receiving end of the market-fundamentalist approach. In the discussion, I pursued the line of investigation of how to make the market work to deliver long-term reductions in CO_2 emissions so as not to exceed the safe limit defined by climate scientists. This seemed of no concern to this economist, not because they were unconcerned about climate change, but because they believed the existence of the market was sufficient and the economic policy did not need to go into further details.

This economist wanted to discuss how the carbon market would operate and how the UK in general, and the City of London in particular, might benefit from the trade. I probed deeper and found that there was a deep and well-intentioned wish to deal with climate change and an unshakeable belief that the existence of the market would do the job. I struggled to get this person to shift ground and embrace a discussion about achieving the long-term environmental objective. To the economist, this was not part of the economics of the market; environmental policy would have to deal with that.

To see up close how market fundamentalism can divert analysis into a cul-de-sac was useful. My discussion was with an intelligent, highly qualified and respected economist doing what they do best, dealing with economics without fully factoring in the real-world context. It was actually enormously helpful because it taught me not to expect too much from the current generation of economists and not to trust statements from economists at face value.

Carbon dioxide will come under the spotlight again in Chapter 17 when examining energy. For now, we can note that market mechanisms will be of limited value to effective action to address global CO_2 emissions.

Markets for Labour

The economics of labour markets is the foundation of personal livelihoods so it is important that it works well. A challenge we will face in the not-too-distant future is how to retain the relevance of employment in the age of robotics and automation. It is becoming possible to automate more and more jobs as the technology of automation becomes increasingly affordable. It is not just the simplest jobs, such as shop check-out operators, which are at risk, but even professional management jobs are under threat as developments in artificial intelligence (AI) gather pace. An example is language translation services. This used to be secure professional employment but the work of translators has been transformed by the Internet. Customers wanting translation services can choose between a range of options including free automated services or human translators based anywhere in the world. This competitive market is tough with downward pressure on fees and the competition is no longer just between people but also includes robots.

The automation challenge will not be solved by the economist's rule of thumb to increase consumption to boost jobs. When factories and work places are staffed by robots, increasing consumption will lead to more robots, not more jobs. We could end up with a dysfunctional society of a few well-paid managers managing the robots, and a huge underclass of unemployed living on welfare handouts. To prevent this, we will have to design the way the economy works to require the active engagement of humans. We can expect government to offer incentives to employ people and for innovative ways of working to evolve. Through my career, I have examined many business cases for capital investment in automation based on eliminating head count. As I look forward, I can see that it will become a valid exercise to reverse the analysis, by working out how to employ more people to take advantage of government incentives and avoid capital investment. This might seem odd now, but I suggest such analysis will become a normal aspect of human resource management.

The new world of work will be different, and how the economic model is crafted will determine whether this will be divisive and corrosive for society, or a renaissance in drawing people into new ways of working with only the most mundane and dirty jobs given to robots. There are choices to be made, not driven by the simple economics of eliminating expensive workers with automation wherever possible, but a much more nuanced process of embedding the corporation into the fabric of society, through cultivating a workforce supported by automation. Quite how this evolves is hard to predict but careful application of the tools of economics can ensure that people remain central to the corporation with robots their servants – provided we get buy-in for this vision of the future of work.

This brief discussion of labour markets has outlined the looming challenge of automation. Further informed discussion is required about what people need from employment and what society needs from the work force. When that has been decided we can think about economic policy which can deliver such aspirations. How the situation can be improved using the concepts of resilient economics will become clear when the policy of universal basic income is factored in (Chapter 11).

Equity Markets

The total value of the world's equity markets amounted to $60 trillion in 2019, down from an apparent value of $100 trillion just four years before in 2015.[23] This illustrates the extreme volatility and uncertainty of stock prices. A large proportion of pension funds and other long-term savings are invested here. How they operate is important to the resilience of the economic system.

The equity markets trade shares in businesses ranging from global corporations down to small aspiring firms and everything between. The emergence of equity markets can be traced back to the 17th century. International trade was a risky business, requiring the financing of a ship and its crew to sail off to far flung corners of the globe. If it came back safe with exotic and valuable cargo there was a good profit to be made. Merchants would put up the money required, taking a share in the venture. When the

---

23   https://data.worldbank.org/indicator/CM.MKT.TRAD.CD [accessed 25 May 2021].

ship returned (if the ship returned) the cargo would be sold and the money paid out to those who had financed the venture. The idea of a limited liability corporation to operate such trade came about with joint stock charters awarded by the crown to monopolies such as the East India Company. There was some concern at the time that the protection for the business through limited liability could cause a drop in standards of probity. There is now total acceptance of limited liability companies, owned by shareholders, as the prime agent for business activity.

A simple example of a company owned by shareholders is a toll bridge which still operates close to where I live in Southern England. It was built in 1792 by a group of investors who put up the capital required with the payback being the income from charging a toll. The toll is authorised by an Act of Parliament (the Whitchurch Bridge Act 1792 and 1988). The bridge structure was renewed in 1852, 1902 and 2014. The original toll was a half-penny each for pedestrians, sheep, boars and pigs, and two pence for each wheel of a carriage. In 2021 it is £0.60 for cars and £4.00 for vehicles weighing over 3.5 tonnes. The bridge is still owned by The Company of Proprietors of Whitchurch Bridge. In this case shareholding was about building a major capital addition to the public infrastructure through private finance providing a secure and steady return to shareholders. It is clear to see the purpose of the company, why a shareholding is appropriate, and the logic of how it operates.

Jumping forward to modern equity markets, it has become a grand game. The game continues to have real-world consequences but close links to society are being eroded. When corporations are judged primarily on their ability to generate money, it can be forgotten that within the business there are real activities, with real consequences, which can be beneficial to society, or not. The equity market is the prime mechanism by which corporations are owned, so it would be beneficial to bring it under greater over-sight by society.

THE PURPOSE OF EQUITY MARKETS

Let us start this examination of equity markets with considering what purpose they serve. Three objectives are considered here starting with the evident purpose to enable businesses to raise the capital they need to operate. Equity markets also provide a home for long-term savings such as pension funds and sovereign wealth funds. These two functions are the primary purposes and are complementary. Investors need a home for their savings and business needs capital. I argue that there is, or should be, a third purpose, one which might seem odd from a conventional economic viewpoint. I suggest that there should be an expectation placed on equity markets, that the market should work in such a way that it facilitates companies delivering benefits back to society. This is not currently the case, but improvements are discussed below which could deliver on this aspiration.

Let us consider the three purposes, starting with raising cap-ital for businesses. Although this was the original purpose of equity markets, modern businesses raise a lot of their capital as loans from banks so this purpose is not as significant as might be supposed. Second, as a home for long-term savings, equities per-form better than bank deposits because companies put the funds to work. This means that a large proportion of long-term invest-ments are funnelled into equities. Money flows in, and shares increase in value in a positive feedback loop of good returns reinforcing the strategy of holding equities. The third objective is to facilitate companies delivering benefits back to society. In a sense they do, because failure to do so would put their license to operate at risk and dent their reputation in the eyes of custom-ers, which could be detrimental to the bottom line. However, the way equity markets are structured means that the delivery of benefit to society is not a direct requirement (I will return to this when considering possible improvements).

THE EXTENT OF EQUITY MARKETS

Next, let us consider the extent of equity markets. In theory there could be local equity markets but in general equity markets are national, operated under regulations overseen by government.

Multinational corporations can have their shares traded widely by being listed on more than one stock exchange. The freeing up of international capital flows since the 1990s allowed investors to switch between markets to chase the best returns. Listed companies are for sale to whoever purchases the shares. Unless there are special safeguards to keep a company national, they can be bought and sold across the world.

Governments might have supported national champions with grants, aid and training support to help the business flourish, but listed businesses are not owned by government; ownership is brokered through the market. Any investor, from China or elsewhere, can buy a listed company.

PROBLEMS WITH EQUITY MARKETS

One problem with equity markets is the tendency towards short-termism. As investors decide which shares to buy (or hold) and which to sell, they try to maximize their financial return. Investors will grill the management on their immediate plans and examine closely the quarterly results. Active investors shift ownership often, looking for shares on a growth trajectory and selling shares which seem to have stalled. Such market behaviour can be detrimental to the steady long-term management of corporations.

The more fundamental problem with equity markets, much more difficult to fix, is the focus they have on shareholder value.

My colleagues in the business school would castigate me for suggesting that focusing on shareholder value is anything other than good management. For decades business schools have placed a strong emphasis on the primary role of executives to deliver value to shareholders. This is seldom questioned and has a strong influence on corporate behaviour. We find again the virtual world of finance being cut adrift from the real world. To have real value for society, equity markets should be anchored as servants of society, facilitating corporations to serve all stakeholders.

The equity markets are the mechanism by which we (everyone in society) own a large proportion of corporations and businesses. This ownership is indirect, using the cash in our pension funds. The managers of these pension funds decide where to invest on our behalf. We expect them to deliver a good financial return. They, in turn, expect the executives of the companies in which they invest to run the company to deliver shareholder value. We have ended up with a system where shareholder value is how we manage our ownership of the corporate world. We may hope the corporations deliver benefit to all stakeholders and to society (and there is growing interest in ethical pension funds), but the system is skewed heavily towards a blinkered focus on financial return. For something as important as equity markets this is a mighty limitation on their usefulness. We accept this because we do not know how it could be done better.

IMPROVEMENTS TO EQUITY MARKETS

One problem with equity markets is short-termism. There is a fairly straightforward measure which can be taken to improve this, although resistance to it is likely to be strong. All that is required is a tax on share transactions (McManners 2008: 178–9). If an investor pays a significant fee to change ownership (say 2–5%) it would suit the investor to hold a share for longer and trade less often. The questions investors could ask executives would be more about long-term plans rather than how the next quarterly figures look. This is much more conducive to sound management of the firm in the long term.

The problem with share transfer taxes is that they do not suit those who manage the equity markets. Changing ownership generates fees from each transaction. A market of relatively stable ownership may support long-term investment, but will reduce the income of those who manage the market. Opposition to share transfer tax is a clear case of those who manage the markets looking after their own interests. Through the 20th century, governments were persuaded to reduce or remove share transaction taxes to free up the markets. In the 21st century we need to rediscover the value of a share transaction tax to reduce volatility and bring greater stability.

AN ALTERNATIVE TO EQUITY MARKETS

The fundamental problem of equity markets is the narrow focus on shareholder value. The way this distorts business performance and the allocation of capital is only now being understood as a problem. Changes are needed to switch the focus of investment in business to be more suited to 21st-century challenges. This requires lateral thinking and new ideas. Taxing share transactions would tweak the current system to at least support a longer-term horizon, but more is needed. To support open lateral thinking let us consider again the purpose of equity markets. I suggested earlier these were threefold: raise capital for business; provide a home for long-term savings; and deliver value to society. What sort of market could deliver this nexus of expectations?

Let us start with the third objective – delivering value to society – about which current equity markets are weak. I do not want to be too harsh on listed corporations, as they do deliver value back to society, but this is almost incidental to the current system rather than a required objective. There are a number of ownership models for business which work directly to deliver value to society. I shall describe these as Society Embedded Enterprises (SEEs). Examples are mutual companies, cooperatives, Community Interest Companies (CIC), and the US equivalent structure of benefit corporations. An alternative to such huge reliance on equity markets would be to shift the focus of big investors such as pension funds to support many more SEEs and encourage the formation of more types of SEE. At the time of writing, this might seem like a bold proposal (which will be resisted by those who benefit from trading equities) but it illustrates that the current limitations of equity markets can be overcome.

Within the proposed changed corporate landscape with far more SEEs, let us consider the primary purposes of equity markets to raise capital and to provide a home for long-term savings. How can SSEs supplant corporations? This appears to be problematic in that most types of SEE do not generally release ownership to external investors. Let us consider that instead of selling shares such companies issue fixed interest bonds. The rate of interest would reflect the perceived risk inherent in the business. A stable and predictable business could sell bonds with a low interest rate, and an ambitious but risky business would offer higher interest rates. It may not seem likely now, but it is possible to envisage a wholesale shift in investment such that SSE ownership models become the preferred corporate vehicle across the whole breath of the economy, from high tech and advanced engineering, to energy, transport, manufacturing, construction, and services. The SEE gets the capital it needs and the investor holds bonds rather than an equity share. This is a much less volatile investment market but some investors would be unhappy that there would be less scope for rapid high returns. I suggest that such a market could serve the overall needs of society much better, not just because of financial stability but because of the way SEEs would be able to operate to broader aims than bottom-line results.

For a snapshot of how a corporate landscape might change with more SEEs, let us consider the UK retail business John Lewis and how it survived the COVID-19 pandemic crisis (see Box 7.1).

Box 7.1 John Lewis during the COVID-19 pandemic

John Lewis is a UK-based SEE owned by its staff. It was established by the far-sighted John Spedan Lewis who in 1929 relinquished ownership to place the business into a trust for the benefit of the Partners (all employees). During 2020–21, the retail high street was decimated by the shift to online shopping, which was accelerated by the pandemic. This kept physical shops closed for long periods, putting retailers under enormous financial pressure and leading to a wave of bankruptcies. This included John Lewis's main competitor Debenhams. Other casualties included Philip Green's Arcadia retail empire including Topshop, Topman, Miss Selfridge, Burton, Dorothy Perkins and Wallis. As Philip Green built his retail portfolio, he extracted over £1 billion in dividends in 2005 saddling the group with huge debts. This left the group exposed to a downturn. John Lewis had not been subject to such pressure to strip out cash for its shareholders, a benefit of its ownership structure. That did not make it immune to financial stress. It would have to navigate the crisis and remain solvent. The amount it could borrow from the banks would be limited by the assets available for collateral. It would not have the option of raising cash in the way listed corporations can by tapping the equity market with a discounted share offering. In good times these might be seen as limitations, but in a time of crisis John Lewis has been a beacon of stability. Its ownership structure has required a prudent and resilient financial model, the benefits of which were highlighted by the crisis.

In a model of business finance more reliant on bonds than equity, SSEs such as John Lewis could issue bonds instead of tapping shareholders. These could be offered to investors and discounted for staff to be able to buy into the security of their employment and share in the collective success. A corporate world dominated by SEEs would have less scope for quick financial returns and less opportunity for the sort of financial engineering which brought down Philip Green's Arcadia group. Such an upheaval in the corporate landscape would require investors to be persuaded of the benefits of stability and long-term steady returns.

If the balance of business ownership is skewed more towards SEE, let us consider what this would mean for pension funds needing a home for long-term savings. These large influential investors could shift focus to buying a portfolio of SEE bonds. People who like to manage their investments directly could select which bonds to buy and let their choice steer towards businesses that relate to their interests and needs. In such a 21st-century corporate model, many people would work for a SEE and/or be a customer of a SEE. If this idea were to take root it would become normal for people to expect their pension pot to be invested in SEE bonds and for pension managers to look very closely at how well the SEEs are managed as they monitor the portfolios they manage.

A FUTURE FOR INVESTMENT MARKETS

In this chapter I wanted to convey a way of thinking about markets which breaks out of the market-knows-best mindset to a mindset of thinking carefully about what we want the market to achieve. The particular idea, to reduce the scale of equity markets in favour of a market for SEE bonds, will be seen as radical and perhaps controversial. To recommend such a shift away from conventional equity markets, would require considerable further analysis and careful thought. Rather than claiming to have *the* solution, this shows how adopting the new mindset can challenge the status quo. Let us go a little bit further and sketch some thoughts on this proposal for investment markets. At this early stage, it is necessarily incomplete.

Pension funds need stable long-term investments. Shifting focus to SSE bonds could serve their needs rather well. Business would be freed from pressures to continually grow profits and drive down costs. Well-run SEEs could build up reserves in good times to help them weather downturns without pressure to return cash to shareholders. Critics could complain that without the tough discipline of the equity markets such businesses could become lazy and inefficient. One person's view of failure to sweat the assets could be another person's example of stable and careful stewardship. It is a judgement call. Management would continue to be expected to do a good job and there would be no excuse for incompetence or waste. This is where business schools can have an important future role. The universal qualification for senior management is the MBA. Currently the MBA curriculum is skewed heavily towards promoting management practices with the primary objective of increasing shareholder value. The MBA could return to the original intentions of the qualification to train people to be 'pillars of the state, whether in private or in public life'.[24] Such noble intentions are betrayed when managers are trained to manage businesses to operate like cash machines.

For this tentative new model to take hold it would need to be possible to transfer a listed corporation into a SEE. In the current prevailing mindset, it would be very odd for a corporation to seek such a change of ownership, but it would be feasible. The corporation could propose to its shareholders that it would sell

---

24 According to founding principles of one of the oldest business schools, the Wharton School of the University of Pennsylvania, established in 1881, founded initially as the Wharton School of Finance and Economy.

sufficient bonds to buy the company. Existing shareholders could be given the choice of bonds or cash. This would only work when substantial funds are steered towards SEE bonds. This altered market would not be attractive to speculators or those out to make a quick buck. That is of course a positive attribute rather than a weakness.

I accept that my proposal for changing the nature of investment markets is too radical for the current state of investment norms. Whether my proposal stands up to further analysis depends on how discussion unfolds. I have taken the risk of presenting such a radical proposal to replace the current dominance of equity markets because it exposes a whole new way to approach investment. Whether this particular outcome ensues, it outlines the thought process to demonstrate the value of challenging current economic thinking and testing new ideas.

Conclusions

The invisible hand of market forces can be useful in the efficient implementation of policy, but markets do not automatically deliver desirable outcomes. Markets have to be designed with care and regulated accordingly. Where a market is small, the procedures are transparent, and participants behave honestly, regulations can be minimal. At the other end of the spectrum, large markets with opaque procedures, where gaming is the normal behaviour, should be treated with caution and regulation needs to be tight. Between these two extremes, markets of appropriate scale, with transparent procedures, and participants using the market for the purpose intended, sensible light-touch regulation should suffice.

The market is capable of basic tasks, but it needs clever, well-crafted policy to provide a framework for how it operates. Instead of putting the market first, it should be put last. Economic efficiency should be our servant, not our master. We should dictate the outcomes using the market to aid delivery. Conventional economic thinking encourages a market-first mindset leading people away from complex and nuanced analysis to an unsophisticated and blinkered approach. This can appear to work in the short-term but ends up eventually failing unless proper control is exerted from the outset. By the time a market has failed, the damage has been done. The challenge for policymakers is to bring markets to account before they fail, before the problems become hard to fix, and perhaps even before the market is allowed to begin operating.

CHAPTER 8

PRINCIPLE 3: RESILIENT TRADE

The economics of resilient trade
are framed by sustainability
and security of supply.

The theory of free trade underpins present-day macroeconomic policy. The challenges the world will face in the decades ahead means that this central plank of conventional economics will have to be abandoned. Resilient economics replaces 'free trade' with the principle of 'resilient trade'. The former is based on pure economic efficiency; the latter is based on sustainability and security of supply. This chapter presents a set of trade rules to flesh out what resilient trade means in practice. This approach to trade will need debating and adjusting as it is adopted to ensure it is effective. By outlining specific proposals, I provide the debate with substance. I do not claim to have nailed precisely the rules of resilient trade, so aspects outlined below may need adjusting as the concept is tested and the ramifications are accepted.

The essence of trade is to keep society supplied with sufficient resources. The safest and most secure resources are those available locally but when this is insufficient, we rely on trade. Some trade is frivolous such as out-of-season asparagus flown into the UK from Peru. This is stuff we don't need, but we have become accustomed to supermarkets stocked with a wide range of foods and all manner of things, regardless of seasonality or local circumstances. Amongst this tsunami of desirable but often unnecessary stuff, there are real needs to satisfy to enable people to live secure, healthy and sustainable lives. There are people who cannot feed themselves from their own means; or they can, but not throughout the seasons. There are countries which have few commodities or raw materials and need to import them. There are other countries with ample labour but without the wherewithal to make high technology products. We can agree that trade is vital, but not all trade is sensible and sustainable. Prising apart the case for trade, and examining the economics of trade, produces interesting insights into the future for trade.

Current thinking about the economics of trade is dominated by the perceived benefits of free trade. This has a long heritage in trade economics, based on a robust and logical argument, but long-term consequences are starting to become apparent. This includes environmental overload and resource depletion (Heydon 2019). This is another example where the real-world consequences of particular economic policy have become less desirable, meaning the policy needs to be reviewed. Going forward, the world needs a resilient model for trade which allows society to be sustainable in the decades ahead.

In this chapter, there will be extensive discussion and analysis of free trade. This is necessary to understand why free trade has had such a stranglehold on policy, before confining it to the dustbin of obsolete ideas. This leads to setting a new direction which is better suited to current challenges. To many people this will be a radical change, but all I have done is to capture a common-sense approach. The resilient rules of trade are based on society's needs and are designed to help steer the world economy back onto a sustainable path. First, let us consider why free trade has been such an attractive policy.

Free Trade

An enduring mantra used by politicians and policymakers is that free trade is good for the economy. Free-trade agreements are seen as a prize to seek. In this section, I will consider the case for free trade and examine whether it should continue to be regarded as the cure for our economic woes. It should be noted that whether it is concluded that free trade is good or bad in principle, in reality all trade agreements are the result of political negotiations. The politicians involved ensure they get the best deal they can. The more powerful the country they represent, the stronger the negotiator's hand. So, when the United States strikes a trade deal you can be sure that it is in America's interests. The same applies to China and the EU; these are powerful trading entities and the negotiators will protect Chinese or European interests, respectively. Small and poor countries get the trade deal the powerful countries will allow them to have. They are reliant on fair and equitable behaviour by the countries which hold the power. This might work well where there is good will, such as a trade deal with an ex-colony which allows preferential market access into the economy of the old colonial power. In other cases, poor countries can be exploited with trade deals presented as free trade but designed by powerful countries to suit their ends.

In general, trade negotiators hold an economic brief and altruistic behaviour should not be expected. It can be argued that if the political wrangling could be put aside, and impartial free trade deals were put in place, all countries would benefit. The widely accepted argument is that despite negative consequences for some industries and some people, overall free trade is beneficial. Let us start with examining the core theoretical argument in favour of free trade.

The line of economic thinking which leads to favouring free trade starts with the father of economics, Adam Smith, who wrote:

> *If a foreign country can supply us with a commodity cheaper than we ourselves can make it, better buy it of them with some part of the produce of our own industry employed in a way in which we have some advantage.*

The Wealth of Nations, 1776: Book IV, Section ii, 12

This seems entirely sensible. Countries should specialize and export goods that they are skilled at making or commodities with which they are well endowed, and import goods and commodities from other countries in exchange.

David Ricardo took the idea further to develop the theory of comparative advantage (Ricardo 1817). He argued that it was not necessary to have an absolute advantage to make trade worthwhile provided there is a comparative advantage. A country which is better and more efficient at making everything should trade freely with another country which is less efficient at making everything; provided each country is comparatively better at making one product compared to another. The theory of comparative advantage says that both countries will be better off as a result of such free trade. When first encountered this is counterintuitive, but the argument holds up as demonstrated by David Ricardo in his original hypothetical example of trading cloth and wine between England and Portugal (see Box 8.1).

Box 8.1 Ricardo's example of comparative advantage

David Ricardo explained the principle of comparative advantage with a hypothetical comparison between England and Portugal over the production and consumption of cloth and wine, where the parameters are:

Hours of work required to produce one unit of cloth:

England – 100   Portugal – 90

Hours of work required to produce one unit of wine:

England – 120   Portugal – 80

The figures he used show that Portugal has an absolute advantage in both the production of wine and the production of cloth. In England, 220 hours of work are required to produce 1 unit each of cloth and wine. In Portugal, 170 hours of work are required to produce the same quantities. However, England is comparatively more efficient at producing cloth than wine; and Portugal is comparatively more efficient at producing wine than cloth. So, if the countries specialize in the good for which they each have a comparative advantage, and trade for the other good, then the total production of both goods increases.

Without trade, for 220 hours of work England can produce and consume 1 unit of cloth and 1 unit of wine. For the same amount of work, Portugal can produce and consume 1 unit of cloth and 130/80 (1.625) units of wine. With trade, England could apply 220 hours solely to making cloth producing 220/100 (2.2) units of cloth. Portugal could apply 220 hours solely to making wine producing 220/80 (2.75) units of wine.

In this example, without trade, both countries can produce and consume altogether 2 units of cloth and 2.625 units of wine. With trade, both countries can produce and consume altogether 2.2 units of cloth and 2.75 units of wine. Production is greater by 0.2 units of cloth and 0.125 units of wine. Exactly who reaps the benefit will depend on the prices agreed when making the trade, but the example shows that there is a net benefit by freely trading despite the fact that Portugal has an absolute advantage in both cloth and wine.

David Ricardo's explanation of the theory may be dated, but it is hard to better. I reuse his example for two reasons. First, if you are an economist, you will already be familiar with Ricardo's example so are likely to have jumped past the box without reading it. If you are not an economist you can see for yourself the evidence which has influenced economic theory of trade for the last 200 years.

Comparative advantage is the fundamental theoretical basis of free trade. If you are a trained economist this is something that will have been drummed into you and will have entered your DNA. I shall tread carefully through the minefield of the theory of comparative advantage, respecting the theory because on one level it is sound. This is an example of robust economic theory which stands up to mathematical scrutiny, but following the maths can get you caught in a virtual trap. The economic theory of comparative advantage is mathematically correct; the question is whether it is useful.

David Ricardo's maths continues to add up, but it is worth examining the model of comparative advantage in more detail. This is the most important concept in trade economics and hugely influential so we need to understand why. As with all economic models, it is based on a set of assumptions:

+ The goods or commodities produced are of identical standard;

+ There is full employment in each country;

+ The cost of transportation is zero;

+ There are no restrictions or impediments to switching production from one product to another;

+ There are no requirements from social or environmental policy to undermine the theoretical model.

These are substantial assumptions which clearly will not apply in the real world. If we reflect, it is doubtful that a theory based on such assumptions could continue to have relevance applied to a modern economy threatened by job losses from automation, facing the prospect of limits on resource availability, and struggling to deal with environmental overload. The theory may not be wrong but it is irrelevant to economics at this point in history. For a theory which is so central to the economics of trade, and so influential to trade policy, this insight has huge implications. I can envisage some economists wanting to engage in a sterile debate about whether the policy laid down by David Ricardo 200 years ago could still have relevance today under a new set of carefully crafted assumptions. Pragmatists who want to make progress should push forward past such 19th-century ideas to develop a theory of trade which fits 21st-century challenges.

To clarify the consequences of the insight presented above, let us follow the logic chain. Let us start by accepting that comparative advantage is now largely irrelevant. As comparative advantage is the foundation of free trade policy, this means free trade no longer makes sense. I don't challenge the theoretical argument for free trade, but it is now almost completely irrelevant to the real world. Without free trade to lean on, policymakers will have to think carefully about how to craft trade policy going forward. Resilient trade policy should serve society, maintain employment, safeguard the environment, and take us forward to a sustainable economy. This is a tall order but achievable.

The Basis of Resilient Trade

The concept of free trade has been allowed to dominate trade policy for so long that the world has lost touch with the fundamental basis of trade which should be to satisfy real needs in a sustainable manner. It should never have been otherwise, but a narrow focus on the economic perspective has confused the real impact of trade with the virtual economic model. To move trade policy forward, we need to develop the basis of resilient trade, defined here as:

> *Resilient trade is the exchange of goods and commodities to supplement self-sufficiency on the basis of reciprocity and according to the appropriate regulations to ensure the sustainability of trading arrangements.*

The rules of resilient trade presented below may seem new, but not so. These are restatements of established and well-proven attributes of effective trade policy which need to be allowed to regain the importance they deserve. To accept and apply these rules, it is necessary to accept first that the concept of free trade is an idea which has run its course.

The consequences of a number of decades of free trade policy are an increase in the raw economic numbers for trade. On the face of it, this is welcome. It is assumed that greater volumes of trade increases GDP, and growing GDP is assumed to correlate with progress. We should pause and reflect whether this is actually so. It seems clear that volumes of trade have little correlation with weightier issues such as health, security and sustainability. So, quantity of trade is nigh on irrelevant to the measures that really matter. It is quite amazing that we continue to see and hear media reports focus on quantities of trade on the assumption that more is better. The real news is that the volume of trade is not important. In fact, the world would have a greater chance of dealing with accelerating depletion of resources and environmental overload if there were to be less international trade. Instead of being driven by the counterintuitive idea of free trade, we need to trust our intuition more and adopt rules which bring trade back under control, in support of real needs, not of the economy (it is a rather strange concept that an economy has needs) but of society.

RULE ONE: TRADE SHOULD SATISFY REAL NEEDS

Real needs for trade are commodities you don't have, goods you can't make, or food you don't have the climate to grow.

Under current trade policy, huge quantities of goods, materials and commodities are shipped around the world bearing little relationship to society's real needs. Trade takes place because a profit can be generated. Some of the profit-earning opportunities of international trade are mind-boggling and an affront to common sense. For example, prawns are a food which can be caught or farmed in many localities. Global supply chains have evolved to search out the cheapest source and so Thailand has become a major supplier of prawns to global customers. Disease is rife within many Thai prawn farms (Peel et al. 2013) and slave labour is commonly used to shell the prawns (Mason et al. 2015) but the prawns enter the major supermarkets' global supply chains packaged and looking pristine. This should concern us for three reasons. The first is the health of consumers. The second is the morality of being complicit in slave labour. The third is the carbon emissions of the transportation. We should be ashamed to have allowed an economic system to evolve in which health, morality, and climate impact are sidelined.

An even stranger example is a Scottish seafood company that supplies supermarkets and other large retailers. It decided to ship prawns caught off the coast of Britain more than 5,000 miles to China to be shelled by hand, then shipped back to the River Clyde in Scotland to be packaged for sale in Britain. The company said it was forced to make the move by commercial pressures. 'This seems a bizarre thing to do but the reality is that the numbers do not stack up any other way,' said Andrew Stapley, a director. 'We are not the first in the industry to have had to do this. Sadly, it's cheaper to process overseas than in the UK and companies like us are having to do this to remain competitive' (Ungoed-Thomas 2007).

The current economic system is stacked firmly in favour of incentivizing many such bizarre activities. It is not reasonable to expect corporations to forgo profit to fix a broken system. As a society we need to act to change what is normal in trade policy to ensure that trade satisfies real needs. In the example above, to ship prawns caught off the coast of Britain to China and back, sacking seventy British workers and generating carbon emissions in transportation, makes perfect economic sense. Economic sense is clearly not the same as common sense.

Closely aligned with satisfying real needs is the second rule of resilient trade: self-sufficiency.

RULE TWO: SELF-SUFFICIENCY

The default trading position should be self-sufficiency.

For commodities, where the country has a resource, it should be second nature to conserve the resource for the future and exploit it in a sustainable manner. Public health, working conditions, and safeguarding the environment are under the country's control. Through the era of globalization, rich countries have found high environmental standards more affordable through exporting dirty processes to countries far away. Self-sufficiency replaces this recourse to blind global economic efficiency with the responsibility to ensure safe and sustainable local supply. Countries will have to accept that a pristine environment comes with the cost of investing in ultra clean processes. Poor countries should be helped to resist exploitation by states or corporations seeking to circumvent tight environmental regulations in their home markets. The price of commodities would be expected to rise in many cases, but prices could fall in countries well-endowed with resources. The exception to self-sufficiency is where there is overwhelming difference in circumstances such that national production does not make sense.

For goods, local production allows for the development of production methods based on the emerging concept of cradle-to-cradle manufacturing, applying full lifecycle design and total recycling. This is very different to current norms, and the implications are significant. For example, supply chains will be completely reconfigured. Instead of making in China, shipping to Europe, and ending up in landfill; products can be made in Europe, serviced in Europe, repaired in Europe, and eventually recycled into the next generation of products with zero waste. This is the future of manufacturing and we should embrace it now.

For food, local production is secure, safe and sustainable, relying on the natural oversight of local markets backed up by national regulations and a national inspection regime. Few countries could be self-sufficient throughout the year, but economic policy should favour seasonal produce from the locality or region. It is worth noting that longer supply chains could regain favour when sustainable shipping is introduced powered by solar and wind.

Self-sufficiency is not an absolute requirement but the default position. It makes sense for trade to depart from the default position when local production cannot deliver or makes no sense.

RULE THREE: RECIPROCITY

The concept of a balance of trade should be resurrected.

Trade has lost touch with the fundamental basis of the

exchange of goods. We can now import and consume any amount of goods in exchange for a promise to pay, building up huge debts within the international financial system. The idea that there should be a 'balance of trade' is seen as old-fashioned. I argue that it is not old-fashioned but should be a fundamental principle of trade which we ignore at our peril. The imbalance in the world economy brought about through ignoring this principle is hugely destabilizing. If we need something, we have to have something to export in exchange. Currencies avoid direct barter of an export for an import, with the value of currencies allowed to adjust to find an equilibrium which delivers overall a balance of trade.

Restoring reciprocity into the trade policy package is not a new innovation but an old established idea which makes sense. Balance of trade had gone out of vogue during decades of economic exuberance. It now needs to be brought back into play to help deliver resilience.

RULE FOUR: COORDINATED REGULATIONS

Coordinated regulations are needed in circumstances where frictionless trade is negotiated and agreed. National regulations will vary, particularly as the principle of subsidiarity becomes widely adopted. Within a national economy, there will be a level playing field with regulations which apply to all. When it comes to international trade, open unfettered trade will tend towards exploitation of regulatory differences between countries. This could be dangerous as resource limits are reached (see later). This means that where there are trading areas where there is little friction to trade, such as within the EU or bilateral trading corridors, there needs to be close coordination of regulations. This will include, as a minimum, product standards and environmental regulations.

Implementing Resilient Trade Rules

The rules of resilient trade can put trade back in support of society and open the possibility of building a sustainable global economy. In a world economy conforming to this set of trade rules, all countries can prosper according to their circumstances, priorities, and culture. Framing trade in this way is distinctly different to seeking maximum economic efficiencies from free trade. Where current economic policy encourages states to export polluting activities and import commodities without looking too closely at the source, this set of rules should put trade on stable foundations. For multinational corporations, where they currently engage in unsustainable trade, they do so because of the trading system they are required to navigate. It is for governments on behalf of society to change the system. Adopting and implementing this set of rules would set an economic framework in which it makes commercial sense for business and corporations to orchestrate sustainable supply chains.

Ideally there would be agreement at world level to establish a framework for resilient trade. Without such a mechanism, poor countries with weak governance could be exploited. Such a framework may be welcomed because countries may like taking back national control. Politicians have had to work hard to extol the virtues of free trade, pushing back against the populism which favours protectionism. It should be easier politically to promote economic policy which aligns with the populist perspective.

Currently, the main international forum for trade policy is the World Trade Organization (WTO), so this is where I turn next.

The World Trade Organization

The precursor to the WTO was the General Agreement on

Tariffs and Trade (GATT) launched in 1948 after WW2. It came about with good intentions to use trade to enhance prosperity and cement global peace. This was replaced by the WTO in 1995 based on the 1994 Marrakesh Agreement in which 124 nations agreed rules to facilitate global trade. The WTO provides a framework for negotiating trade agreements and a dispute resolution process.

The WTO is the world's highest-level body to regulate global trade so the principles it espouses and the way it operates has huge influence on the world economy. According to the WTO, the 'overriding purpose is to help trade flow as freely as possible… because this is important for stimulating economic growth'. The 2019 Annual Report adds to this: 'so long as there are no undesirable side effects' (WTO 2019: 10). This is the beginning of an acknowledgement that there may be more to consider than simply freeing up trade. Noting the possibility of undesirable side effects is not enough; there needs to be a change of approach.

In the context of shifting the focus of policy towards resilient economics, the WTO now looks like an organization from a bygone era. The whole raison d'être of the WTO is to ensure that trade flows as smoothly and as freely as possible. The time has come to challenge the intellectual foundations on which the organization is built. Instead of an organization to facilitate free trade, the ethos of managing trade should be to facilitate sustainable trade in ways which reinforce security of supply whilst minimizing negative environmental impact.

The Principles of Trade according to the WTO (WTO 2020a):

+ Trade without discrimination;

+ Freer trade: gradually, through negotiation;

- Predictability: through binding and transparency;

- Promoting fair competition;

- Encouraging development and economic reform.

There have been a series of international trade talks seeking to advance these principles over the last seventy years, the most recent being the Doha Development Round, which was launched in 2001 with an explicit focus on developing countries. Agreement has been elusive due to conflicts between the developed and developing countries, particularly over the agricultural sector.

Criticism of the WTO includes systematic bias toward rich countries and multinational corporations, as well as little interest in issues of labour and the environment – criticisms which the WTO denies (WTO 2020b). The ethos from which GATT and the WTO were born can be understood in the context of the aftermath of a destructive world war and the overriding priority to build shared prosperity and peace. The context has changed; the overriding priority is to rescue the world from dangerous long-lasting environmental damage and to prevent conflict over diminishing resources from taking the world to war again. Within the approach to economics championed in this book, the WTO seems like an anachronism. The organization's ethos is quite wrong for today's circumstances and its aim almost diametrically opposed to building a sustainable world economy.

The future of the WTO must be in doubt for two prime reasons. First, enforcing a completely different rationale for world trade would require a dramatic about-face by the WTO. It would be hard for the existing organization to undertake such a total transformation. Second, the principles of trade presented here would be largely self-enforcing as they are based on encouraging countries to take back control. Countries need not look to the WTO for guidance as they develop trading arrangements to suit their national interests.

If there is to be a global trade organization for the 21st century (McManners 2010: 152–3), the rationale would be to facilitate sustainability rather than facilitate free trade. Its aim and mission would mirror the rules of resilient trade:

+ Promote the principle that trade should satisfy real needs, sustainably;

+ Self-sufficiency as default;

+ Encourage nations to maintain a balance of trade;

+ Where trading zones are agreed there should be coordinated product and environmental standards, to support a circular economy within its boundaries.

Having set some general resilient trade parameters, there are a number of other issues to consider with regard to the economics of trade, starting with the distortions which commodities tend to cause.

The Problem with Resources

A country rich in resources should be a rich country, but commodities are not necessarily good for society unless they are managed with care. For example, Saudi Arabia is a rich country with the world's largest oil reserves but there are also deep social divisions which are partly fuelled by wealth from oil (Cammett et al. 2018). The problem with commodities, and the problem of having commodities, is that they distort the local economy. It's like a person who wins a large lottery prize. A person who is well-balanced, sensible, and thinks about the long-term, can use the win to secure a healthy and enjoyable life. Another person might blow it on fast cars and parties for new-found friends and end up deeply depressed when the windfall is exhausted and the new-found 'friends' disappear. The problem is partly about attitude. If you have a healthy mindset, which sees money as a facilitator of life's administrative necessities, you are well placed to benefit from a lottery win. If you view having money as an aim in itself, and see friendship as something you can buy, a lottery win could destroy your life. What applies to people applies to countries. For a country whose government is concerned with maintaining the quality and cohesion of society, where the standards of governance are high, and economics is understood to be a facilitating function, commodities are a great bonus.

Lottery winners face a problem because other people would like a share of their winnings. They receive begging letters, offers of friendship, and perhaps even proposals of marriage. It is hard for the lottery winner to separate good intentions from selfish exploitation. The same applies to countries with the resources which are needed in increasing quantities to provide for a growing world economy. A resource-rich country will be courted by MNCs and states such as China which require commodities. Altruistic intentions should not be expected. In fact, both MNCs and states make no secret of acting in the best interests of their shareholders or their national interest respectively. Those who are fortunate to possess commodities have to be very careful in their dealings with interested outside parties.

How the world deals with the exploitation of commodities in the 21st century will decide the state of the planet we bequeath to our grandchildren. Let us consider how the current international economic and trade policy norms facilitate the extraction and trade of commodities.

International mining corporations prospect around the world for where they can open new mines. They focus on countries with resource potential and those most likely to allow them to operate. They seek permission to open mines expecting to pay for extraction rights and offering employment to people in the communities close by. Governments often receive advice from influential advisers such as the IMF and the World Bank that such Foreign Direct Investment (FDI) is beneficial. When the mines and facilities are operating, the country earns revenue from the export of the commodity extracted. Where governance is weak, as is the case in many less-developed countries, deals will be agreed with the local ruling elite. It is these people who become rich, with local people and communities given little say and receiving less benefit than they should.

China is a country in search of resources. It approaches other countries with offers to build roads, ports and railways, in exchange for extraction rights. This provides jobs, although China has a reputation for importing its own workers in preference to employing local labour so the benefit to the local economy may be limited (Taylor 2012). The world community should be concerned on behalf of poorer countries whether such activities are of true long-term benefit. All too often this is not the case. Such 'development' is rife in the poorest African countries. We are all complicit in the unfair exploitation of the wonderful continent of Africa as we stand by and watch as inappropriate trade and economic policy is foisted on countries without the necessary strength of governance to push back.

The effect on the local economy can be perverse. With funds flowing in to pay for the commodities being exported, the local currency strengthens. Under the ethos of free trade, the country can afford to import lots of goods but they cannot export anything other than the commodity because locally produced items are too expensive due to the strong currency. Local businesses find it hard to compete with cheap imported goods. The country becomes dependent on commodity income with the local economy based on selling imported goods. A local inclusive economy of local production for local needs can be totally undermined. This economic situation is termed the 'resource curse' (Ross 2015; Venables 2016).

The resource curse can be lifted by applying an approach to trade policy which is better suited to the challenges of the current era. Following the four rules of resilient trade (presented above), pushes back against current policy norms. This is not a radical proposal, but rather common sense.

First, the income from commodity exports should be applied to real needs; not replacing locally produced products or undermining the local producers and manufacturers. Imports should be particular goods and services which the country requires in addition to, and complementary to, what is available in the local economy.

Second, self-sufficiency should remain the default objective of the local economy, in tune with local culture, needs and geography. This retains the character of the country and protects the long-term sustainability of the economy.

Third, the aim should be to achieve a balance of trade, such that a resource-rich country only exports the amount of resources needed to balance against the need for imports. This avoids the economic distortion of excessive exports, as well as ensuring the resources are conserved to serve the country well into the future.

Fourth, it makes sense to open up trade with other countries close by with similar circumstances and closely aligned social and environmental standards. It also makes sense to establish trading corridors between pairs of countries with complementary needs. An example of a pair of trading countries is

Australia and China. The former is resource-rich and the latter is a major centre for manufacturing. An Australia-China trading relationship makes economic sense. Australia and China both have mature governance arrangements and are strong partners without one exploiting the other. Australia and China may not be close neighbours, but a sea journey of 7,000 km between Shanghai and Perth is short compared with many of the other long snaking supply chains which currently crisscross the globe.

It need not be a curse for a country to have resources, provided the country uses them well and retains tight control of its economy. Natural resources can be a major economic advantage, as Norway demonstrates. This country in northern Europe has used its substantial oil reserves to build a strong economy and a substantial sovereign wealth fund to underpin a sustainable future beyond the era of fossil fuel. Well managed and tightly controlled resources are part of the foundations of a sound economy. The importance becomes clear when considering global resource limits.

Global Resource Limits

Current economic policy does not factor in the fact that global resources are finite. The closer we get to resource limits the more urgent it becomes to alter the economic model.

Maintaining an open global economy, operating according to WTO free trade rules, will deal with resource limits in a particularly pernicious way. Rich countries which can afford to pay higher prices will continue to get supplies; poor countries who cannot afford to pay high prices will miss out. People living in rich developed countries might feel confident that they will be on the safe side of the divide, but it is not that simple. First, let us examine the current economic model to understand the consequences of its continuance.

Open global markets ensure the efficient exploitation of global resources. The easiest to locate and cheapest to extract will be used first. The idea that some reserves might be conserved, or left unexploited, does not gain traction. This is a consequence of choosing to allow market forces free reign at global level. The market would be doing exactly what you would expect it to do, running down the world's resources to depletion, extracting the maximum for the least cost. There might be some people who genuinely believe this would be appropriate, but if you are a reasonable person and reflect, it soon becomes clear that beyond the immediate short term this would be utter folly.

Our complacency about global resource limits is understandable because we have never before faced limits on global resources. There has always been another place, another oil field, another deposit of copper ore to be dug out.

Oil is a prime example, where for decades there has been talk of the end of oil. As a young engineering graduate in the early 1980s, I had job offers to enter the oil industry but I decided that the industry could not offer a full career as the industry would be closed down before I reached retirement age. How wrong I was. The engineering challenges in the oil industry have increased as companies seek to exploit more difficult fields in deep offshore waters or seek to extract tight oil from unconventional sources such as oil shale rock. For engineers, these are stimulating challenges but the real challenge for the oil industry is the politics.

The end of oil will be when we as a society decide to close the industry, not because oil runs out. This can be a smooth and orderly transition, provided we do the right thing and close down demand before reserves are depleted. I have climate change in mind, when I write 'do the right thing', but we should do it anyway to ensure resilience so that the end of oil is not another economic shock. The action required is to build an economic model and adopt trade policy which steers society away from crashing into resource limits. Economic policy should encourage and support the careful management of resources for the long-term.

To understand why global resource limits have such huge economic significance, let us consider what happens when there is an imbalance of greater demand than available supply. In the short-term the price increases as world markets adjust. Those who can afford the higher prices will still have access to resources. However, there comes a point when this adjustment mechanism is no longer enough.

Academics have explored what would happen as resource limits are approached. Research by economist Petros Sekeris provides a deeply worrying insight into how the world might respond (Sekeris 2014). He applied game theory to the situation where shared resources are being exploited – which is the situation in a globalized world where resources are traded freely. The logic is clear; the best outcome is for the players to cooperate over exploitation of the shared resource. Sekeris tested this logic by grafting onto a standard natural-resource exploitation game the possibility to appropriate the resource through violent means. He found that conflict emerges as a natural consequence. The equilibrium observed is that players exploit cooperatively the resource when it is abundant, and they revert to conflict when it becomes scarce. This leads to accelerated exploitation in the period leading into the conflict. One conclusion relevant to the short-term is that scaremongering over resource limits may bring forward such accelerated depletion. However, the conclusion for the long-term is that early action is vital to resolve resource issues well before resource limits are reached (McManners 2017).

Whilst resources are plentiful, cooperation works well and everyone gets the resources they need. To relate this research to the real world; this is where the world is now. We still have sufficient resources, but as resource limits are approached exploitation gathers pace until – as the research shows – the situation descends into conflict. This should worry us deeply, because this is the future into which we are heading driven by current economic and trade policy.

We have a choice to make. We can let the current open trading policies encourage a rush to exploit as much as possible, as quickly as possible, and let the consequences unfold. When resources are no longer sufficient to meet demand, countries will take action to retain the resources they have and fight to obtain the resources they need. We have seen that in a small way in 2008 when the price of rice on the world markets doubled. India curbed exports of rice to the global market to conserve rice supplies for local consumption. Such situations will become more frequent and more serious. Without a change of policy, it would be highly likely that the world descends into yet another round of global conflict.

The alternative to crashing into resource limits is to shift economic and trade policy to a sustainable system, adopting the rules of resilient trade.

Protectionism

Protectionism has negative connotations within the current economic discourse, but within resilient economics it is overwhelmingly positive.

The conventional view is that protectionism should be avoided. Although it might be tempting to protect a country's home economy, this will impact negatively on other countries whose governments then respond in kind, so that protectionism ends up coming back to bite the initiator. In the tussle of political manoeuvring, the best outcome would be to protect the home economy whilst having the freedom to export freely to other economies. If every country tried to do the same, then no one would be able to export freely. So conventional economic thinking would say that protectionism is bad and every country should be open to every other country to enjoy the shared benefits of free trade. In practice, those most skilled in trade negotiation, or representing the most powerful countries, will profess support for free and open trade whilst ensuring there is selective protection for their national industries – in so far as they can get away with it. Protectionism is practised, but it tends to be underhand, often unfair, and resisted by those who believe in an open global economy.

The term protectionism became a pejorative term within the lexicon of those promoting free trade and economic globalization. This comes from a different era of economic thought, and the term is set to be rehabilitated as we embrace resilient economics. Protectionism has a positive feel to it when focused on protecting the health and welfare of society. If through protectionism we can also prevent over exploitation of resources and safeguard the natural environment, protectionism seems to be something to aim for rather than avoid. This is a complete reversal of how protectionism is currently framed.

As we understand the advantages of embracing the concept of resilient trade, and back away from the short-termism of the free-trade agenda, economic protectionism starts to look like a description of a better way to deal with the economics of trade. The trade we need is sustainable trade. Tariffs and controls which put friction into the trading system, to ensure that trade is used to satisfy real needs under the default of self-sufficiency, are protectionist. Absolutely they are protectionist, but that should be the intention. We need protection of national and local economies to ensure they serve society and communities. Such protection is likely to reduce the headline numbers for GDP, and in some cases squeeze consumer prices higher, but these are of little real consequence when the greater prize is a sustainable economy which fits the needs of the society it serves.

Conclusions

Trade has lost touch with the fulfilment of real needs; and trade policies have become ensnared in obsolescent economic theory. We have allowed the situation to arise where trade is seen as intrinsically good, and growing trade adopted as a specific aim of policy, with few caveats. This could be the most damaging example of blinkered adherence to economic theory without careful examination of whether it remains appropriate to today's circumstances.

The time is overdue to hit the reset button and put trade back in support of human needs according to fundamental common-sense principles. The resulting agenda of resilient trade is radically different to the concept of free trade. However, there is little that is new, unusual or particularly radical about the principles presented in this chapter. Trade should satisfy real needs; self-sufficiency should be the default option; trade should be reciprocal; and trading areas need consistent rules and standards. These guidelines are simple and intuitive but because they conflict with long-standing conventional economic thought their adoption will be resisted.

To accept the common sense of resilient trade policy requires backing away from free trade. To attack such a core pillar of conventional economic theory means the argument presented here will be tough to sell, and the message will be exceedingly slow to propagate. A whole host of people with vested interests will resist, ranging from academics and trade experts deeply steeped in free-trade theory to policymakers in the powerful countries defending a system which favours their multinational corporations. Such a formidable array makes a gigantic opponent blocking the way forward. This short chapter loaded into my slingshot is unlikely to slay the Goliath which threatens our future. If it were to hit just the right spot, and be accepted by a few forward-thinking and influential policymakers, this could be the beginning of resuming forward progress and reforming trade for the challenges of the 21st century.

CHAPTER 9

LEVER 1: MONEY

Money, money, money makes the world go around.

Liza Minnelli, *Cabaret*, 1972

Money does indeed make the world go around but the pursuit of money has become an aim in itself. This fixation has grown in importance to the extent that greed and avarice are no longer thought of as vices. People are respected for having money and admired for their ability to make money. This obsession with money is getting in the way of real progress in improving lives.

Everybody wants money, money.

Riton, 'Money', 2017

Using quotes from popular songs to communicate the central role of money might seem flippant in a book about economics, but it suits the ephemeral nature of money. Money is no more real than a song is real. The days of gold coins with real intrinsic value are long gone. Money has value only in so far as we believe it has value. Even so, money is the raw material of finance and the lifeblood of the economy. For a healthy economy, money needs to flow to where it is needed, transferring value from one person to another, one organization to another, one generation to another. For something as important as money we need to be in control and alert to systemic problems which could infect the system.

International finance has become so interconnected and interdependent that problems in one part of the system can propagate quickly as money sloshes around without tight controls. To improve resilience requires taking back control. National currencies should circulate freely within the economies they serve to ensure a buoyant home economy, whilst inter-currency transfers should be subject to close scrutiny and tight controls. This might be seen as a radical change of policy but is little more than bringing money back under the proper oversight of national governments. Applying resilient economics reinforces the role of money and extends its reach to include local currencies. Before going into further detail, it is worth reflecting on the history of money.

A Short History of Money

The history of money goes back many thousands of years. Livestock and plant products were used as a form of money as long ago as 6,000 BC (Davies and Davies 1998). Salt and tobacco have been used as currency, being valuable commodities and long-lasting. Interestingly, this form of barter continues today with cigarettes used as an informal currency in some prisons. An example of the first use of something akin to a modern currency is the bronze shapes of small knives and spades used in China during the Zhou Dynasty, around 1000 BC. The first standard coins seem to have appeared separately in India, China, and Greece between 700 and 500 BC (Graeber 2014). Paper money was first used by the Chinese during the Tang Dynasty (AD 618–907) but did not get established in Europe until over 500 years later. In 16th-century Britain the goldsmith-bankers began to give receipts for gold coins deposited with them. These receipts, which were the forerunner of paper currency, promised to pay the depositor (or bearer) on demand the amount of gold recorded in the note. As paper currency was introduced, the amount in circulation was matched to the amount of gold held in the vaults of the

Bank of England. This provided stability but also limited the supply of money. After the 1930s financial crash, the UK abandoned the gold standard (with the US following shortly after) to increase the supply of currency. All currencies are now fiat currency which means there is no link to intrinsic value. The currency has value only because the government authorizes its use and people accept it has value. The notes are just printed sheets of paper but we trust the issuer of the notes, and trust that they will be accepted in payment and have enduring value. We return again to the issue at the heart of finance; currencies are all about trust.

Modern currencies no longer have intrinsic value, which is eminently sensible. Tobacco would get stale; salt is no longer worth much and is too heavy to use; gold and silver coins wear out with the valuable metal spread around as dust. The fact that contemporary money has no intrinsic value clarifies the nature of the value we ascribe to it.

The historic path for money has gone from commodities with intrinsic value, to printed notes, to become simply numbers in computer systems. Money has made the transition from a means of facilitating real transactions to a complex financial game operating in cyberspace; from a simple system where it is obvious how it operates, to a complex network run by computers. The purpose of money used to be simple and obvious; it is now complex and opaque. Returning to basics and defining the purpose of money is how to ensure that money has real value for society.

The Purpose of Money

The purpose of money, when you try to define it, is as elusive as money itself. Money is something we all want, need and value. If we do not have money, we feel powerless. If we do not have much money, we feel disadvantaged. If we have enough money, we feel good. If we have more than enough money, we feel even better. If we have all the money we could ever need, that would be nirvana. For something so obviously connected to our welfare and well-being, it hardly seems necessary to define the purpose of money. Feeling good when you have it, and feeling bad when you don't, may be our reaction to money, but why? Could it be that holding a wad of bank notes or reading a bank statement with a considerable balance is a pleasurable activity? Perhaps in the modern world, our feelings and emotions have been so subsumed in the pursuit of money that there is real pleasure from having a lot of money. That would indeed be a sad reflection on modern life.

It is rational to like having money, because of what can be done with money. We can buy what we need, do what we want, and no longer need to worry about how to afford it. The thing we cannot do with money is buy love, health or happiness; but we rely on money for the day-to-day transactions of life. The important stuff sits above money, but the routine matter of how we administer our lives is totally dependent on money.

It is clear that money is important but what precise purpose does it have? It is widely acknowledged that money has three purposes: as a means of exchange, as a store of value, and as a measure of value (or unit of account).

MEANS OF EXCHANGE

The fundamental importance of money as a medium to exchange value is illustrated by considering life without money. Without money to buy and sell, we would need to resort to barter. To get the food we need we would have to offer something in exchange, something which the provider of food wanted. If we did not have something to offer which the food provider wanted, or which the food provider already had enough of, we would need to find another party who wanted something from us and could provide something which the food provider wanted. It would soon get very complicated and difficult to set up a network of barter arrangements to keep society operating. Using money to facilitate exchange of goods and services is a necessary and important part of maintaining the fabric of society.

STORE OF VALUE

Another important role for money is as a store of value. By saving money, we can build up enough for major purchases, to spend at some point in the future, or for peace of mind so if we need something, we know we can afford it. For the money which is put into pension schemes that future may be many decades hence. For this purpose, we need to be sure that the money will retain its value over time. This might be through buying investments, the value of which is accounted for in terms of money, leading to the third purpose of money as a measure of value.

MEASURE OF VALUE

The role of money as a measure of value is problematic because an apparent monetary value may not be a real value.

The classic example of a speculative bubble (where apparent value is disconnected from real-world value) was tulip mania in Holland in the 17th century. Speculating on the value of tulip bulbs reached a point where one bulb had a notional value of 2,500 florins at a time when a skilled labourer could earn only 150–350 florins a year.[25] So a skilled labourer would need to work for ten years to buy one bulb. People who bought into the craze

---

25 The Tulipomania, Chapter 3, in Mackay, C. (1841), *Memoirs of Extraordinary Popular Delusions and the Madness of Crowds*, London: Richard Bentley.

early made a lot of money but those owning bulbs when the price crashed were left only with tulip bulbs, which have limited real value.

It was obvious soon afterwards that tulip mania had been a ridiculous socio-economic phenomenon. It is interesting that more recent research examined exactly what was going on within the market for tulips and concluded that 'Tulip contract prices before, during, and after the "tulipmania" appear to provide a remarkable illustration of "market efficiency".' (Thompson 2007). This analysis by the economist Earl Thompson is an interesting and scholarly examination of the role of futures contracts. To my mind this is another example of the esoteric world of economics distancing itself from reality. Even though Thompson's paper appears to be sound in its economic analysis, to describe tulip mania as a remarkable illustration of 'market efficiency' is astonishing. I apologize for this deviation from my argument in this section, but when I came across this in research for the book, I had to include it because of the insight it gives into the esoteric world of modern economics. This fits so neatly into the central argument of this book that economics has to be brought back to reality.

The key point about monetary value is that it is set by the transactions which take place. Where there are many similar assets and only a few are traded at any given time, the apparent value of the assets is set by these few trades.

The monetary value which has most relevance to people's lives is the property market. A house is likely to be the single most valuable asset that people possess. Its value is of great interest when prices rise and a huge concern when they drop. It is the nature of the housing market that only a few houses come on the market at any given time. The apparent monetary value of a house is calculated from recent transactions. These houses have real direct value to people as places to shelter, be secure and live their lives. There is every reason to suppose that with the right policy, the monetary value of houses can align with real value and be stable and predictable. (The economics of the housing market is considered in greater detail in Chapter 15.)

Overall, the monetary value we ascribe to things far exceeds the money in circulation or in bank deposits. Things have a monetary value and more importantly a real value. Food has real value because it can be eaten; houses have real value as places to live; anything with a real-world role has real value. Real value is tangible, whereas monetary value means nothing except at the point when ownership changes. The divergence between apparent and real value can be considerable, as the art market demonstrates.

The Strange World of Money and Art

The art market is a good example to draw out the differences between real and monetary value.

There are a fixed number of artistic works by Picasso. When they come to market wealthy buyers compete to own one. There may be a few extraordinarily wealthy people who accept the price as the true value of being able to look at, feel, and touch these wonderful works of art. However, almost all participants in the high-end art market believe the art they buy is a good investment. Whilst this belief remains, the owners of Picasso's work increase the valuation each time there is a transaction in the market at a higher price. It would just take a change of sentiment to reverse the market. If owners of Picasso's art need the money and try to sell, when there are few people with enough money, or inclination, to buy, the price of Picasso's art could collapse. I am not predicting a collapse in the price of Picassos because he is such an iconic artist, and no more are being made, so it is a closed market. This is not the case with artworks by the modern artist Damien Hirst (Box 9.1).

Box 9.1 The art of Damien Hirst – investment or economic bubble?

Damien Hirst was one of the YBAs – Young British Artists – who came to prominence during the 1990s. A symbiotic relationship with influential art collector Charles Saatchi helped launch his career. Saatchi paid £50,000 for Hirst to manufacture the shark suspended in formaldehyde (*The Physical Impossibility of Death in the Mind of Someone Living*), one of Hirst's most memorable early pieces. Saatchi bought Hirst's work, increasing his reputation and the market value of his art. As Damien Hirst cemented his place as an established artist, the relationship soured and Charles Saatchi sold his collection (for a considerable profit). Once the band wagon got going, owning a Damien Hirst became a symbol of affluence and wealth. Initially there was a limited supply and Hirst's work continued to escalate in price, reinforcing the idea that it was a good investment. Three decades later, Damien Hirst is still alive and uses a team of people to manufacture works on an industrial scale making him the world's richest living artist. Are there enough people who believe in Damien Hirst to keep prices high? If a relatively small number of influential art collectors/dealers were to decide that the artist's actions are putting their investment at risk, so decided to sell, and such thinking propagated through the market, a collapse in prices could follow.

Real value can be hard to discern within the art market, but this hardly matters. Trading art can be seen as a form of grandstanding and gambling amongst the rich, so the real-world consequences are limited. We should be wary of owning things which don't have real value and only have monetary value (such as a work of art by Damien Hirst) because such value can evaporate into thin air.

Currencies

Money takes the form of currencies issued by a central bank. For money to achieve its purpose it is important that it is widely accepted within society and holds its value, so the bank which produces the money and controls its supply should be an organization which can be trusted. Let us consider the role of currencies and how they are managed at three levels: local, national, and global. I will start with the national level which is the level at which most currencies reside.

NATIONAL CURRENCIES

National currencies reflect the culture of the country which administers them. It is very important to any country that its currency is widely accepted and that it retains its value. Printed notes and coins are designed with symbols of national significance engendering pride in the country's currency and trust in its value. There will be a central bank charged with managing the currency. This might act with a high degree of independence from government, as is the case in the UK and the USA, or be tightly controlled by the government and the country's leadership. For well-managed countries, the enduring value of the currency is seldom questioned. For countries with corrupt rulers who use the central bank as their personal cash machine, the local currency could become debased.

Currencies exist in three forms. The first is a physical note or coin. This is something to hold, safeguard and feels like it has enduring value. The second is bank deposits. How secure these are depends on the extent to which the bank can be trusted. A deposit in a dodgy bank could be lost if the bank were to fold. Many governments operate a bank deposit guarantee scheme so that balances up to a certain value are covered by government compensation if the bank fails. The third form is investments denominated in the currency such as bonds or shareholdings in corporations. Whether this should be counted as money is doubtful because these only become money when sold, but people think of such investments in terms of the money tied up so I believe it is reasonable to regard them as a form of money. These can be highly volatile and could lose all their value. People select which form of money they prefer. Cash feels secure but is at risk from robbery and provides no return. Bank deposits are secure from physical robbery and provide interest, but you need to trust the bank and be aware of the risk of online fraud. Investments offer the best return but carry the highest risks.

The proportion of national currency in these three forms is hard to assess but a rough comparison for the UK between cash, bank deposits and money in listed shares is: £71 billion of cash (Bank of England 2020); an order of magnitude greater as bank deposits; and the shares on the London Stock Exchange apparently worth more than three times bank deposits. If the net is cast wider, to include the housing stock of the UK, this is estimated to be worth about £7 trillion. The owners of these houses would each expect to be able to convert these into cash. This shows that for the three purposes of money, national currencies serve primarily as a reserve of value and a means of saving for the longer term. The role of currencies as a means of exchange seems tiny in comparison. This is a potential problem because the prime reason why society needs money is as a means of exchange. When there is the potential for a lot of money to be pumped into the economy or sucked out, from these other forms of money, it could mean that the economy overheats or is starved of cash in ways which are hard for policymakers to predict or control. Rather than suggest that we use national currencies any less as a store of value, I propose that society needs other complementary currencies, designed to be primarily means of exchange, to support greater stability in everyday affairs. This is the rationale for local currencies, which will be discussed in more detail below.

TRADING CURRENCIES

National currencies do not sit in isolation but are traded and exchanged with other national currencies to enable international trade and other cross-border transactions. The simplest trade is cash, where currency traders hold notes in a number of currencies and buy and sell, taking their commission. International banks have the ability to trade and exchange currencies electronically. Numbers are swapped within computer systems under arrangements of trust between the global banks. This is needed of course to enable trade in goods and services. A simple economic model of currency transactions and how they relate to trade is like this. When there is an imbalance between the demand and supply of the currency this implies there must be an imbalance of trade. The relative values between the two currencies adjust accordingly. The country which has been importing more than it exports finds that its currency weakens. Its exports become more affordable and imports more expensive. This supports the maintenance of a 'balance of trade'. If the way currencies are traded is kept simple and used only in support of real transactions this simple model can apply.

The modern international currency markets have become much more complex with vastly more currency transactions than required to support real transactions. One view is that currency markets are now more 'sophisticated' but this gives them too much credibility. Current currency markets are described more accurately as 'excessively complicated' having lost touch with their true purpose. To allow a market to evolve which is suited to the speculators and traders breaks a fundamental rule of market design, which is that they should be run for the benefit of those who need the market for transactions with a real purpose.

People, businesses and organizations trading internationally need to be able to exchange between currencies. There is a clear need to recapture currency trading to bring it back in support of society. This idea will not be liked by those running the system, such as the big international banks dependent on currency trading to generate profits. To even begin a dialogue with an international bank which asks the bank to put aside the profit motive would be seen as laughably naïve. It is only naïve because no one believes that the international banking system could be brought under control. In truth, governments have the power and could rein in international finance. They don't because they dare not. Even quite large countries have become beholden to the international financial system and would not choose to pick a fight with the global banks. This leads onto whether there might, or could be, a role for a global currency.

GLOBAL CURRENCIES

Ideas about global currencies are worth exploring to investigate if there might be merit, although a convincing case for global currencies has yet to be made.

Let us suppose that a global currency exists with a value based on a basket of the world's major currencies. In theory, such a currency could fulfil the three purposes of money: exchange of goods or services, store of value, and a measure of value.

To use a global currency for exchange, it would be necessary to buy units, presumably using a national currency. If this meant money being swapped into a global currency and then back out into a national currency it might make little sense compared with a direct exchange between national currencies. The circumstances where this could be useful is in a country in dire financial circumstances, whose currency is no longer trusted, where the economy has ground to a halt. The global currency could be introduced as a trusted means of exchange to operate alongside the national currency keeping the economy operating. The US dollar has served this purpose in a number of countries.

As a store of value, a global currency could provide some insulation from volatile exchange rates. Currently, countries hold reserves of other currencies to be able to manage their financial affairs, with the US dollar and Euro held widely. A global currency could be used instead, or as well as, crossholdings of other national currencies.

As a measure of value, a global currency would provide a stable reference frame. For example, global oil prices are quoted in US dollars but a global currency could be used instead for such globally traded commodities.

In this discussion of global currencies, the US dollar has been mentioned a number of times. In the absence of a global currency, the US dollar has been used as the world's de facto reserve currency. The United States has benefited from reserve currency status, being able to borrow cheaply, but over recent decades the US has been building up huge debts. This might put a question mark over continued reliance on the US dollar. Investors may shift preference to holding other currencies such as the Euro or China's Renminbi, or generate appetite for a global currency.

For a global currency to be accepted, it would need to be trusted. To be trusted, it would need to be managed by a trusted global entity. If there is an appetite for a global currency, perhaps the IMF could be the central bank. The concept of a global currency has parallels with the idea of a universal second language.

This was the concept behind Esperanto, designed to be logical, easy to learn and available for everyone to use. It has been around since the late 19th century but has not taken root. This is because language is much more than a means of communication. Language is about national identity and cultural heritage so it is not surprising that Esperanto has not been adopted. National currencies are also about national identity and cultural heritage so it is not surprising that there has not been demand for a global currency. I do not detect support from national governments for a global currency due to deep reluctance to cede control to a global central bank.

DIGITAL CURRENCIES

Digital currencies, such as Bitcoin and Ethereum, have huge potential to disrupt finance. There are concerns which will need to be addressed, particularly how to regulate them. Governments worrying about losing control could respond by setting up their own digital currency backed by the central bank. These could prove popular, and bypass retail banks, so care would be needed not to undermine the structure of the national banking system (*The Economist*, 8–14 May 2021).

The most well-known digital currency is Bitcoin. It is transnational and does not fall under the control of any country or global authority. The currency exists in cyberspace allowing the transfer of value across the Internet anonymously facilitated by cryptographic technology called the block chain. Some people see Bitcoin as the future of finance freed from the shackles of government control. This is a dangerous idea which makes about as much sense as trading Dutch tulip bulbs.

Bitcoin was invented by a computer programmer (or group of programmers) under the pseudonym of Satoshi Nakamoto. It was released as open-source software in 2009. Trading with other currencies began soon after and by 2011 each Bitcoin was valued at US$0.30. Over the next decade, Bitcoin trading has been highly volatile peaking at over $19,000 in 2017 as people observed its rising apparent value and jumped on the bandwagon. Its popularity then waned dropping back to below $5,000. In 2021, it regained upward momentum to break through $50,000 influenced by comments made by people such as American financier Anthony Scaramucci, who claimed that bitcoin could be trading at $100,000 in the next 12 months (Bambrough 2021). Anyone buying Bitcoin in the early years could now be exceedingly rich, particularly if they sold out when the Bitcoin bubble was fully inflated. Buying Bitcoin now should be regarded as risky, only providing a return on investment if demand for the currency holds up.

There are aspects to Bitcoin which explain why it still exists and is still traded. Not every dealer in Bitcoin is a speculator. The Bitcoin market has a real purpose facilitating real transactions, such as people who need to transfer cash without leaving an audit trail. No honest venture should worry about leaving an audit trail. These 'genuine' users of Bitcoin include drug dealers, underworld criminals, Chinese nationals evading their government's currency controls, and perhaps white-collar criminals avoiding tax. We cannot tell from the outside how much of the trade in Bitcoin is pure speculation and how much is secretive financial dealing. When we pause and consider, Bitcoin would seem to have two uses, as a means for speculation, and to transfer cash anonymously. There seems to be little here which has true value for society. Perhaps the reality is that currencies like Bitcoin can be set up in cyberspace and cannot be controlled. Even so, it seems odd that policymakers don't make it crystal clear that Bitcoin and similar unconventional currencies do not have the support of government. The places where Bitcoin is traded for real currency should be outlawed and, if possible, closed down to protect naïve punters and remove a money transfer mechanism for criminals. Anyone who gets involved with Bitcoin should know exactly what they are dealing with so as not to be ensnared in its web of deceit.

Where respectable investors have been drawn into the Bitcoin web, they should be aware that they are gambling and supporting a system of shady transactions. Another concern is the colossal energy requirements of the network of computers employed to crunch transactions, estimated at more than the power needs of a medium-sized country. My advice if you own Bitcoin is sell now before the bubble bursts. If you are thinking of joining the bandwagon, don't. I predict that Bitcoin will crash and burn and people, in hindsight, will wonder why society turned a blind eye for so long.

The technology of digital currencies is interesting, and could be useful where underwritten by a central bank. A Wild West of currencies outside the control of government looks more like a gambling den with little relevance to sound financial management.

Local Currency

I will now turn to local currencies, which are often regarded as a curiosity but have huge potential to reinforce economic resilience. They can have real purpose, with considerable potential to improve the economic health of cities or regions nestled within a national resilient policy framework.

The purpose of a local currency should be to grease the wheels of the local economy. Of the three roles of currencies, the prime role is as a means of exchange. The idea is to keep cash flowing rather than held static in saving accounts. Its potential role as a store of value can be deliberately degraded by not paying interest on savings. This disincentive to save can be strengthened by applying negative interest rates so that hoarding the currency means that the balance in a local currency account slowly erodes. This provides a strong incentive to spend rather than save. For the third role, as a measure of value, it is often pegged to the national currency, but to hold local currency is not equivalent to holding national currency. It makes sense when designing a local currency to restrict (or penalize) the transfer of funds back out to the national currency to ensure that its role is focused on facilitating exchange.

To examine why local currencies can be so beneficial, let us consider the local perspective. It is often the case that a locality has requirements which need to be met, together with the capacity to do so. There are people with needs, and people with the ability to work. An example best illustrates how a local currency can help. Let us say that in a particular locality there is a building in need of repair. The locality also has workers able to repair the building who are available to work. Let us consider that the building's owner may not have the cash to pay for repairs. Meanwhile the workers are unemployed. The building needs repair and there are workers willing and able to repair it, but no cash to make a transaction and get the job done. Introducing local currency can provide the building owners with the means to engage workers to repair the building, using the local currency as the means of exchange. The currency needs a central bank which issues a loan to the building owner. The building owner pays workers to repair the building. The workers spend the local currency in the local economy on food and services. Let us say that the owner of the refurbished building is now able to rent out a room to someone providing such local services, paid for in local currency, enabling the building owner to pay back the loan in instalments. Thus, the local currency circulates, connecting capacity to work with people's needs. The locality is invigorated enabling the mobilization of local resources. This is a microeconomy within the national economy with these circular flows of currency being complementary to the official national currency.

EXAMPLES OF LOCAL CURRENCIES

The potential of local currencies is seen most clearly in places where there is a shortage of cash to run a vibrant local economy. There may be demand for products and services, and capacity to satisfy the demand, but one cannot be connected with the other because of the lack of cash to facilitate transactions. A successful example is the WIR Franc, an electronic currency which operates in Switzerland alongside the official currency the Swiss Franc. It was established in 1934 by businessmen Werner Zimmermann and Paul Enz. It operates between commercial companies to encourage participating members to put their buying power at each other's disposal and keep it circulating within their ranks, thereby providing members with additional sales volume. At the time it was founded, there were severe currency shortages and global financial instability. Swiss companies had capacity and needed goods and services but lacked cash. The formation of the WIR connected companies providing a means to exchange their goods and services. Originally there were sixteen members; now there are 62,000. It is designed as a means of exchange and does not charge interest on obligations/loans.

A number of local currencies have been established in the UK in recent years each designed to serve its community.[26] An example which has gained wide support is the Bristol Pound. The

---

26 Places in the UK with a local currency are Brixton, Bristol, Cardiff, Cornwall, Exeter, Kingston, Lewes, Liverpool, Plymouth, Stroud, Totnes, and Worcester.

Bristol Pound is a not-for-profit partnership between the Bristol Pound Community Interest Company (CIC) and the Bristol Credit Union (Bristol Pound 2020). In this city in the west of England it is widely accepted by shops and is even accepted for the payment of Council Tax. Bristol City Council has committed to spending 100% of the value of Bristol Pounds they receive with local, independent businesses, supporting local jobs, keeping more money in Bristol and making the local economy stronger. To generate full benefit, these currencies need to be embedded into local communities and used by local people, traders and suppliers. A perceived problem is that they may become a threat to the government's tax raising powers. The local currency can become a way to formalize a black economy operating outside the reach of the tax authorities. In the case of the Bristol Pound, this is solved by treating all Bristol Pound transactions for tax purposes as if they were made in pounds sterling.

The UK experience of local currencies has been confined so far to relatively affluent areas with leadership from middle-class people with a green perspective. When local currencies are used to repair the economies of places with severe economic and social problems their true value will be appreciated. Broken and dysfunctional communities may not have the wherewithal to establish a local currency. It will require the government to shift from tolerating local currencies to championing their benefits for the full potential to be realised.

MANAGING LOCAL CURRENCIES

A requirement of a local currency is that a local bank needs to underwrite the currency and be the trusted guardian of the currency and how it is managed. The ideal bank for this purpose would be a local mutual bank which is owned by its members and is therefore already embedded in society. It may be that as the benefits of local currencies become understood, renewed support for mutual banking grows in parallel.

It is early days for the emergence of local currencies. Considerable variety can be expected in how they are set up and operate. Good ideas will be widely copied and other initiatives will fail to deliver and fade out. To give a flavour of the possibilities of how this might develop beyond a simple means of exchange, we might consider a local bank which underwrites the local currency offering mortgages denominated in the local currency. This could be an adjunct to a policy of affordable homes for local people. Let us suppose that a new development is given permission on the stipulation that they are for people who live and work locally. A local currency mortgage could be a mechanism which supports enforcing this. The local bank would provide the mortgage to people who could demonstrate their ability to pay the instalments in local currency. The risk of outsiders gaming the system would remain. It would therefore make sense for there to be tight controls on money being exchanged out of the local currency to restrict the speculators. Anyone purchasing local currency to buy an affordable local house would need to accept that when they sell, they would be paid in local currency which is not easily converted. The idea of a local housing market for local people facilitated by a local currency would need further thought and experimentation. It would be interesting for such a housing scheme to be established to test the concept and work out the detail of how it could operate successfully.

There are two ways to approach the issue of taxation. One is to draw the currency inside the national tax regime but this complexity may undermine the purpose of a local currency. The other is to allow it to operate outside national taxation accepting that mobilizing local economies is inherently good for society. For this to work, it may be necessary to rethink the parameters of national taxation so that local and national taxes work in harmony with the national and local currencies. Local shops, traders and tradesmen could operate using local currency and be exempt VAT (which is already the case in the UK for businesses below the threshold for VAT). This would give them an advantage compared with the big supermarkets where efficiency is derived from economies of scale and their ability to be tough on suppliers to deliver low prices. The local currency could help small local traders dealing with local suppliers to deliver similar prices and facilitate vibrant local economies.

Whilst considering local currencies, it is important to understand that the purpose is different to the national currency. Local currencies are for facilitating transactions within the locality. Such money is to be spent, not saved, hence the use of zero or negative interest rates. In my view, transactions should remain beyond the reach of the national tax system, providing local suppliers with advantage and allowing the local economy to thrive. From a conventional economic perspective, this could be seen as negative, formalizing a black economy. From a resilient economic perspective, recognizing the advantages for local communities will make it worthwhile for governments to adjust national taxation policy to support local currencies. Governments should provide freedom to operate remaining alert to potential abuse providing appropriate oversight of the sponsoring banks.

A Special Case – The Euro

Currencies should be managed to match the society which they serve. The formation of the Euro is an example of applying economic analysis without first deciding the political dimension. There is a mismatch between how the currency is managed and the ability of European nations to run their affairs. The currency is now well-established but there are lessons to learn and apply.

Let us start with noting the benefits of the Euro. Within the Eurozone, businesses no longer have to pay to change currency or carry the risk of exchange rates shifting. Buying and selling becomes as easy as a transaction within a single state. The population can move between countries without carrying multiple currencies. The simple economic justification is that the Euro reduces bureaucracy and increases efficiency.

The problem with the Euro is that it was established out of sync with the politics. For a single currency area there needs to be close coordination of fiscal policy. The political aspiration of deeper and closer union was behind the establishment of the Euro, but the Euro came first. Again, the economic case was put first, when it should have followed progress with the higher order decisions about political union.

In a single currency area, there will be strong and weak regions. Within the UK, economic strength is concentrated in the southeast region around London. There are therefore cash transfers to weaker regions such as the North of England, Scotland and Wales. It would be politically impossible for the southeast to argue that they keep wealth to themselves. It is normal for there to be differences between the economic performance of regions within a single currency area; and normal that there would be compensating cash transfers.

The Eurozone is by definition a single currency area, but it is not consistent with a single European state operating as a single entity. This might be an aspiration to be achieved at some point in the future, but the Euro exists now, in advance of such political and cultural integration. It is normal to expect some countries in the EU to have stronger economies than others. It should therefore be normal for cash transfers from such strong countries to weaker countries. Europe's northerly countries tend to have strong economies and those in the south relatively weak. It should be normal for cash to flow from north to south to compensate for the imbalance. To consider a specific example, Germany is strong and Greece is weak. There is a valid discussion to be had about different standards of probity and different taxation policies, but the fundamental need to transfer cash from the strong to the weak economy remains. Eurozone politicians resist such transfers for political reasons even though the economic case is sound. Greece has huge debts it can never repay and high unemployment causing social unrest. It has seemed for some years that Greece will either have to default on its debt and leave the Eurozone, or the Eurozone will have to behave much more like an integrated state and accept cash flows from economically strong regions to those which are weak.

The lesson to draw from the Euro is that currency design and management should match the political aspirations and social needs of the entire region which it serves. The Euro should serve all its members as a cohesive European economic block. National currencies should be managed to serve the entire country. Local currencies should be designed to serve a city or region within a country.

Conclusions

Money is the lifeblood of the economy. In the context of resilient economics there is a strong case to extend the reach of money to promote local currencies alongside national currencies. How money is managed and where it is allowed to flow is crucial to economic health. Local currencies need to flow freely within a locality. National currencies need to flow freely within a national economy. Inter-currency flows need to support trade between countries. In all cases the focus should be on currencies supporting real-world transactions.

Restrictions on inter-currency flows make sense, enhancing stability and putting governments in control. Such restriction may also reduce the potential for short-term economic growth, but the benefit of stability is the greater prize.

Reminding ourselves of why currencies are needed leads to taking back tight control to ensure they serve the needs of society. This is simple common sense, but may be seen by some in the financial community as retrograde. The changes outlined in this chapter may reduce the scope for making profits from gaming the financial system, so will not be liked by those who pocket the proceeds, but society would be correct to take such action. The benefit of this approach to currency management is stability and sustainability. Instead of lurching from crisis to crisis, such an approach would support countries in maintaining control of their economies and ensure that local difficulties are isolated and do not infect other economies.

CHAPTER 10

LEVER 2: TAX

In this world nothing can be said to be certain, except death and taxes.

Benjamin Franklin (1706–90)

Governments need revenue to fulfil their responsibilities including building and maintaining national infrastructure, defence and public services. Taxation is therefore necessary and desirable. No one would want to live in a society devoid of public facilities, without security and without a safety net for the most vulnerable people. Whether extensive high-quality public services and high taxes are better than limited basic public services and low tax, is a political choice. This chapter avoids the political debate to examine the core principles of taxation which should always apply.

The design of the tax system, and how it is implemented, can have significant consequences. Regarding taxation as simply a mechanism to raise income for government is unambitious. This leads to designing taxes to raise money with the greatest ease. It is important to do more than this and use taxation as a lever to drive change.

Easy Taxes

The art of taxation consists in so plucking the goose as to obtain the largest possible amount of feathers with the least possible amount of hissing.[27]

Jean-Baptiste Colbert (1619–83)

---

27 Quoted in: McKechnie, W. S. (1896). *The State & the Individual: An Introduction to Political Science, with Special Reference to Socialistic and Individualistic Theories.* Glasgow: James MacLehose and sons: p.77.

The tax authorities prefer taxes which are easy to collect. These are taxes which are precisely defined, collected automatically, and evasion is difficult. Value Added Tax at point of sale is an example. The government sets the percentage to apply and requires retailers to collect the tax and remit the money to the Inland Revenue. Politics might add complexity such as exemptions or categories of goods charged at different rates. All the government has to do is set the rate(s) and have a system of spot inspections to ensure compliance. Income taxes have similar characteristics with employers required to calculate the tax, take it off pay and submit the funds to the tax authorities. A political process sets the levels of tax to be applied to different levels of income. Big ticket items, like car sales, are another candidate for easy taxation, with car dealers required to collect the tax.

Of course, there will always be tax avoidance and evasion. In some countries the black economy is large and the loss of tax significant. An ideal taxation system would be designed such that there is little incentive to avoid the tax and limited scope to evade it.

If tax policy, and the authority which implements it, remain focused on the amount of tax collected, then an important role of tax is not being utilized. This is the way that taxes can be used as a lever for change. Understanding this role can make the taxation system doubly effective, driving change and raising revenue.

Using Tax to Drive Change

The simplest way to understand the role of taxes in driving change is to think of it as taxing 'bad' activities. Obvious examples are smoking and alcohol. Society does not judge that they are so bad that they should be banned, but their consumption has negative consequences for people's health and the healthcare system. The taxes provide a disincentive to consume, together with a useful revenue stream, so are doubly effective. If something is seriously bad, such as some drugs, prohibition is the appropriate response. Where a ban is implemented and widely ignored – as is the case with the soft drug marijuana – the pragmatic solution could be to legalize and tax. This shifts income from criminals to reputable suppliers protecting people from access to an illegal supply chain which may also include hard drugs like heroin. The prime objective would be to protect public health with the additional tax income being a convenient side effect.

One thing to be borne in mind when taxing bad activities is that when the tax succeeds, the tax revenues will drop. When taxes are used to drive change, it is important not to become reliant on the revenue, or the perverse incentive arises to maintain continuance of the bad in order to retain the revenue.

A prime example of taxing bad activities is to tax pollution, but care is required. If the pollutant is particularly toxic and persistent when released into the environment, then tight control is the correct course of action. It would be quite wrong to allow such chemicals to be released and morally corrupt to raise revenue by taxing them. This is the case with the fluorocarbons that were found to be destroying the ozone layer. The Montreal Protocol is an international agreement to ban the production and use of this category of man-made chemicals. This is the correct response for such a damaging pollutant, and taxing would not be appropriate.

An example of a situation where pollution taxes can be a useful option is carbon dioxide emissions.

TAXING FOSSIL FUEL

Carbon dioxide is a natural part of the processes of life and the planet. It is not a toxic and damaging pollutant. The danger is excess emission of CO_2 above a safe level. The activity which is the bad in this case is the burning of fossil fuel.[28] It is clear that something must be done, and that something is to shift our energy systems from fossil fuel to other sources (discussed in detail in Chapter 17). Tax can be a useful tool to support this transition.

Taxing fossil fuel makes it more expensive compared with other energy sources – heavy tax on fossil fuel makes it much more expensive. The tax lever can be applied without being dependent on detailed plans for the best mix for future energy supply. In fact, it might be better not to attempt top-down planning in such a complex and uncertain situation. The simple tool of taxing fossil fuel can force through the required change – without quite knowing the final solution. The rate of tax can be advertised in advance, escalating over a number of years from an initially low level to a level which becomes significant in investment decisions. The economic rules of the game will have been altered deliberately to force change, not only in energy generation but also in energy consumption. The detailed outcome cannot be known in advance, nor predicted with certainty, but taxing fossil fuel is an appropriate economic tool to drive down consumption.

Unfortunately, politics gets in the way of the simple tax solution to deal with fossil fuel. Politicians do not like having to make the case for more expensive energy, this being the inevitable short-term consequence. Politicians therefore take the politically easier option of applying subsidies to renewable energy in

---

28 Burning fossil fuel is causing climate change. This carbon has been locked up in the Earth's crust since the Carboniferous period in the late Paleozoic Era of geological time about 300 million years ago. Unlocking this fossil carbon is changing the planet including making more intense storms more likely and a slow but steady rise in the sea level which will continue well beyond the time when we find the collective will to stop burning fossil fuel. Many cities will be flooded and low-lying countries inundated. These are 'planet changing' alterations to the human living space.

an attempt to achieve a similar outcome. There is a role for subsidies in the short-term, to initiate customer demand and kickstart new industries, but this should be replaced by the hard lever of taxation. Not only does this give renewable energy an advantage but it also makes energy efficiency more cost effective, providing the dual benefit of reducing energy demand and cleaning up energy supply. Such clear thinking and political courage could move the situation forward at pace. The beauty of taxing fossil fuel is the combination of driving change coupled with raising revenue to pay for related improvements to public infrastructure.

TAXING LAND

Tax on land can be used to drive change in the way land is managed and used. This is a straightforward tax to apply. The owner is easy to identify and the tax has to be paid or the land forfeited.

An example of using tax on land to deliver outcomes other than simply generating revenue, is an idea I floated for a tax applied on urban land to retain a proportion of land for nature. This would help to recognize the intrinsic value of nature and allow people to enjoy being close to nature (McManners 2008: 198–9). The idea is for tax on urban land to be offset with a tax rebate for contiguous land kept for nature. Landowners would then have an incentive to retain part of the land they own for nature. Such a mechanism would ensure that stewardship of space for nature becomes ingrained in how land is used and managed. Again, this can be outside any formal system of land protection. If the tax exists, land would be saved for nature in places and ways that we do not need to know in advance and cannot predict. I use this as an example of the type of thinking which this approach to taxation encourages without reigniting the argument for or against my particular proposal.

TAXING PEOPLE AND ROBOTS

Taxing employment can have huge influence on the availability of jobs. Taxing robots can influence decisions about automation. Balancing the two taxes can help society to navigate the new world of work.

Advances in automation have the potential to make our lives easier but are also a threat to jobs. Applying resilient thinking to the challenge of employment in the age of automation provides pointers to possible future developments in taxation. It is becoming feasible to automate many more jobs and replace people with robots. As robots get cheaper, employing people gets relatively more expensive. If government fails to act, there will be fewer and fewer jobs.

The conventional economic rule of thumb to increase employment, is to boost consumption. This breaks down when most work is carried out by robots. This rule of thumb needs to be removed from the economic toolbox and replaced with measures to retain people engaged in the economy. It is clearly good that dirty or dangerous jobs can be delegated to robots; but a healthy society needs people to be engaged, valued and incorporated into the fabric of society and the economy. The general way forward is clear enough, which is to recognize the value of employment to society.

In order to maintain employment in the age of automation, one idea is to tax robots. This has its merits, but is too simplistic to be enough on its own. Another is to shift the burden of taxation from employment to taxing expenditure and material inputs, so that employing people remains cost effective. If employing people cost less it would be natural to retain jobs.

Recognizing the value to society of employment, governments can be expected to use the tax system to incentivize business to recruit and retain a large workforce. Currently within the business world, there is a blinkered, almost unthinking, drive to increase efficiency and productivity through investing in capital equipment to eliminate human workers. A more nuanced approach will be required. Instead of working out the numbers for capital expenditure to eliminate jobs, it should be equally valid to work out the numbers for employing people to save on capital investment. We should use automation of course to enhance people's lives and improve society, but within an economically viable plan facilitated by taxation policy designed to support maintaining a workforce.

Additional measures could include reducing the cost of employing people through repealing minimum wage regulations. This would be politically toxic at the moment, but this will change when the benefits of a universal basic income have been factored in (more on this in Chapter 11). Such joined-up policy can help retain jobs and protect the least well off. This is a very different approach, requiring complete reconfiguration of the system of taxation. This is likely to be resisted until there is widespread understanding of how the new economy should operate.

TAXING AVIATION

I will close this discussion of the role of taxation as a lever of change with how it might apply to the tricky environmental challenge of aviation. This short section summarizes a decade of detailed research into a complex dilemma (McManners 2012, 2017 and 2020).

Aviation is trapped in an outdated economic model which is over seventy-five years old. In 1944, towards the end of World War Two, a convention on civil aviation was held in Chicago. Over a period of seven weeks the rules which govern aviation were agreed. The intentions could not have been healthier – to use aviation to connect the world and help to cement the post-war peace. Seventy-five years on this agreement has had unintended consequences.

Article 24 of the Convention on International Civil Aviation prevents countries from levying taxes on fuel carried on board aircraft arriving in a country. If any country were to introduce a tax on aviation fuel for international flights, the airlines would be within their rights to arrange their schedules to refuel elsewhere. For example, if the UK took a lead in taxing aviation fuel, airlines would move their long-haul operations to Charles de Gaulle or Schiphol airports demoting Heathrow to short-haul flights. The consequence is a tax stalemate where tax-free aviation fuel is hardwired into the industry's economic model. This skews decisions away from initiating the transformation the industry needs to respond to the environmental challenge of emissions.

Taxation of aviation fuel is what the aviation industry needs to move forward, but the only way countries can implement the tax change, without suffering economic disadvantage, would be through international agreement. The United States is resolutely opposed to any such suggestion. I know also through my research that in general passengers are not aware that aviation fuel is tax-free and they do not appreciate how much better aviation could be. Passengers, therefore, are not demanding change and are not putting pressure on politicians.

My research found that politicians in Europe see the logic for a tax on aviation fuel but are not willing to expend political capital on moving aviation policy forward. So, decisions with regard to planning the future of aviation, including the development of aviation technology and airline operating models, are predicated on tax-free fuel. This is holding back progress in the development of better more efficient air vehicles. The stalemate is so deeply engrained that aviation fuel tax is seldom discussed. When I talk with people inside the industry, they are confident that government will not change the status quo. I speak also with many people outside the industry who have no idea that aviation fuel is tax-free and find it hard to comprehend that such a long-standing exception remains even now. In this polarized debate, few people take the pragmatic middle ground to consider how 21st-century aviation could be significantly better for people and the planet (McManners 2012 and 2016). It is absolutely possible to transform aviation but nothing substantial will change until there is a significant tax on aviation fuel to drive forward the transformation.

Tax-free aviation fuel is an outrageous affront to common sense. Whilst the politicians are locked into the mindset of the fossil-fuel economy, and bow to lobbying from the aviation industry, nothing happens. It is true that when the transformation gathers pace, a large part of the current aviation industry would face bankruptcy. This is because all decisions over many decades have assumed that fuel will remain cheap. It is for society to light the blue touch paper, agree to tax aviation fuel, and watch the industry go up in flames. There will be disruption in the short-term but then a sustainable model for aviation will rise like a Phoenix out of the ashes (McManners 2012).

We had a foretaste of the consequences of transforming aviation when the COVID-19 pandemic gripped the world from 2020–21. As the world's aviation shut down, burning much less fossil fuel, people could start to experience a cleaner future (Le Quéré et al. 2020). The economic consequences for aviation were severe with large parts of the sector facing bankruptcy. This could be the opportunity to relaunch the industry into a low-carbon future. Following the idea of never letting a good crisis go to waste, the key response by governments should be to make any support contingent on significant emissions reductions. The crisis could be used to convene an international convention on civil aviation to rescue the industry, with the taxation of aviation fuel on the agenda, something which would not have been possible prior to the crisis. Through the lens of resilient economics, there is a bright future for aviation provided policymakers have the courage to grasp it (McManners 2020).

An interesting insight into how tax experts can offer advice without seeing the broader perspective came to light as I researched this section. An examination of tax on aviation fuel was carried out for the IMF and published as a working paper (Keen & Strand 2006). In the paper, it was explained that the application of a tax on aviation fuel would lead to 'distortion' of production decisions in the direction of less aviation fuel use. For revenue generation, the tax would need to be low (around 20 US cents per litre) otherwise the tax revenue would fall as the airlines would change how they operate to burn less fuel. Although the authors noted that reduction in aviation fuel use would be beneficial given the environmental damage caused, they had fallen into the trap of regarding the tax solely in terms of revenue raising. The potential for tax on aviation fuel to drive environmental performance improvements was entirely incidental to their analysis. The conclusion that the tax should be low to ensure that airlines do not avoid the tax by cleaning up their operations to burn less fuel is completely at odds with common sense.

The resilient approach to taxation of aviation fuel tax is to follow common sense and target emission reduction. The mental barrier, if you are a tax expert, is the assumption that your role is to maximize revenue. From this perspective, it makes perfect sense to argue for a *low* aviation fuel tax to ensure fuel burn remains high to maximize revenue. The authors of the analysis are clearly expert, their paper is well-written, and there is nothing inaccurate in what they write. It is true that from a revenue-generation perspective, aviation fuel tax would need to be low or the aviation business would arrange its affairs to burn less fuel. When such thinking is exposed it becomes clear that more common sense is needed in economic analysis and the urgency of adopting the resilient economic approach is underlined.

Applying the mindset of resilient economics, the purpose of a tax on aviation fuel would be less about revenue generation and much more about transforming the industry. The revenue in this case is not the prime objective. In fact, as in all cases where tax is used to drive change, the revenue will drop off considerably as the tax succeeds in driving a step-change towards more efficient flight. Through the transformation, when tax receipts would expect to be high, the tax could be hypothecated to speed up the rapid development of low-carbon aviation. The drop off in tax when the transformation is under way would not then be a problem, as the tax would not have been factored into core government spending.

Incentives, Subsidies and Tax Breaks

Having considered the role of tax in driving change, it is also worth considering the flip-side of using subsidies and tax breaks to incentivize positive behaviours. Here the government pays out money to provide the subsidy or sacrifices revenue by offering a tax break. In an economic sense, applying tax as a driver is almost always more effective than spending on subsidies. The reason subsidies are useful is to kick-start change, to support the development of new technologies, and to introduce capabilities into the market to educate customers about what is available. Subsidises often have a political dimension so care is needed that this does not undermine the economic rationale.

Examples where a subsidy or incentives can have sufficient value to overcome the revenue downside are where the objective is to plant the seeds of change to set up the right circumstances before applying the tax lever. Research into technology might be required, or other actions to overcome initial resistance and pump-prime the change process. Such subsidies and incentives need to be carefully targeted and withdrawn as soon as possible. The danger of targeted subsidies is that government selects which technology to use or decides which process to employ. Governments have a poor record of selecting winning solutions. Using tax to drive change is preferable because it is neutral about technology or process, allowing the freedom for the best solution to emerge on its own merits.

SUBSIDIES FOR RENEWABLE ENERGY

The promotion of renewable energy in the UK is an example of the application of subsidies. As a way of kick-starting the renewable energy industry it has been a good approach but there were perverse outcomes as people exploited loopholes in the complex system. For example, in Northern Ireland there was shameful incompetence with regard to the Renewable Heat Incentive (which encouraged the burning of wood and other renewable fuels instead of fossil fuel). The system was such that the subsidy was greater than the cost of the fuel. Some buildings were heated all year round with the windows kept open to maximize the subsidy which could be claimed. The scheme was shut in 2016 after burning through £33 million of taxpayer's money (BBC 2019). I am not sure who is worse, the policymaker who designed the incentive system or the building owners who knowingly exploited its flaws for financial gain.

Subsidies almost always have a political dimension. Politicians tend to be timid to apply the tax lever, fearing that they will be blamed for the initial increase in energy prices. Prices would indeed be higher until renewable energy generation prices dropped through economies of scale, and bills reduced because less energy was needed as efficiency improved. Economists can be complicit in providing politicians with convenient excuses, through presenting complex subsidy regimes instead of promoting the simple solution of taxing the 'bad' and letting industry navigate towards solutions. Some short-term incentives and subsidies are useful to sow the seeds of change but this should advance quickly to pulling firmly on the tax lever.

For the renewable energy sector, the best way forward comes from examining closely the desired outcome. The reason to want more renewable energy is in order to burn less fossil fuel. The most appropriate economic action is to apply the tax lever to fossil fuels. This has a trio of advantages. First, it makes renewable energy viable without needing to second-guess which form of renewable energy to support. Second, the tax incentivizes investment in efficiency thus reducing energy demand. Third, the tax provides a revenue stream to invest as the government sees fit, which could be in improving the energy efficiency of public infrastructure. Taxing fossil fuel is hugely more effective than paying subsidies – but politically more difficult.

THE PERVERSION OF ONGOING SUBSIDY

It is important to withdraw subsidy when its purpose has been achieved. An ongoing subsidy reinforces the status quo, protecting the economy as currently configured and preventing creative destruction from taking place.

For example, the current economy is based on energy derived from fossil fuel. To defend and protect the economy is taken to mean ensuring that it continues to operate much as it does now. Through the application of subsidies, incentives are provided to replace fossil fuel with renewable energy. The invidious side to this approach is the objective to protect the current economic model, rather than replace it. The subsidy helps to retain an economic model structured around cheap fossil fuel. A resilient economic analysis would seek to shift to an economy structured to suit renewable energy. This will be a different economic model, in which energy has greater value.

Instead of adding subsidies into the current economic model, economic policy should be adjusted, according to circumstances, to orchestrate the changes required to build a new economic model. If you pause and reflect this is obvious and common sense.

Enforcement

A tax which is not enforced fails in its purpose and brings the tax system into disrepute. A tax which is fair and sensible (and therefore attracts public support) is easier to enforce than an unpopular tax. It therefore makes sense to have a tax system which is fair and sensible – and demonstrably so. When avoidance for a particular tax becomes widespread, this can quickly degenerate as tax dodging becomes pervasive and people think it only fair to join in. Breaking such a vicious cycle might need changes to the tax to improve clarity, fairness, and ease of collection.

An important perspective on enforcement, which can be easily overlooked, is to decide what is to be enforced. Taxes have two purposes: to raise revenue and drive change. For the former, enforcement is about maximizing the tax collected; for the latter, enforcement is about delivering the required change. These can be quite different, as the discussion earlier in this chapter about taxing aviation fuel showed. When the purpose of the tax is to drive change, the tax should be as high as politically palatable to match the pace of transformation required. Inevitably there will be arguments about who should collect and retain the tax revenue, but this should not deflect attention away from the primary objective to drive transformation.

For another perspective on confusion over the purpose of tax, we can consider James Tobin's proposal for a tax on international currency transactions. He presented the idea in a lecture at Princeton University in 1972. As a proposal to tackle the problem of excessive speculation in international currency markets it made sense (Tobin 1978). This was a reasonable suggestion to bring currency markets back closer to reality. The purpose of the proposed tax was to drive change. It was unfortunate that the transaction tax was also identified as a source of revenue to help fund UN development work (Haq et al. 1996). This confusion of purpose between the intention to improve how the market operates, and the generation of revenue, helped to kill the proposal. It would have been hard to win the argument for such a tax in the face of opposition from those who run the markets, but to also expect governments to hand over the revenue to the UN alienated the prime stakeholders who would have the task of collecting the tax. The Tobin tax was effectively killed off because of the confusion over its purpose.

Taxation Guidelines

Some guidelines are offered for taxation as a lever of resilient economics. The intention is to cut through the complex interplay between the two objectives of raising revenue and driving change.

1. *Clarity of purpose*: a particular tax should be designed to either raise revenue or drive change.

2. *To raise revenue*: a tax designed to raise revenue should be consistent, long lasting, easy to implement, and hard to evade.

3. *To drive change:* a tax designed to drive change should steer decisions towards desirable outcomes with the revenue applied in support of the change.

4. *When to use subsidies and tax breaks:* these should only be used as short-term measures to initiate change.

5. *When not to use subsidies and tax breaks:* subsidies and tax breaks should not be used for purely political purposes unsupported by sound economic analysis.

Tax can provide revenue as well as drive change, but it is important that the design of the tax is focused on one or the other. The primary purpose must be specified because the design parameters are different.

To drive change, tax should be levied to discourage the 'bad' and reward the 'good'. The revenue cannot be relied on to fund the government's core budget, so it would make sense to apply the revenue to support the desired change. This could be related public infrastructure or measures to ameliorate the impact on people or organizations that might be affected by the change. As change takes place, revenue drops, hand-in-hand with less need for the support measures funded by the tax.

Subsidies and tax breaks make sense to kick-start research and development or initiate customer acceptance. Long-term subsidies only make sense when there is a tax-neutral plan linking an ongoing subsidy with a related ongoing tax. For example, governments might decide to subsidize companies to employ larger workforces, linked to a tax on robots. Another example could be to provide a tax break on land retained for nature, linked to an additional tax on urban land. There are all sorts of possible tax doublets which fit this pattern.

When considering using subsidies and tax breaks, it is

important to understand when they should not be used. For example, it is common across the world in many countries to subsidize fossil fuel to ensure it is affordable. Such political expediency is the height of folly. This reinforces reliance on fossil fuel and soaks up government funds which could be better spent. If the political intention is to make energy affordable, then subsidy should go to renewable sources (and energy efficiency measures), funded by tax on fossil fuel. In poorer countries where the political pressure to subsidize fossil fuel can be intense, a better approach would be to subsidize alternatives. For example, instead of kerosene subsidies for household lighting in India, subsidy could go to small-scale solar power and battery systems (Lam et al. 2016). The desired political outcome of affordable lighting would be delivered but without the negative environmental impact.

Conclusions

Taxation is vital to pay for civilized society. At the core of the tax system are easy-to-collect taxes, such as VAT, with rates set to balance government finances. The other purpose of tax is to leverage change, with revenue generation as a convenient bonus. In this case, revenue should be allocated to support the desired outcome, so that the drop in revenue as the tax succeeds does not open up a hole in government finances. The tools of subsidies and tax breaks should be used with caution. These reduce revenue, so should have a very narrow short-term role in initiating change. Ideally, there should be clarity of purpose, fairness in how tax is applied, and enforcement with the minimum of bureaucracy and the maximum of effectiveness. Complex unenforceable taxes are not helpful, particularly where the purpose is not plain to see and revenue generation gets confused with the process of driving change. Appropriate taxation is a powerful economic tool provided the five guidelines presented above are followed.

CHAPTER 11

LEVER 3: UNIVERSAL BASIC INCOME

Such a proposal will strike many readers as mad... it is no longer clear where the boundaries of economic sanity lie.

Financial Times, 14 March 2016

The concept of a universal basic income is that every adult is paid a low-level income by the state regardless of their circumstances. Universal basic income was described by the Financial Times as a proposal which will strike many readers as mad, but went on to conclude that it is 'an idea whose time may finally have come' (Thornhill 2016). Employed or unemployed, rich or poor, everyone would be eligible to receive it.

I first came across the idea of a citizen's income (an alternative term for universal basic income) in 2004 at a conference convened by the newly founded Institute of Green Economics. The delegates were an eclectic bunch of people from a wide range of backgrounds. As a management consultant and business school academic, I was a bit of an oddity. I had chosen to dress appropriate to the sort of business conference with which I was familiar, whilst others were wearing home knitted jumpers and eco sandals. Despite a certain amount of mutual distrust, it soon became clear that what we had in common was the desire to improve economics. Over the two days of the conference, I listened to impassioned pleas for better economic policy and a range of ideas. One of these was the concept of citizen's income – which initially seemed to be completely unworkable.

It took me some time to come around to support the idea of a universal basic income. In my mind it had to pass the test of pragmatic reality before arguing for its introduction. I support it, not because I have become an idealist, but because as a pragmatist I have worked out how it can operate in support of society and its current challenges. Universal basic income can be the catalyst for effective policy provided it is implemented for clearly defined logical reasons. I believe that the mechanism of citizen's income, if designed well, can invigorate local economies, cement social cohesion, and reduce people's reliance on the state. It can set people free to take control of their affairs and reward those who accept the responsibility. It can be set up to be cost-neutral with associated changes to income tax and social welfare expenditure. To deliver the full benefits, it would have to be implemented in conjunction with other policies including wholesale structural change to welfare support.

A trial of the concept began in Finland in 2017 and lasted two years. Finland has generous unemployment pay and faces the problem that people have little incentive to work in low-paid or part-time work. A random sample of unemployed people were paid €560 per month without any stipulation on whether they work, or not, or how they spend the money. The trial was set up in a rush on a limited budget which goes some way to explaining the disappointing results (Hiilamo 2019). It would be wrong to write off the idea from the results of this real-world experiment because the income paid was not universal and was not part of wider changes to the employment and welfare system. Policymakers will have to be more ambitious in testing whether it can be implemented in such a way that it delivers on its promise. This early setback might be used to justify ditching this promising idea; that would be a shame.

The concept is also being tested in the United States. The Stockton Economic Empowerment Demonstration (SEED) was launched in February 2019 in the city of Stockton, California. A total of 125 randomly selected residents were given a guaranteed income of $500/month for 24 months. The cash was completely unconditional, with no requirement to work. The aim was to address problems of inequality, income volatility, and poverty:

> *We believe that SEED provides an opportunity to imagine a fairer and more inclusive social contract that provides dignity for all. Everyone deserves financial stability – SEED proves that a guaranteed income is one way to achieve it.*

> West et al. 2021

The interim report published in March 2021 showed a 'causal connection between guaranteed income and financial stability, and mental and physical health improvement.' (West et al. 2021: 22). This project demonstrated the social benefits of financial stability and security, but was overlaid on the existing economic model, without changing other aspects, so it was not a true test of its potential to empower people and change the world of work.

In this chapter, the potential benefits of universal basic income are explained to give pragmatic policymakers the confidence to deploy it understanding the positive role it can play in a resilient economy.

Resistance to Universal Basic Income

Universal basic income does not sit well with a conventional policy mindset. Those on the right of the political spectrum can see it as money for nothing and a scoundrel's charter. Those on the left of politics worry that it could be used as an excuse to pay less in welfare benefits. Such concerns mean that initial resistance is likely to be universal.

There is a fundamental barrier to realizing the wider benefits of a universal basic income. This is the policy of a 'minimum wage' which has become a foundation of employment policy in many countries including the UK. Such legislation ensures that people in work are paid at least the minimum wage. This is a fair and equitable concept, but the problem with the policy is that it makes employing people expensive. In the current age of automation, enforcing minimum pay levels gives the robots the edge and accelerates the destruction of jobs. The good intentions of minimum wage legislation are thus undermined. In explaining how universal basic income can leverage wider benefits, it will become clear that minimum-wage legislation should be withdrawn (or amended) to deliver the benefits outlined below.

It would be politically difficult to withdraw minimum-wage regulations. If its removal could be coordinated with the introduction of a universal basic income, it could become politically palatable. Such combined action could expose the full potential of the policy.

The Way Forward

There is no consensus on how universal basic income should be implemented – or even agreement on why it should be implemented. The argument liked by the political left is that it provides every citizen with income. The political right like the way it can be used to cap welfare payments. The politically neutral perspective is that when implemented fully it is good for society. It is only with experiments in the real world that these different perspectives can be forged into good policy. It should not be expected that there will be one blueprint as it makes sense for there to be different versions to suit different societies.

I expect the model of universal basic income I outline here to be adjusted with experience of real-world implementations. I provide enough detail to explain the concept and start to unlock its potential without insisting that the model should be implemented exactly as described below.

I suggest that the prime reason to have a universal basic income is to deal with the dangers to social cohesion of automation. Ways have to be found to adjust models of work to engage people with useful roles in society. This needs to suit both workers and the organizations offering work. One interesting outcome is that it blurs the distinction between employer and employee, helping to foster social cohesion within the work place.

The basic income should be paid to every citizen regardless of their circumstances across the breadth of society. It might seem strange at first, for people in employment to receive it too, but this is important to its potential. Universal income is paid with few restrictions. It is not means tested; nor reduced or withdrawn if people work. Rather than being odd, this is an important part of its attraction. Where chief executives, prime ministers and well-paid people receive the basic income, they would not be better off compared with now, because of the other adjustments in the tax system to pay for it. Making it universal in this way means the bureaucracy can be minimal, so administrative costs are low, with the net benefit flowing to those who need it at the lower end of the income scale. The people who will be worse off are those people not in work who receive substantial welfare payments in the current system. This group will initially receive less cash because the universal basic income is the only direct cash benefit available from the state. It must operate in this way, despite potential political difficulties, if it is to work in the way intended. The success of the whole concept depends on how well it supports people to improve their lives, and the extent to which it encourages people to take responsibility for their affairs.

People can respond to the opportunity of a guaranteed basic income in a number of ways. Some people might choose a frugal lifestyle living within the basic income alone. Such a lifestyle would necessarily be low consumption which might include all sorts of self-help such as growing their own food as the season allows. Such people can take pride in their self-sufficiency and not be looked down on as scroungers. The basic income allows people to live a simple life by choice without stigma. In an age when the future of humanity is under threat of excessive consumption and environmental overload, no one should begrudge people that.

Other people may use the security which comes with the universal basic income to start a small business, or take part-time or low-paid work. Volunteering becomes a viable option as part of people's portfolio of work-type activity. People who are less able, or less capable, perhaps with some form of disability, will have opportunities to work for a rate of pay appropriate to their output. So instead of being excluded from the job market where a minimum wage means only the able-bodied can get work, they can be drawn back into employment. Such work places might be set up by charitable foundations, but all businesses will be able to draw people in at low rates of pay for the mutual benefit of employer and employee, providing some resistance to the march of the robots.

Worries about exploitation I think are overdone. When everybody has a basic income by right, employees have the freedom to leave a job they do not find satisfying or if they feel they are being unfairly treated. Employers will have access to a potential low-cost workforce but they will have to think carefully about the nature of the work they provide. It will be less about making work pay, and more about making work satisfying, even enjoyable.

Citizenship

An obvious ramification of the universal income for all citizens, is that the definition of citizen becomes extremely important – and valuable. Developed countries provide all sorts of welfare support payments, based on need, and the precise definition of citizenship may not be part of the current system. The introduction of the universal basic income will require precise clarification of who is, and is not, a citizen. This will be decided by politics rather than economics. A prudent government would guard citizenship carefully and grant citizenship in a carefully controlled manner. There will be people living in the country who do not have citizen status, such as temporary workers, temporary residents, foreign students, and others who do not meet the criteria to be citizens.

For the economic analysis, temporary worker will be an important category. The existence of the citizen's income should draw many more of the population into low-paid jobs but rich countries would probably still have need of additional foreign workers for jobs shunned by its citizens. In addition, poorer countries are likely to continue to want to benefit from income remitted by their nationals working temporarily in richer economies. It would make sense to allow temporary workers to enter the country for a time-limited period without gaining entitlement to citizenship, or eligibility for the basic universal income.

Funding Universal Basic Income

A complaint about universal basic income is that it would be expensive. Brought in as an additional measure in isolation from other changes, it would be a huge additional burden on government finances. It needs to be part of a rebalancing of government income and expenditure. Part of this could be higher income tax rates for higher earners. Another part would be redirecting existing welfare spending. To make the numbers add up, it would be worth considering rethinking the whole taxation system recognizing that work and jobs are not just good for the economy but are good for society. Perhaps employment in general should be taxed less with the burden of taxation shifted to expenditure. It is not just low-level jobs that are at risk; advances in artificial intelligence mean that professional and middle-income jobs will also be at risk. It could be in everyone's interest to slow down the march of the machines by ensuring the cost of employing people is kept in check.

The funds to afford universal basic income could come from a range of tax changes, including increased sales tax (especially on unhealthy activities or products) and taxes on resources recognizing that we are entering the era of tight resources. Fossil fuel is another area to increase tax, as hefty taxes would be a powerful lever for change; but this would be short-term only until fossil fuel is eliminated from the energy mix. The politicians could consider a wide range of options including taxes on land, property and perhaps wealth. Overall, if universal basic income is accepted as a foundation of government budgeting, it should be feasible to rejig the government budget to pay for it.

A key issue is the level at which universal basic income is set. In economic terms, the higher the rate the more it costs the government. In political terms, those on the left might want it to be a 'living wage', that is enough to live the sort of life people have come to expect. Those on the political right might prefer the rate to be low to minimize expenditure. Putting politics aside, the universal basic income should be set at a rate which suits the term 'basic'. It should be enough for people to live simply in safety and with enough to eat. This makes the policy affordable and means it can serve its purpose which is to provide a financial foundation on which to build an inclusive economy. If it is set too low, government will come under pressure to supplement it with welfare benefits; set too high and people will not have the incentive to work to improve their circumstances.

The universal basic income becomes the heart of the welfare state. This can, and should, be far more than swapping one benefit for another. It will allow and support a complete rejigging of the welfare system to support the less able and most vulnerable people in society.

Building the New Welfare Web

The universal basic income is a simple concept and straightforward to implement. What is really interesting is that something so simple can be at the heart of a complex web of improved welfare support. I will use the analogy of a spider spinning a web. A spider is a small, simple creature that can produce a web which is stronger than anything modern industry can produce. Spider silk is stronger than steel and stronger than Kevlar. We would like to understand how spiders do this to develop industrial processes to make new stronger materials. Thinking about a top-down industrial process, the engineers consider how to mix appropriate ingredients and extrude the mixture through tiny holes to make a fine filament. Top-down thinking has not been helpful; it has been discovered that spider silk is not forced out, but pulled out with the filament almost a liquid but drying and hardening as it meets the air. The pull process does not need high pressure or expensive ingredients just the right system at the microscopic level. For the welfare system, trying to design a comprehensive system top-down which looks after every person's needs fully without anyone being missed, is impossible and unaffordable. The alternative is to implement the universal basic income, and allow people, organizations, and communities to build the welfare web from the bottom up, pulling out what they need as it enters the real world to harden into welfare support mechanisms.

Pulling from the community level against the opportunity of citizen's income, can produce results which no amount of money pushed down from above could achieve. As this is not top-down planning, it is impossible to be precise about how this welfare web would operate. I will attempt to describe the possibilities starting with what the government might provide directly as the default option. I will then examine what non-governmental organizations (NGOs) might offer and finally consider what business can orchestrate.

Governments have responsibility for their people, particularly the vulnerable such as the very young, the infirm or those with disability. It is assumed that there would remain a residual need for basic welfare provision by the state. Where a universal basic income has been implemented it will empower most able-bodied people to help themselves. The rigid view that the basic income is all that is available, although being clear and simple, would not be acceptable in most civilized societies. The other extreme would also not be acceptable – for the state to fund everyone to a high standard of living regardless of whether they are lazy, feckless or accept no responsibility for their actions. The middle ground is where the state implements a universal basic income, together with providing a welfare safety net of last resort. Building on the opportunity of the basic income, NGOs and others will be enabled to do more, as explained below.

The provision of care in institutions, or supporting people where they live, always boils down to affordability. This is where the universal basic income can leverage better social care drawing maximum value from limited resources. People held in state institutions, such as prisons or long-term special residential care, will have their basic income taken to help pay for it. Such provision is expensive, and can be much more expensive, so additional government funding is required. There could also be state-run hostels where people can get shelter and food, which might consist of little more than their own bed space and access to communal washing facilities. For these hostel spaces it is feasible that the basic income would provide sufficient funding. Basic would mean basic. This is where people could end up when all other options are exhausted. Where children are involved, there would need to be additional safeguards and services focused on the children's needs. These would be designed as services rather than cash handouts to ensure that parents cannot steal these for their own benefit. Most parents want the best for their children; but feckless or incompetent parents should not be able to hold the state to ransom.

The social care system typically consists of two broad options: institutions where people are cared for by professional staff, and care in the community where people live in their own homes supported by a care package of carers visiting on a regular basis. Both models are expensive to deliver. The prime expense for institutions is the cost of the professional workforce. For care in the community, people incur normal living expenses plus the additional cost of a care package. There are problems with both models. Institutions can be soul-destroying places, with staff under pressure and inmates without a sense of purpose. Care in the community is always constrained by cost so people can feel lonely and exposed through insufficient support.

New models for care can be developed involving what is called the Third Sector in the provision of public services. These are a range of charitable organizations, neither government nor business. The implementation of a universal basic income allows this sector to do much more. The key aspect is the blurring of lines between the delivery of welfare support and self-help. Such charitable models of social support and care are particularly relevant to people who are less able or less capable but not to the extent of being totally dependent. In the current cash-constrained system this group tends to be marginalized, receiving limited support and often expected to manage their own affairs. The new model which becomes feasible is for charities to build communities where people work to their ability (whatever that might extend to) to contribute to the community and have a place to live which is safe and feels like home. There will be professional staff in charge, but below this level it might be hard to discern who is a member of staff and who is being looked after. The idea is to reach the situation where people feel they are members of the community, and proud to be contributing to the community, as well as enjoying its support.

The basic income underpins care models where significant components of service delivery comes from self-help from within the community. Some people working to the best of their ability may not be at the level where they would be able to hold down regular employment but in these new communities they can be employed. They will be paid a wage which they feel has been earned but in real terms it may be little more than pocket money. Current minimum wage legislation tends to block the development of such models of engaging people in low-paid, low-expectation work.

An issue to be alert to, is the possibility of vulnerable people being exploited. The potential for exploitation is more relevant when such employment models are established in the for-profit sector (see below). If these communities are run by charities with a strong ethos, supported by an inspection regime, that should be sufficient to deal with such concerns.

COMMUNITY BUILDING

There are numerous ways that individuals, groups of people, organizations, and business can participate in community building using the basic income to underpin their finances. Two quite different examples are outlined below to give an idea of the range of possibilities.

Let us consider first a group of people who wish to establish an eco-community. Together they buy some land and build eco-homes, highly insulated, built with sustainable materials and with sufficient renewable energy capacity to cover the community's needs. Their intention is to become largely self-sufficient in energy and food through most of the year. These communities exist now but find it hard to balance their finances over the longer term. A community setup in this way may find that the citizen's income is sufficient external income to purchase key materials and services needed from outside the community. Such communities could be sustainable places to live with a strong culture and the cohesion of shared values. In an era of resource constraints and the potential for persistent unemployment, no one should resent people from having this option freely available to them.

Another example is communities set up by business. This may seem odd from a modern perspective but there is a strong rationale for these to become commonplace through this century. Let us say that the business makes and sells widgets. Currently it has a factory which makes the widgets operated by staff paid at least the minimum wage; or perhaps the manufacturing is offshore and the local operation is sales and marketing only. This is recognisably a late-20th-century business. The enlightened management examine the consequences of introducing basic income for everyone. They conclude that it could be cost-effective to get into the business of community building.

Making and selling widgets remains the profit-earning activity but manufacturing is carried out close to customers in communities orchestrated by the corporation with the corporation seen to be embedded in society with many customers being employees or friends of employees. The factory would have robots for dirty, dangerous or highly repetitive tasks; but the intention is to save on capital expenditure through employing people. This is definitely not a 20th-century business idea, an era when eliminating jobs reigned supreme. This is how business in the 21st century can operate alongside government to counter the danger of mass unemployment through automation. Around the factory there could be a whole community of small businesses and services, operating in facilities owned and operated by the corporation. The interests of the community and the corporation are closely aligned. All of this is possible because every adult has a basic income by right.

I could be accused of wearing rose-tinted spectacles in predicting how such communities could arise on the back of the citizen's income. I feel confident that the policy can deliver vibrant communities which are great places to live. This might sound reminiscent of the communities around the mills or coalmines of the 19th century but there is a huge difference. People with the basic income can choose to work, or not work, where to work, what to do, who to work for. Business will have to ensure that work is satisfying and enjoyable, although not necessarily well paid. It will be the quality of the community which is the big draw for potential employees. There are bound to be failed initiatives where lessons can be learned, but the idea of leveraging the opportunity of the basic income to build eco-communities, care communities and corporate communities, is immense.

Conclusions

Universal basic income has huge potential to reinforce society and underpin aspects of a resilient economy. It provides a workable solution to the challenge of automation and robotics and the impact these could have on the economy and for society. Whether such impact is good for society could be a close call. Freeing people from the drudgery of work would seem to be good but eliminating jobs in ways which undermine social cohesion is not. How this plays out is under our control. We should strive for improving quality of life in ways which conserve the structure of society. Universal basic income can be a prime economic tool to help navigate the transition. Without it, the economic pressure to eliminate jobs will decimate communities leading to polarization between the rich elite served by robots and a huge underclass of the unemployed.

The universal basic income could be the catalyst which allows building a range of vibrant communities. People can be drawn into meaningful and fulfilling activity, engaged in society through new models of work which blur the distinction between paid work, voluntary work, and leisure activity. The economic lever of universal basic income supports a society run by people for people, with robots relegated to menial, dirty or dangerous tasks.

It would be possible to implement universal basic income in a cost-neutral manner without further delay; but the initial benefits would hardly seem to justify it. Over the longer term the real value will show through as a variety of community models are developed underpinned by the foundation of a basic income to every citizen. In the next part of the book, focusing on the application of resilient economics, universal basic income is used in a number of ways showing that it can be an important component of coherent economic policy.

PART 3

APPLIED ECONOMICS

Having defined the characteristics of a resilient economy, and developed a toolbox for resilient economics, we can now explore how to apply the concepts on a sector-by-sector basis.

For each sector, I do not pretend to provide the definitive solution, but the analysis illustrates the mindset of the new approach. Some insights might be seen as controversial, such as my analysis of aviation. However, rather than being controversial, I suggest that the analysis presented provides simple clarity. Aviation policy, for example, has become trapped by its historic path. To shift to a new development path will not be easy but the logic of doing so is clear-cut (when examined without preconditions or worrying about vested interests). The analysis in the chapters which follow should provide confidence that a sustainable, vibrant, safe and better future is possible. Each chapter stands alone, but only makes full sense when seen as part of the bigger picture of wholesale change. Elements of one chapter connect with elements of another to complete the picture of comprehensive change rippling through society facilitated by the principles and levers of resilient economics.

Central to resilient economic analysis are the needs of society and the constraints of resource limits. These are the solid foundations which underpin resilient economic policy. This is not economics focused on the economy, and judged by economic measures. This is economics for the benefit of society, judged by quality of life, aimed at a secure future for humanity on a planet of finite resources.

The expected outcome is a superior economy; not a larger economy, not a growth economy, but a modest economy which serves our human needs. If an economy could be a humble servant, that is the economy required. The economy should not be defined by economic metrics but by impacts on people and society. As I completed this sector-by-sector investigation, I came to reflect on whether the whole concept of *the economy* is misguided. There are people and communities; manufacturing and construction; activities and services; all within the frame of the environment in which we live. These are important because they matter, not because they are part of the economy. This shift of mindset is required to escape economic fundamentalism, and is a prerequisite to the benefits of resilient economics.

Many of the tools of economic analysis which were presented in Part 2 may not be particularly novel. You could hand the toolbox to trained economists, and if they used conventional thinking, very little might change. The toolbox presented in this book might be regarded as a simplification of economic analysis (which it is) lacking the sophistication of more complex methods and theories. This is the point. Once economics becomes the domain of the economist its usefulness to general policymaking diminishes. The straightforward application of economics presented here shows the effective simplicity of resilient thinking.

The six chapters which follow cover manufacturing, services, agriculture, housing, transport, and energy. Although not precise blueprints, they show what can be achieved when resilient economics is applied without preconditions and without being held to ransom by conventional economic norms.

CHAPTER 12

MANUFACTURING

The circular resource economy will require
the transformation of manufacturing.

Manufacturing is changing at a rapid rate as firms exploit new technologies to produce better products more quickly and at lower cost. There have been a number of industrial revolutions in the past, and more to come as advances in technology gather pace. It is common to look at such change through the lens of advances in technology, but there are multiple dimensions. Each revolution has had huge social and economic consequences – for better and for worse. Technology might be the catalyst, but industrial and economic policy overlap and interact to reinforce each other to drive change. Appropriate economic models can turbocharge industrial advancement. The converse can also apply with advances in technology making new economic models feasible. For example, the combination of free-market economics with the Internet and high-capacity transportation has been behind the development of global manufacturing supply chains of incredible reach and huge complexity. The technology and the economic policy mesh like a tight-fitting glove to the invisible hand of market forces, making textbook economic sense. This model of globalized manufacturing is embraced, overriding common sense, because the conventional economic case is so strong.

Before looking forward, it is worth glancing back into history. The Industrial Revolution began in Britain in the late 18th century. Power from watermills, and later steam engines running on coal, made it possible to mechanize industries such as textiles.

Laborious work which had been done by a multitude of individual weavers could now be done by machine in huge cotton mills. Thus, the factory was born. The second industrial revolution came in the early 20th century, with innovators like Henry Ford developing the assembly line, ushering in the age of mass production. We are now well into a third revolution as manufacturing is going digital. A number of technologies are converging: clever software, novel materials, more capable robots, new processes and a whole range of web-based services.

There is no clear dividing line between where one revolution ends and the next begins. Each builds on what went before to take manufacturing to the next level. The first revolution replaced human physical labour with machines; the second shoehorned people into routine jobs on production lines; the third replaces these jobs with robots. It is relatively easy to look back on each revolution with hindsight and work out what happened and why. Looking forward to the Fourth Industrial Revolution is much more difficult.

The Fourth Industrial Revolution

The concept of a Fourth Industrial Revolution is still uncertain and incomplete. The drivers are a range of new technologies capable of fusing the physical, digital and biological worlds. These include: artificial intelligence, robotics, the Internet of Things (IoT), autonomous vehicles, 3D printing, nanotechnology, biotechnology, materials science and quantum computing. According to the World Economic Forum (WEF), 'scientific and technological breakthroughs [are] poised to transform economies and societies' (WEF 2016: 3). Professor Klaus Schwab, Founder and Executive Chairman, wrote in his book *The Fourth Industrial Revolution*:

We are at the beginning of a revolution that is fundamentally changing the way we live, work, and relate to one another. In its scale, scope and complexity, what I consider to be the Fourth Industrial Revolution is unlike anything humankind has experienced before... The changes are so profound that, from the perspective of human history, there has never been a time of greater promise or potential peril.

Schwab 2016: 1–2

To emphasize the last phrase: '...there has never been a time of greater promise or potential peril'. The Fourth Industrial Revolution could build on the revolutions which came before to reach yet greater efficiencies; have even greater throughput of resources; and finally remove the need for humans in manufacturing. It is not just the factory floor which could be staffed by robots; support functions such as marketing, administration and finance could all be automated. People could be removed from the manufacturing process altogether as automation builds supply chains of ever greater efficiency, providing society with every physical good we might want. This promise of such a wealth of affordable riches is a perilous way forward. To deliver 'promise' rather than 'peril' we will need to steer the future of manufacturing away from a focus on outputs to working in support of society. If you have been indoctrinated into contemporary business and economic theory, this might sound strange. Have patience, it takes a while to see the limitations of the current industrial age and appreciate the huge opportunities to make it better.

The Fourth Industrial Revolution could take markedly different alternative directions. We could allow technology free reign to transform the economy and society, or set a vision to steer the development and deployment of new capabilities.

Instead of being slaves to technology, we need to ensure that we are its master.

Industrial revolution is driven by the interplay between vision and technological advancement as illustrated by the race into space. The invention of the jet engine made it feasible to exit the Earth's atmosphere. The vision of a human in space was compelling, driving forward developments using the new technology to launch space capsules and satellites into Earth orbit. This was the birth of a huge aerospace industry venturing into space to exploit the commercial opportunities of each step forward in technology. Vision was again important for the next leap forward, to put a man on the Moon:

> *This nation should commit itself to achieving the goal, before this decade is out, of landing a man on the Moon and returning him safely to the Earth.*[29]

> John F. Kennedy, 1961

The Apollo program delivered President Kennedy's vision, putting a man on the Moon in July 1969. Spinoffs from the program in terms of technology developments according to NASA include: freeze-dried food; recycling fluids for space missions leading to improved kidney dialysis machines; cool suits to keep Apollo astronauts comfortable during Moon walks worn today by race car drivers; space suit technology used in running shoes; foil-backed insulation for buildings; water purification technology; Teflon-coated fiberglass; and much more (NASA 2020). The Apollo program drove the development of such technology. Some of these would have happened in any case, but the Apollo vision gave direction and purpose.

---

29 President John F. Kennedy, speaking before a joint session of Congress, 25 May 1961.

For space technology, the next logical commercial venture with a strong economic case could be space tourism. That would be the outcome of an economic appraisal despite the uselessness and unnecessary environmental impact of such extravagant and conspicuous consumption. Alternatively, the future direction could be set by the vision of Elon Musk to colonize the planet Mars, despite the weak economic business case. The Fourth industrial Revolution needs direction and purpose if it is to deliver promise rather than risk a perilous outcome. This should be set by deciding our aspirations and priorities, rather than letting pure economic analysis work with technology leaving us to experience the consequences.

Rather than acting as bystanders as creative destruction takes its toll, the Fourth Industrial Revolution should be about people setting a vision for what is required of technology, in general and particularly in manufacturing. How should the world of products operate; how should they be made; how should they be used; and what should happen to them at the end of their useful life? This should be much more about people and society than about technology. Technology may not be in short supply, but virgin resources will be; this will change the fundamental nature of manufacturing. The vision I propose is:

> *The Fourth Industrial Revolution should be when we learn to husband resources, protect the environment and start to undo the damage of earlier industrialization; setting up circular resource economies, making, using, repairing and finally recycling the materials for high-quality long-lasting products, produced and repaired in ways which engage with the needs of society.*

To bring in the new, requires destruction of the old, described by the economist Joseph Schumpeter as 'creative destruction' (Schumpeter 1942). Waves of creative destruction ripple through the economy as one technology displaces another. Standing on the shore, watching the waves rolling in, it would be right to be pensive. It is not possible to stop the wave of course but we should be thinking about what to do. To be bold, you would be out riding the swell getting ready to surf the wave as it breaks. The wave might have a nice clean face which can support a long ride if you get the timing right, but not all waves are predictable.

It is certain that the Fourth Industrial Revolution will be accompanied by a wave of creative destruction. We can hope for a smooth and predicable ride but we should not expect it. This could be a dumper wave of the type which occur when waves travel from deep water to shallow water and have to slow down rapidly. If you get caught by one of these, the consequences can be serious. I learnt this as a small boy playing in the surf of Australia's beaches. I never told my parents about an incident on the beach where I was playing in the waves (ignoring my parents' instructions) and got caught by a dumper smashing my head into the sand and knocking the breath out of me. I thought I was going to drown. This incident left me with a deep-rooted fear of the ocean which I only overcame in my twenties after taking up the sport of triathlon. I entered a race held on the coast near Auckland, New Zealand. The swim segment went straight offshore for 750m around a buoy and back. I had to fight to get out past big breaking waves coming off the Southern Ocean. As I returned to shore, the waves literally threw me onto the beach. Coping with such waves overcame my fear and allowed me to enjoy wild sea swimming. When the waves are big and dangerous, and you have learnt how to cope with them, fear turns into excitement. If we get to grips with our current challenges, we should not be fearful of the next industrial revolution but excited for the opportunities it provides.

The Fourth Industrial Revolution will coincide with globalization coming up against resource constraints. The resulting wave of destruction, rolling in from the deep ocean of the globalized and interconnected economy to reach the steeply shelving shore of the limits to resources, could have all the characteristics of a dumper. The economy could suffer a massive wipe out – or we could use foresight to prevent it. This is not an ocean wave outside our control. We can influence how the Fourth Industrial Revolution unfolds by anticipating the need for different economic policy before we are again dumped into crisis. It is possible that the next industrial revolution could have a profile which breaks gently and can be ridden all the way to shore. The revolution is more likely to be beneficial if it is less spectacular, less exciting, more certain, and more secure.

If we stand aside and simply watch, we should be fearful for the future. If we engage with shaping the Fourth Industrial Revolution, a balance can be struck between creative destruction and achieving progress. Each individual person, each business, each government department, has little control, but through sharing an appropriate vision we could pull together to ensure an outcome which looks more like progress than destruction.

The Circular Economy

The idea of a circular economy is the vision needed to drive the future of manufacturing. The concept has been around for some time but policymakers have been slow to appreciate its value. Its merits were explained in a book published in 2002 titled *Remaking the way we make things: Cradle to cradle* (McDonough & Braungart 2002). It opened my eyes to a rosy future for resources and manufacturing, but only a few of us were interested at that time. A decade later, the book was updated and republished under a different title: *The Upcycle: Beyond Sustainability – Designing for Abundance* (McDonough & Braungart 2013). Most people remained ignorant of resource shortages and environmental overload so again, the book generated a limited response. Perhaps the time is now right for it to be published yet again, and the message will finally get through to a wider audience.

The attraction of what has become known as 'the circular economy', and the imperative to adopt it, is so familiar to me that I can forget that these ideas have yet to propagate more widely, and are new to many people. My vision for the Fourth Industrial Revolution is based on this concept. If you are familiar with the concept of a circular resource economy you might want to skim through this section. If this is new to you, take time to read the section carefully reflecting on the consequences. In the short explanation which follows, I cannot capture the fine detail and nuances, but I need to tie down the core concept because it meshes perfectly with the future economic model for manufacturing. I have explained how policies in support of economic globalization, coupled with high-capacity transportation, turbocharged economic growth. Here you will see how policies in support of resilient proximate economies, coupled with circular resource models, can turbocharge resource efficiency.

The concept of a circular economy is that there are two material cycles; one for 'technical' materials and one for 'biomaterials'. The biomaterial cycle is the easiest to explain. At the highest level this is the biosphere of the planet, and its processes, which has been running for millions of years and could continue running into the foreseeable future. Material we grow as crops, harvest from forests, or otherwise extract from nature, can be used, and once we are finished returned to nature. Provided nature is not overloaded with extreme demands, natural processes can deal with such waste. Biomaterials, and products made from them, can be part of a sustainable economy which could continue indefinitely. Cotton clothes, wooden furniture, leather shoes, wool or hemp-based insulation are all examples.

The other cycle is for technical material. These are man-made materials not found in nature, or not in the form used in industrial processes. These man-made materials should be part of a cyclic system designed so manufacturing can continue indefinitely. Currently, much technical material is made from virgin resources which are dug out of the Earth's crust, refined and incorporated into products. Although there is some recycling, it is ad hoc with much technical material ending up in landfill. For the most valuable metals such as copper it makes commercial sense to reclaim it, but too often this involves environmentally damaging procedures, especially when shipped to countries with lax regulation (see Box 12.1).

Box 12.1 The hidden filth of the linear industrial economy

Modern manufacturing does not implement closed material cycles. This will be seen by historians in the decades ahead as dirty, unsustainable practices which society should not have tolerated. We look back at the awfulness, filth and social upheaval of previous industrial revolutions without appreciating that our current third industrial revolution has environmental impact and social disruption much greater in scale than anything before.

40 million metric tonnes (Mt) of e-waste were generated worldwide in 2014 increasing to 50 million Mt by 2018. The proportion of this which is properly recycled and disposed of is only between 10–40% (UNEP 2015). Considerable quantities of junked electrical and electronic equipment are exported from developed country markets, such as Europe, to destinations in Africa and Asia where legislation and enforcement is lax. The methods employed include breaking apart with hand tools and setting alight old electrical cables in the open air by people with no respiratory protection in order to be able to pick the copper out of the ashes. We need to find a better way. Such processes should not be part of a modern industrial economy.

Once we understand the circular economy, to implement it requires a different mindset and a different economic model. The new mindset is product lifecycle design, in which materials are handled within two separate cycles, one for technical material and one for biomaterial. This means avoiding making what McDonough and Braungart term 'monstrous hybrids'. These are products such as Formica-topped wooden tables. Not an attractive product in any case, but the incorporation of material from both material cycles mean it cannot be recycled. It cannot be put into bio recycling and the technical material cannot be extracted for reuse in the technical cycle. Its end-of-life destination is either landfill or the incinerator. Adopting the circular economy changes this.

The orchestration of material flows becomes a key aspect of product manufacture. This can be challenging and has consequences for the design of future products. When the costs and consequences of recycling are factored in, it makes commercial sense to produce high-quality long-lasting products. There is a strong incentive to repair rather than junk and replace. Refurbishment becomes an affordable option compared to producing a new product. Designing quality long-lasting products, with regular refurbishment planned in advance, instigates a sticky relationship between manufacturer and customer. Corporations relying on distant factories and one-way supply chains will be at a huge disadvantage.

Each component, or subcomponent, of a new product should be made from either biomaterial or technical material so it can be easily dismantled and the material recovered; but only after the options of repair and refurbishment have been exhausted. Full commitment to total lifecycle design for products can eliminate entirely the concept of waste and make landfill completely unnecessary. Implementation will require legislation about waste of course, but more importantly legislation about how things are made. This simple common sense has been incinerated in the economic model focused on growth. The throwaway society, encouraged by one-way global supply chains, will be seen in hindsight as an inexcusable deviation from sensible manufacturing policy. The focus should be on resource efficiency and facilitating a circular economy requiring different economic policy to the current pro-globalization stance.

As the attractions of the circular economy are better understood, demand will increase for appropriate regulations and suitable economic policy. Tight national regulations will be needed to prevent technical materials being 'lost' into the natural environment. Suitable economic policy will include taxes on virgin materials to reduce their use (and lessen the environmental impact of extraction) as well as reinforce the value of recycling. Taxes on landfill should escalate over time to the point where landfill sites are priced out of existence. The new model of manufacturing will consist of circular material flows such that there is no waste. There will only be materials at different stages in their lifecycle. As for the wider economy, changes in global governance will mean countries will seek to localize production applying appropriate tariffs and taxes to do so. Both governments and corporations will see the benefit of localized production reversing much of the current unsustainable global manufacturing infrastructure.

From Products to Services

Lifecycle design and total recycling are concepts for industry to implement with little impact on customers in the early stages. From a consumer perspective, products will continue to be for sale, with the notable difference being higher quality and improved longevity, with repair and refurbishment readily available. The consumer mindset does not have to change to start the transition, but once the transition is underway consumer attitudes are likely to alter. When the manufacturer is responsible for ensuring that the product has a complete lifecycle plan, it makes sense to lease rather than buy. A leased product will have all the advantages of ownership but none of the responsibilities. The manufacturer remains responsible for maintenance, repair, refurbishment, and finally taking back the product at the end of its useful life.

The migration away from cheap throwaway products to better quality products, backed by good service, is attractive to governments, corporations, and customers. For government, this provides a sustainable response to the impending resource crisis. For corporations, this allows a business model which enhances stable long-term relationships with customers. For customers, they get high quality long-lasting products backed up by good support services. This is not a utopian idea but the result of a hardnosed analysis of the future of manufacturing. It will be sustainable, better, and different to now. This is not a peril to fear but a promise to embrace.

Synergies with Social Policy

As the new economic framework evolves, manufacturing should not be seen in isolation. Now we tend to think of manufacturing as a linear process of discrete factories making things which are shipped to market and sold to customers. Current manufacturing systems are designed to maximize production efficiency, drive down costs, and ensure affordable prices to consumers. Future manufacturing systems will be judged by different parameters, such as maximizing resource efficiency, driving down the need for virgin resource inputs, and ensuring sustainable value to customers. Elements of this system are less amenable to total automation. Factories for new products could be largely automated, but the functions of maintenance, repair and refurbishment require either skilled people or robots much more advanced than the current generation of technology. I assume that in due course we will be able to make robots clever enough for such tasks, but there is a more fundamental issue. We need to ask ourselves whether the current drive to remove people from manufacturing is sensible or desirable. The stakeholders here are: society represented by government, corporations, and customers.

GOVERNMENTAL PERSPECTIVE

Government has responsibility to ensure the cohesion and quality of society. Partly this is provided by the provision of services but also through setting rules and regulations. From a governmental perspective, jobs are good for society. Engaging people in work provides a means of support, pride in what they do, and a sense of belonging. If jobs were to be eliminated from manufacturing, where and how would people be employed? Perhaps there will be plenty of work in services, but one way or another government will be very interested in ensuring that there are jobs available in the economy. Direct and indirect incentives to employ people are likely to be part of the governmental response. Whatever the detail, governments will be interested in having a manufacturing system which deals efficiently with resources and needs the involvement of people.

CORPORATE PERSPECTIVE

Before the Industrial Revolution, manufacturing consisted of skilled tradespeople making bespoke products and providing repair services as required. Compared with now, this was not efficient and the modern concept of brand had not yet evolved. The key to success was the reputation of the skilled tradesperson and direct relationships with customers.

As the Industrial Revolution transformed manufacturing, the customer relationship changed. The Ford Motor Company realized that in the altered corporate landscape, to sell cars to a wider market they would have to be affordable. This required maximizing efficiency, ushering in the production line which required uniformity of product. Hence the well-known statement attributed to Henry Ford that 'customers can have any colour they want so long as it's black'. Over the last century there have been huge strides forward in the efficiency and flexibility of manufacturing. These new capabilities mean that the customer relationship is set to change again.

Customer relationships continue to evolve as corporations continue to drive down costs as well as build the value of brand. The focus has moved from simple affordability to desirability. Where, or how, a product is produced is less important than the combination of value and brand. Protecting reputation and brand are important considerations as we enter the Fourth Industrial Revolution.

Resource shortages are looming, and environmental overload within the supply chain is putting the reputation of corporations (and their brands) at risk. Corporations will have to work hard to maintain their license to operate. Focus will shift from selling stuff to recruiting customers and building long-term relationships. To succeed, corporations will need to be embedded in society. Value and brand remain important, but cultivating customer relationships becomes critical to success. This is already apparent with corporations such as Apple. People choose Apple products not because they are the cheapest or the best value, but because they want to. The sale process is more like joining a community of Apple users than a simple purchase. The Fourth Industrial Revolution will enhance and exaggerate such corporate strategies as customers regain their power.

CUSTOMER PERSPECTIVE

Before the Industrial Revolution, customers were in control and tradespeople had to cultivate relationships with people requiring their services. The Industrial Revolution transferred power to the corporations with customer choice limited to the products offered by the corporations. The Fourth Industrial Revolution returns power to customers. Corporations will succeed by recruiting customers, and customers have a choice as to which corporation they trust. The workforce acts as a recruiting agent, blurring the distinction between worker and customer. I work for corporation X so I will buy from corporation X to protect my job. For the same reason I want my friend to be a customer of my corporation. My friend works for corporation Y so I want to buy from corporation Y to protect my friend's job. Manufacturing becomes an integral part of building a corporate community of workers, customers and supporters. I expect a shift from linear production processes, dominated by advances in technology, to circular processes dominated by relationships. We will seem to have travelled full circle. Over the last two centuries we have reaped the benefits of efficient manufacturing technology to the detriment of relationships. As society and the economy move forward, instead of technology driving change, technological innovation will fall back into its proper place as a facilitating function.

What is manufactured, how and where, has social impact. There has always been a social aspect to work, so when automation and robotics take work away, it removes something from society. Unless other work is generated, society is poorer as a result. Currently, manufacturing responds to the needs of two prime stakeholders: the manufacturing company's sharehold-ers, and their customers. Shareholders want the business to make profits; customers want to purchase at least cost. It is in both their interests to use automation and efficiency to reduce costs and keep output prices low. As more stakeholders take an active interest, the situation changes. Government has to think about overall impact on society. Their concern will be for effi-cient use of increasingly scarce resources as well as maintaining employment opportunities. For corporations, manufacturing is only a part of what they do. They will want to build long-term value from enduring relationships with customers. As for cus-tomers and workers, their concerns will start to converge into a shared interest in the success of the corporate 'family' as new community-orientated corporate models emerge.

At the start of this section, the title suggests that there could be synergies between manufacturing and social policy. I hope the discussion which followed, despite the lack of precise predic-tions, has outlined changes which could benefit all stakeholders. Harping back to the words of Klaus Schwab, talking about the Fourth Industrial Revolution, there are perils to avoid but there has never been a time of greater promise.

Conclusions

It would appear that manufacturing has never been more advanced, but what has been seen so far is just the beginning. It is eye-opening when you realize the scope of change which scientific and technological breakthroughs could facilitate. We can allow technology to drive the changes, framed by share-holder demands for profit and customer demands for low price. Alternatively, we can take an active role in ensuring there is a renaissance in manufacturing which fits the needs of society and responds to the broader challenges of resource limits and environmental overload. Appropriate economic policy can influence which direction wins out.

Through the lens of resilient economics, it is clear that sustainable manufacturing requires a different approach to economic policy. The policy of free trade supports the product-centric model: make it, sell it, junk it. Protectionist economic policy favours local production and associated repair and refurbishment support systems. For manufacturing there is enormous peril in sticking with the outdated policy of free trade. Instead, the promise of adopting protectionist economic policy should be embraced to make a successful transition to a circular economy.

In the developed world, manufacturing has shifted abroad where labour is cheap and environmental legislation less onerous. The advent of the circular economy will draw manufacturing back closer to home with quality products manufactured using tightly regulated processes. This is a major economic rebalancing with short-term disadvantages. This is likely to include higher prices for many products, but once the circular economy beds in people will come to appreciate the greater overall value. Manufacturing in each country can utilize levels of automation appropriate to their circumstances. All economies can be better balanced, more self-sufficient and at less risk from external shocks.

The same pressure to automate in manufacturing will also shake up services, which is where I turn next.

CHAPTER 13

SERVICES

People are doing it for themselves.

Services are an important part of the economy, ranging from insurance and banking to hospitality and personal services such as hairdressing. The delivery of services will change as advances in artificial intelligence make it possible to automate many more tasks. The current march of progress seems to be favouring automation, replacing people with robots. On one hand, this should save costs compared with expensive people and provide consistent quality without the unpredictable human factor. On the other, services without the human factor could lead to society operating with machine efficiency but without soul.

The dialogue is beginning about the appropriate balance between automated service and service with a human face. The pure economic analysis compares the cost of the computer or robot with the cost of employing a person. Robots will inevitably get cheaper and cost pressures to automate can only increase. Of course, there is more to this than the direct cost evaluation. Assuming that over the coming decades it becomes possible to automate just about any task, we need to start to think about the tasks we want to keep for ourselves and those we will pass to the robots. The current default position is that if it can be automated, and the cost of purchasing the technology costs less than employing someone, then the automation proceeds. This is taking us into a future run by machines. Caution will be required to strike the appropriate balance between humans and machines. A dystopian future where the machines take over the world may be science fiction, but we will need to ensure that everyone in society gets the chance of a productive and fulfilling life. We need to become rather cleverer and more nuanced in our decisions, taking into account what customers really want and value, as well as thinking through the soft benefits of maintaining a workforce that can act as advocate for the corporation.

An example to illustrate the challenge is human procreation. Whether to auto-mate or not to auto-mate has huge implications for the concept of what it is to be human. We can already make embryos in test tubes; it may not be long before scientists are able to build a life support machine in which they can grow.

It is thought-provoking to follow a logical analysis of what would be technically feasible for raising the next generation. The test-tube embryos could be screened for any genetic abnormalities, and perhaps the DNA altered to add desirable characteristics (if ethics in the future allow). After the 'birth', when the baby leaves the life support machine, he or she could be fed and raised by robots. No more sleepless nights and tired irate parents. This could extend to schooling where robots would always have the right answer and always teach exactly what the curriculum requires. It is possible to imagine that to start a family, the man hands over a phial of sperm and the woman has a set of eggs extracted. Eighteen years later, the parents can meet their children, fully grown and perfectly schooled, without going through two decades of heartache. This will not be the reality of course but makes the point that we need to move beyond automating whenever we can, to thinking deeply and carefully about what we want from automation. We need to decide which services we are happy to hand to the machines and which we do for ourselves.

Delivery of a Service

To automate, or not to automate: that is the question: Whether it is better to suffer unemployment by embracing the outrageous fortune which robotics could bring, or to take arms against the robots and by opposing end their hold over society.[30]

The delivery of services is at the start of a transition. There is a choice to be made between automated services which are quick and efficient but inflexible and impersonal; or people providing personalized and flexible service which may have more variable quality. It need not be so black and white. Perhaps we can have services which are personalized, flexible, quick, and efficient using an appropriate mix of people supported by first-class automation to assist them in their work. We could use people to make customers feel welcome, bring a smile to the service, react to problems, and insulate the customer from the technology. Navigating this transition, customers may not be able to explain precisely what they want but they will certainly complain if it is wrong. The design of service delivery has to consider customer reactions, testing, adjusting and, finally, rolling out. As people get familiar with the new way services can be delivered, what they are willing to embrace will evolve. Designing services will be like trying to hit a moving target.

We might consider two objectives: to automate as much as possible to minimize costs, or to focus on the human interface to deliver an excellent customer experience. Focusing on the former, exploiting advances in automated systems for maximum machine efficiency, could alienate customers. As business finds that this is what their advanced systems are doing, there will be

---

30 With apologies to William Shakespeare (*Hamlet*, Act III, Scene I).

a greater focus on enhancing the customer experience. The aim will be to delight customers in a cost-effective manner.

An example to consider is the automated systems for telephone inquiries which are fast becoming ubiquitous. From the system perspective, a logical pathway can be designed with nested menus of options. Being an automated system, it matters little from a cost perspective how long it takes to deal with a customer query, provided it can complete without needing the input of expensive human support staff. From the customer perspective, it is slow, frustrating and almost impossible to get to talk with a real person. Such systems are efficient, well-executed, and save money, but the customer experience is lousy. Thinking about customer experience first leads to systems using natural language and which learn with experience what customers really need. The automation is designed around people rather than the database of possible questions. There should be access to a real person for the most important enquiries and at key points in the enquiry process. Such systems are harder to design and more expensive but have better outcomes. The business case should be based not simply on costs saved by automation but on the quality of the customer experience perhaps measured by customer retention figures.

Call centres are a simple example. Let us apply similar thinking to a whole range of services from banking and building services to personal care and retail. The analysis should focus less on comparing the costs of human delivery with automated delivery and focus more on striking a balance between efficiency and the quality of the customer experience. Where customers value and expect a human-to-human experience, corporations need to be wary of automation. The question becomes how to provide a cost-effective human-to-human experience.

It is interesting in this examination of services, in a book about economics, that the economic case has been sidelined.

This is quite right. If the delivery of a service is approached as primarily an economic analysis, this means focusing on cost savings from automation. If the delivery of service is actually about delighting the customer in a cost-effective manner, we should think about what the customer needs from the service, and only then design an economic model or business case to deliver it.

Exploring how these ideas about service delivery shape different sectors is a good way to appreciate the logic of resilient economic thinking, starting with the delivery of care.

The Delivery of Care

Advances in medicine mean that people are living longer, leading to an increasing number of older people in need of care. In addition, there are significant numbers of people with differing degrees of disability. These people need, as a minimum, food, shelter and treatment for any ailments. Resources are always limited so authorities need to think about how to provide care efficiently. From the perspective of a recipient of care, people need to feel secure, feel they belong, feel useful, and feel loved. Currently, care is provided in two ways: in institutions run by professional staff, and through a policy of 'care in the community' where people live in their own home supported by visiting care staff. Both models of care are expensive, so in a budget-constrained world care teams have limited time to devote to each recipient. The basics of shelter, food and water are provided, and good staff within the current system try their best to make people feel safe, and in rare cases even loved, but there is not much they can do about making people feel useful or feel they belong. An improved model of care is needed which is affordable and helps people to live, rather than simply survive.

Resilient economics can help to break out of the straightjacket of tight budgets and minimum acceptable levels of care. Food and shelter might be the minimum but these are the easy things to provide. The tough challenge is making people feel useful, feel safe, feel like they belong. If these are regarded as the icing on the cake, in times of tight budgets, there is little chance of the provision of care with such characteristics – unless a cost-neutral method can be found.

We need to formulate a different recipe for the basic care cake. I propose that such a recipe could be broad-based care communities. Instead of recipients of care being housed in institutions run by professional staff, communities can be set up around the needs of people who require support. The focus is on making people feel useful and feel that they belong. Each person has a job of work in the community appropriate to their ability. Someone with a learning disability may not be employable in a conventional job, but could be quite capable of straightforward physical work. Older people may have a useful role talking with younger, troubled people. Some of these ideas are already being tested, for example locating care for the very young and very old in the same place, finding synergies between nursery care and making older people feel useful to the benefit of both (Rock 2017; Sheppard 2017). Some people in need of support might only be able to work part-time or have few qualifications to make them attractive within the wider labour market. Such people would still have something to offer within a carefully designed care community. Instead of struggling to make ends meet, living alone in their own flat with limited support, they can come into the community, have their own room, and the advantages of joining a close social group – not an inmate of an institution but a member of the community. The activities which take place inside the community could include growing food for the community and a whole range of support tasks. I list some possible ingredients of the new care cake without being specific about the precise care recipe, which could vary considerably, particularly between countries with different circumstances.

Care communities would be hard to set up now because of economic barriers. Minimum wage legislation blocks the idea of blended definitions of work. If someone is not capable of doing a full job it is uneconomic to employ them. The removal of minimum wage legislation and the introduction of a universal basic income make care communities possible. If you add in developments in artificial intelligence and robotics these could be vibrant communities. Instead of trying to automate all the easy tasks; the focus would need to be on automating the difficult, important, and safety-critical tasks. So, the community does as much as possible for themselves with the technology monitoring and supporting with a focus on protection and safety.

It would not be possible to totally de-risk such communities but the benefits of making people feel useful and that they belong outweigh such risk. It is well known that if you protect children too much it is bad for their development. I suggest that risk-averse care is bad for people's mental well-being. Consider how different this is to a current care institution which is forced by commercial factors to employ the least number of professional staff to balance the books. Again, thinking about human outcomes works better than thinking about automation. The professional team within such care communities would provide leadership, orchestrating rather than controlling direct delivery of care. It should be possible to enable everyone in the community to feel that they belong and that they are useful.

I am not a care professional, so cannot offer a precise blueprint. All I have done is to share a different way to think. This leads to a different approach which breaks out of the conventional economic straightjacket constrained by economic barriers such as minimum wage legislation. I argue that the economic model outlined here would give the care profession many more options to apply their expertise to deliver advanced models of affordable care for the vulnerable and least able members of society.

Repair Services

Repair services used to be available widely. Each high street would have a small business where broken appliances, such as radios and toasters, could be taken for repair. These are almost non-existent now because they are uneconomic. They are uneconomic because products are designed to be produced at least possible cost with a limited life. The advent of the circular economy favours products of higher quality where repair becomes again worthwhile.

Currently, manufacturers have become so well-tuned to defending their sales pipeline that products are designed to make repair impossible. Many smart phones are now assembled using glue so that dismantling is not an option. Customers therefore have to buy new products thus keeping sales buoyant. Some manufacturers design deliberately for early obsolescence. It is suspected that one product manufacturer inserts code into routine software upgrades for older models which reduces the battery life forcing customers to buy a newer model prematurely. I will not name the company accused, as these are unfounded rumours, but within the current economic model such behaviour would make commercial sense. Producing longer-lasting products which could be repaired or whose components could be upgraded would result in higher-quality products, but may be less profitable as sales of new replacement products decline. This current economic model works for shareholders of the manufacturing corporations, and works for current customer attitudes because we are all being persuaded to take pride in always having the latest gizmo.

In Chapter 12, I predicted a renaissance in manufacturing during the transition from the linear product economy (buy, use, junk) to a circular economy. This will transform repair services. It is hard to know exactly how government will legislate for a circular economy, but let us assume that a product rating system is introduced akin to energy efficiency ratings. An AAA sustainability rating would indicate high quality, ease of repair, and modular component design for easy replacement and simple end-of-life recycling. Manufacturers will be required to offer repair, refurbishment and recycling processes, but customers will be able to choose whether to use them. There will be opportunities for small businesses and repair shops to take up the task. The new product might be made in automated factories, but repair and refurbishment are likely to need human expertise for many decades to come. It will be easy for a local tradesperson, who is already receiving universal basic income, to set up such a small-scale repair shop. This is not a reversion to the past, but the application of an appropriate economic model which works at local scale with a personal standard of service.

We do not have repair services any longer because the current economic model favours mass production of cheap products according to a one-way pure sales model. Repair services will return as resource efficiency is allowed to shape how products are made and used. The economic model for the circular economy requires taxes on virgin resource extraction, tight regulations for lifecycle design, and protectionist trade policies to allow the potential of the circular economy to bloom in every country according to its circumstances. Customers will have different options, with the default option being quality products which will likely cost more but last longer. There might be initial resistance as the throwaway society is reformed, but the outcome is so obviously better that I expect customer attitudes to shift quickly in favour of better, longer lasting and repairable products.

Banking and Financial Services

Banking seems to be heading towards total automation. Getting money over the counter from a bank teller is obsolete. Money is now from automatic teller machines (ATMs). These may become obsolete as we ditch cash in favour of cards for all transactions. The COVID-19 pandemic has given a big push towards cards instead of cash. Even bank cards may be abandoned if enough of us agree to have a chip surgically inserted somewhere convenient under our skin. The future of banking could be a small number of managers and IT professionals to maintain the automated systems.

A totally automated integrated banking system would be technically feasible – but highly dangerous. It could be argued that automated control systems could be used to ensure stability. This would be a fundamental misunderstanding of the nature of banking. Banking is about behaviour and trust. People get into debt by their own choices and actions. People need advice and the bank has to decide who can be trusted when making loans. Automation will replace routine tasks but I believe a person-to-person component will remain important.

The number-crunching of banking can be automated of course, but the bank-manager-to-customer relationship is important. Physical bank branches are redundant as places to store cash but remain important as places to meet for advice and to agree transactions such as significant loans. There may be an increasing role for local banks and local currencies based on people-to-people trust as discussed in Chapter 9. Automation can support a range of functions but the heart of banking should remain the bank-employee-to-customer relationship. The future of banking looks bright but it has to be remembered that banking is about people and trust, more than it is about computers, artificial intelligence, block chain and other emerging financial technologies.

Building Maintenance

The state of repair of the infrastructure can tell you something about a community. Walking through an affluent community, we might observe that buildings are in a good state of repair; the walkways clear of rubbish; parked cars are newer models; the shops are up-market including health food shops and delicatessens. Compare this with a rundown neighbourhood with derelict buildings; graffiti on the walls; rubbish lying around; parked cars looking old and battered; and shops from low-end chains with windows protected by steel grills.

People in the affluent community are likely to have well-paid jobs, can afford to keep their houses in a good state of repair, and pay tax which ensures the local authority has the funds to keep the streets clean and the infrastructure well maintained. Such communities can support a wide range of hospitality and retail. In poor communities a large proportion of people may be unemployed and dependent on welfare payments. The local authority is likely to be short of cash so is reliant on the generosity of central government to remain solvent. Such poor communities might have little more than a convenience store, a few bars and a pawnbroker. This is how it is throughout the developed world, but it does not need to be like this.

The current cure for rundown communities is to bid for government funds for regeneration, drawing in new businesses so there are jobs. These measures have some effect but are like throwing banknotes onto a fire to keep warm; when the money is gone the wind is as cold as ever. The real cure is so obvious that it seems amazing that city officials, government representatives, and residents often do not seem to see it. The solution is staring them in the face but they look at the jobless figures, look at the state of the buildings, and despair. Give us jobs; give us money; give us hope. It is assumed that help will come from somewhere outside the community. These failed rundown communities have plenty of unemployed people and plenty of repair work to be done. Connecting one with the other is the solution.

Once again, the key change is better economic policy, facilitated by the implementation of the universal basic income. When every resident of a rundown community has the basic income, they will still be poor but they will be free to work. This could be voluntary work or low-paid work. There is the means for the community to draw together to repair itself. The economic model does not deliver leaders, nor change attitudes overnight, but the community has the economic wherewithal for renewal. No one wants to live in a sink community, so most people would be willing to engage in making it better.

Poor communities are likely to have old buildings showing wear-and-tear and outdated design, but they can be clean and well-maintained. The streets can be clear of rubbish; and parked cars, although old models, can be clean and carefully maintained. There can be vibrant small businesses and local food for sale, facilitated by a local currency which is used widely. A lot of this economic activity may come under the radar of the higher authority. The universal basic income will come off the national accounts but there is no need for additional financial resources. Where additional support is provided, this might be materials, tools and expert advice, with people doing the work for themselves.

Affluent communities of the future may have robots to keep the place clean, driverless taxis to get people around, and all sorts of high-tech gizmos – if that is what people choose. Poor communities need not be run down but will operate differently. They might be teeming with people, providing local self-help, repairing, cleaning and keeping the place in good shape. They might be less modern, a bit worn, less automated, less sterile, more alive, places with soul. You might detect in the words I choose that in my view, a well-managed poor community might be a rather more interesting place to live than many affluent rich communities. A relatively rich place with grand houses, security gates and cars for every journey is likely to be less of a community than another place where people live close by, rely on each other, and walking and cycling are the norm.

If we get the economic model right, people can have the freedom to live well according to their means. The current economic model discourages such self-help and may lead to polarization between affluent gated communities and ghettos of deprivation. Rich versus poor is the way of the world; but this does not need to be polarized between the privileged and the downtrodden, when people are empowered to make the best of their circumstances. This applies between countries, between regions, and between cities with rich and poor areas. Rich and poor places can have different attributes; not better, not worse, just different.

General Retail

Retail is being transformed by economic forces working with the opportunities of technology to allow shoppers to browse and buy over the Internet supported by high-capacity logistics. We can buy anything we want and have it delivered to our front door the next day. The Internet allows people to find the lowest price and delivery is cheap. When a sale is made in a shop or showroom, you decide whether to trust the salesperson – or not. We now put our trust in corporations like Amazon, or for smaller retailers we rely on their customer feedback ratings. We are well advanced in building the most efficient retail system ever devised, but it is far from perfect and it is worth reflecting on whether this is what we really want. The first problem is that this is a one-way system. There are return mechanisms for clothes that do not fit, things which are not right, or products we do not like when we get hold of them. However, once we have accepted the product, the transaction is complete. There is no ongoing repair and maintenance relationship. Retailers avoid such complications. Products are made and sold as cheaply as possible to win the sale in a highly competitive market.

Online retail is wasteful of resources as the delivery process clocks up transport miles and uses substantial quantities of packaging to protect products whilst in transit. Roads are becoming clogged with white vans delivering items which were clicked yesterday. These multitudes of journeys would be unnecessary if retail operated differently. When it comes to packaging, this should at least be biodegradable or recyclable. Advanced packaging, which can be used and reused again and again, is in its infancy. The product could be delivered in a strong easy-to-open container which the delivery agent retains and returns for reuse. The final weakness of online retail is not being able to see and feel the product and discuss it with a salesperson.

The economic tools we can apply, to bring retail back onto a sensible track, include increasing tax on transportation and regulating or taxing packaging. The aim is greater resource and logistic efficiency. Each community could have one or more collection points, perhaps local shops, where ordered items can be collected. Rather than multiple delivery journeys, business could be incentivized to arrange deliveries with the minimum of vehicle movements. Advanced reusable packaging could be deployed.

These changes would take place alongside the shift to a circular economy (discussed in Chapter 12). The closer relationship between manufacturer and customer which this entails would trigger the resurgence of showrooms with products to see and feel together with people to offer advice. It would also be logical to have hubs within communities for product repair, refurbishment, and end-of-life recycling. Where the current economic model has decimated the high street, a new economic model for retail could steer towards rebuilding it.

Food Retail

It is possible to envisage how general retail will evolve as part of a circular economy, but food retailing is more challenging. Currently this is dominated by the supermarket chains. They run efficient operations (in a commercial sense) and claim to keep consumer prices in check, but the system is flawed. There are concerns about excess packaging, unnecessary food miles and a lack of transparency putting safety at risk. First, every item is packaged and barcoded; this allows supermarkets to operate with machine efficiency, but customers end up with a tsunami of packaging. Second, this 'efficient' system has considerable food miles. On average food in UK supermarkets is transported 1,937 miles to reach the supermarket shelf (Food Miles 2020) – plus the customer's driving journey. Third, the only basis customers have to judge food quality is the packaging, and what is written on it. In the long and complex supply chain between the farmer and the customer, dubious practices can be hidden as each trader within the chain seeks to maximize their profit.

To improve food retail, it is necessary to look past the stale economic argument focused on the economies of large scale and instead scale down. Local food markets offer freshness, quality, and transparency; but customers have to get used to and accept seasonality. Such short supply chains have less need for formal regulations benefiting from the natural oversight of the community. In the UK there are local farmers' markets, but there is a near total disconnect between supermarket supply chains and the local food economy. This imperfect model needs to change but the solution is not to focus on local (as some green campaigners argue) but to seek synergies between supermarket systems and local supply.

For some years, my family has had a weekly bag of vegetables from our local organic farm. The farmer told me a story about having a glut of plums. Knowing the manager of the small local supermarket, he offered the plums at whatever price the manager suggested, otherwise they would go to waste. The local store manager consulted head office to be told that the only way would be for the plums to be delivered to the central depot some distance away to be checked and packed and then returned to the store. This farmer baulked at the idea of generating such unnecessary food miles so the offer was not pursued further. The current food retail system cannot handle local produce even though it is inherently fresh and produced to transparent quality standards. The system needs to change to accommodate local food supply as well as supply food from further away. This would reduce food miles, reduce the need for packaging, and apply the natural oversight of the community as a quality and safety check.

To develop an advanced food retail system which serves society better, we need to think carefully about the economic model to deploy. I propose that a safe and sustainable food supply system should have the following attributes:

+ Organic and local given priority;

+ Operate with the minimum of packaging;

+ Where there is packaging, it should be biodegradable or returnable;

+ Local shops supplied with local produce are given economic advantage using tax breaks and less onerous regulation.

Unless action is taken to change the economic model, the current system will become even more entrenched. As a society we have to decide whether we want industrialized food production, centralized depots and long complex supply chains; or safe and healthy food from a more localized system. I would fully expect the current food retailers to be able to rise to the challenge – if we, the customers, demand change. It need not be a battle between the supermarkets versus the farmers' markets. All stakeholders could benefit from the supermarkets implementing advanced computer systems which can handle local produce to be sold alongside produce from further afield. This does not mean reversion to old-fashioned retail but a leap forward to a new sustainable retail system.

Marching Forwards

Better retail is not about returning to rural village life of home-grown crops and limited choice. Technology has to become our servant. Currently, retail systems are designed to deliver a narrow focus on commercial efficiency. The future could be to exploit the opportunities of technology to orchestrate a circular economy of safe food supplies. A brief example follows of how technology could be applied to assist with delivering such an aspiration.

Let us consider a community where local retail has been retained. There will be people without the time or the capability to get to a shop. Assuming there is a shop within their community, the customer could order online, via phone or video link.

The customer would then dispatch a small battery-powered autonomous food transit buggy. The customer's empty food containers can be placed inside it. When the buggy arrives at the shop the shop staff can load the order and dispatch the buggy to find its way home. If the customer is not at home the buggy can enter the house by its own access door, park up, plug in, and stay refrigerated until the customer is ready to unpack. For security, the buggy would be equipped with cameras and access to the buggy's contents controlled via a keypad. Over time these slow-moving buggies could become a common feature on the streets of our communities.

The future model for services should aim for vibrant communities based on human relationships supported by a range of services. Many of these will be automated, not because they can be automated, but because there is a real advantage to society. In the paragraph above, I have tried to paint an example of the application of technology to illustrate what might be possible. On reflection, with regard to the high-tech example above, I wonder if a delivery person on a bicycle might work better. The cyclist might enjoy employment on their bicycle getting exercise and meeting people. As they receive the universal basic income, their pay can be low and competitive with the automated alternative. These are choices for us to make depending on what we decide is good for the community. Services could be high-tech, low-tech, or no-tech provided it suits the community.

Conclusions

Services are being transformed, driven by the economics of keeping costs and prices down through exploiting the possibilities of automation. This is wasteful of resources, detrimental to jobs, and puts clinical efficiency before soul. It is in our power to change direction. I believe we are capable of acting responsibly to steer innovation towards improving services according to altered priorities. We need a much closer fit with the needs of people and society. Quality, safety and sustainability should be valued more than the current economic model allows. In new models of services, machines will operate behind the scenes but the interface between customer and supplier should have a human face.

Communities have been decimated by the twin retail evils of the hypermarket with its huge car park, and streets filled with white vans delivering stuff ordered online. There is a wonderful opportunity to rebuild vibrant living communities, through shifting to an economic model of local facilities where it is easy to buy local produce, have items repaired and interact with a human salesperson who is a member of the local community.

Services cannot sit in isolation but are a core part of society. How we move forward with services is closely aligned with how we move forward as a society. The changes could be significant and perhaps not what might be expected. Overturning the logic of the industrial age can radically improve this important sector.

CHAPTER 14

AGRICULTURE

Agriculture should feed us
and provide renewable commodities
without degrading the environment.

Agriculture is vital to human society, not just for the obvious reason of providing one of life's necessities, but also because the management of agriculture has huge implications for the health of the planet. Our myopic focus on industrial efficiency is causing increasing environmental overload as land is farmed more intensively and nature pushed aside to increase agricultural capacity. The potential damage to the planet and its climate is significant. The need for change is becoming urgent if we are to rescue the future of agriculture whilst there are still easy options available. It would indeed be relatively easy to set agriculture on a different path but progress is blocked by the current focus on raw economic efficiency.

There seems little point in allowing conventional economic ideology free rein and hoping that improvements can be overlaid on fundamentally unsustainable agricultural economic models. It is imperative to think about what we expect of agriculture first and foremost, and only then apply economic tools to help facilitate its operation. Of course, agricultural products are grown for profit and markets are needed to facilitate trade, but such activity has to be framed within the context of higher order sustainable agricultural policy. This chapter is mostly about agricultural policy more than it is about economic policy. This is as it should be.

In this chapter, the broad outlines of resilient agriculture are identified. The analysis is framed by the need to provide food and other agricultural commodities using methods which are secure into the long future, without degrading the environment. From such analysis, three objectives emerge which set the context for developing an appropriate economic model: sustainable indefinitely, conserve nature, and rebuild rural communities. First, agriculture should be sustainable indefinitely, serving society with agriculture produce and operating so as not to undermine climate security. Second, agriculture should work with nature to use nature's mechanisms to serve human needs and rebuild biodiversity to correct the damage caused by industrial farming. Third, sustainable agricultural practices are more complex and require greater human involvement to achieve the same high yields as industrial farming. This means that a larger workforce is desirable so that economic models should facilitate rebuilding rural communities and increasing the proportion of people employed in the agricultural sector, reversing the decline of the last century.

Before examining how alternative economic policy can support the resilience of agriculture, let us consider how current economic policy undermines it.

The Rise of Industrialized Farming

In the developed world, fewer and fewer people are employed in agriculture as it becomes increasingly automated and increasingly efficient – in terms of reduced costs and increased yields. People have moved off the land into better paying jobs in the towns and cities. The rural landscape, agricultural communities, and agrarian economies have changed. Spending time on a working farm in my youth provided an insight into some of the changes (see Box 14.1).

Box 14.1 A comparison of two farms

In the 1970s, I would spend my summers on my uncle's farm in southern Scotland. He was the continuation of a long line of farming generations. He had left school aged 14 to work on the family farm which grew a range of crops and also had both cattle and sheep. The fields were managed in rotation to keep the soil healthy and avoid the expense of fertilizer. As a young farmer in the first half of the 20th century he had learnt to plough using horses and operate the farm blacksmith shop to make running repairs on farm equipment. It was second nature to him to be as self-sufficient as possible. There was a part of one field where vegetables were grown. These were not for sale, but were for the family and the farm workers to take as they needed to feed their families. Those who depended on the farm were not making high incomes but they had a lifestyle with benefits. To them it was a vocation rather than simply a job.

I would go with my uncle to sell livestock in the local market. By tradition, the farmer would go into the sales ring with the animals being offered for sale. I would accompany him – trying, and I suspect failing, to look like a young farmer. There were local butchers who always bought his animals, paying a premium, because they knew the farm and the farmer and that the produce was top quality. He was clearly a well-respected farmer and proud of it. I saw first-hand the natural oversight of farms supplying a local market where buyers and sellers know each other, and know who to trust.

It was interesting to see up close such a traditional sustainable farming system operating. It was also interesting to hear my uncle discuss the neighbouring farm. The previous owner did not have family who wanted to continue working the land, so when he retired the farm had been sold. It had been bought by a young farmer fresh out of agricultural college who was intent on modernizing and 'improving' the farm. The entire farm had been turned over to growing barley. This young farmer and his wife were delightful people, but my uncle expressed sadness about what they were doing.

As there were no longer animals to tend, the farmer's family could take regular holidays (something my uncle had been denied whilst tending his modest farm). This was not the focus of my uncle's displeasure. His complaint was that growing the same crop year after year, using fertilizer to maintain yield, would over the years degrade the soil. He explained to me that decades into the future the soil will be worked out. This young farmer was using modern methods to maximize profit to keep his family, pay the mortgage, and have a lifestyle that did not tie him to the land 24/7. Like many farmers he had joined the industrial farming revolution. My uncle, with little formal education, was seen as the face of the past which needed to be superseded.

Current economic policies, such as minimum wage legislation, make workers expensive and investing in automation increasingly affordable. The current economic model directly facilitates mechanized farming. Today's farms might have a lot of capital equipment and very few workers. Fields are large and crops are uniform so they can be planted, sprayed and harvested by machinery. Hedgerows have been removed to increase the area for crops and to give the machinery a clear run. Advances in artificial intelligence using data from satellite systems are leading to the development of automated tractors. In the near future, it will be possible for the farmer to drive the tractor whilst it is on a public road but once in the field it can be left to do a day's work with little human intervention. If this trend continues the future of farming will be even bigger farms with control rooms and TV screens keeping an eye on the robots. The fields will be securely fenced off to ensure people do not stray into the world of the machines.

A particular model of industrialized farming I want to highlight is the feedlot system for producing beef used extensively in the United States. It is economically efficient and the business is profitable. Cattle are kept in enclosures and fed with maize and soya bean protein; it is easy to administer and cattle put on weight quickly. These feedlots can be located close to railway lines to minimize transportation costs for both animal feed and to send the cattle to market. A major source of soybean feed is Brazil where growing conditions are good and gigantic fields keep costs low. The economic pressure to clear rainforest in Brazil to supply US feedlots is intense. From a conventional economic perspective this makes sense; Brazil earns foreign income; US beef producers make solid profits; US consumers can buy cheap beef. It makes perfect economic sense and everyone seems to be a winner – except of course we all lose as climate security is compromised by the loss of the rainforests of Southern America.

These are brief snapshots of modern farming. There are worse examples of industrialized farming where economic efficiency is put before animal welfare and human health. The misuse of antibiotics as growth promoters is one example. Another is the way chickens, pigs and calves may be crammed into pens or crates and force fed. These processes are wrong on many levels but can be seen to make economic sense. That should make us question the economics. Few people, apart from those with strong green views or those concerned about animal welfare, question the industrialization of agriculture. Even those who do object, argue for regulations and inspection regimes rather than confront the economic model. There is no need to accept the current situation as the irresistible march of agricultural progress. We should have the courage to adjust the economic model.

The prime misconception which allows this to continue is framed within the narrative that the world needs increasing yields of food to feed a growing population; and industrial farming is the only way. I may not be an agricultural expert, but when I discuss agriculture with people who are, this framing is exposed as quite wrong on many levels. First, the challenge of world hunger is generally not a food supply issue but an issue of access to food by the poorest people (FoodPrint 2020). Second, industrialization is not the only way to achieve high yields. Intense sustainable agriculture can deliver high output. The real issue is that this takes substantially more effort. Third, although industrialized farming can provide increases in terms of both profitability and output, this is short-term gain which is damaging soils and changing the climate, putting long-term agricultural output at risk. It is common to discount future anticipated cash flows because of the uncertainty. A pound in the hand today is worth more than an anticipated pound in the hand next month. Applying such thinking to agriculture may make conventional economic sense, but what we are discounting is the future of humanity. Farming is the essence of human survival; and farming is how a large proportion of the planet is managed. Agriculture is too important to allow short-term economic pressures to undermine long-term sustainable practices.

Industrialized farming is cheaper (within the current economic parameters) than sustainable farming. The bottom line is that currently agriculture is managed badly in order to keep the economic model in good shape. This is an example of dysfunctional economics. Fixing this situation requires acknowledging that the overwhelming priority is to secure supplies of food which are safe, sufficient for our needs, and sustainable into the long future. This is a statement of common sense, and should not be controversial. However, it challenges the deeply ingrained economic policy for agriculture based on cheap prices for consumers and profit for agribusinesses. I accept that to change such policy requires acceptance that the sustainable supply of safe and nutritious food is likely to cost more. It may also mean that the opportunities for multinational agricultural corporations to generate easy profits may be reduced. These are consequences to accept; not barriers to progress. Policy for safe sustainable agriculture should always override raw economic efficiency.

Agriculture and the Ecosystem

Feeding people may be the primary short-term aim of agricultural economic policy but no less important is the need for sustainability over the long-term. We need to be able to feed people now and in the future by retaining the ecosystem services which are vital to our survival. The crux of the problem is our failure to appreciate that the shift from hunter-gatherers to farmers appointed us as architects of the ecosystem. This was not obvious when the scale of farming was small compared with the vastness of the areas occupied by nature. Farming a few fields cut from the forest is not going to change the planet, whereas chopping down vast swathes of rainforest will.

For rainforest, there are three obvious options. First, we can accept the current rate of deforestation and accept that the rainforests will probably be gone by later this century. Second, we could slow down the rate of deforestation and push the date of destruction further into the future. In both cases, as the area of rainforest contracts there will come a point when the microclimate fails. The final death of the forest could be rapid, as rain fails and the forest dries out to then be consumed by forest fires some years earlier than extrapolating trends would indicate. The third option would be to stop further deforestation. We could then wait to see whether this was enough to stop the forest from self-destructing from microclimate failure, understanding that there is delay in the climate system. It is worth considering whether there may be a fourth less obvious option which provides greater certainty of a successful outcome.

The only sure way to retain the rainforests would be to reverse the rate of destruction from negative to positive. Having become accidental ecosystem architects, we need to take responsibility to design an economic model which facilitates reversing the rate of destruction. It would be unrealistic to expect countries which have cleared rainforest to take action to reinstate it to its original state. However, there are sustainable agricultural practices which can mimic the rainforest which could be implemented on the land which borders the rainforest, such as permaculture. Such forest-like agriculture managed around the margins of existing areas of rainforest could provide a commercially viable alternative to conventional cropping or grazing. It would have the benefit of effectively expanding the forest in terms of its contribution to the microclimate.

This focus on rainforest is a narrow look at one aspect of ecosystem maintenance. It illustrates well the general observation that we are at a transition point in agriculture every bit as great as the transition from hunter-gatherer to farmer. This is a shift from industrial farming to becoming stewards of nature, able to harvest nature's bounty with methods that mimic the ecosystem. The next agricultural revolution will not be about industrial efficiency, but should be based on shifting agriculture to a resilient model.

Resilient Agriculture

It is proposed that to be resilient, agriculture should operate with three objectives working in concert.

SUSTAINABLE INDEFINITELY

Agriculture should be sustainable indefinitely, serving society with agricultural produce and operating so as not to undermine climate security.

CONSERVE NATURE

Agriculture should work with nature to use nature's mechanisms to serve human needs and rebuild biodiversity to correct the damage caused by industrial farming.

REBUILD RURAL COMMUNITIES

Agriculture should draw in people to rebuild rural communities to provide the workforce needed for high yield sustainable farming – and a high quality of life for the people involved.

These three objectives clash with the current economic model. For that reason alone, they will meet resistance, until the concepts of resilient economics become widely accepted. The resilient approach is to set objectives and only then design an economic model to deliver them. To test whether these three objectives are appropriate, let us consider the nature of an advanced agriculture system which could result from their adoption.

Future Advanced Agriculture

The current path of industrial agricultural leads to rural a dystopia of uniform landscapes dominated by autonomous machines. A better future for agriculture can be framed by forgoing pure industrial efficiency to focus on delivering stable and resilient agriculture. It becomes possible to envisage an agricultural nirvana consisting of vibrant communities of people living on the land, harvesting the bounty of nature and acting as stewards of the natural environment.

Future advanced agriculture would not require reversion to a romantic ideal of what in the past has been back-breaking work. It would require rediscovering the principles of sustainable agriculture. New technologies and new capabilities can be used in support of sustainable human communities managing sustainable agricultural practices. In a world where machines are eliminating jobs in factories, there could be a migration of people back to the land to manage the complexity of sustainable high-yield farming. The ideas presented here can apply to all places and all countries in a wide range of different ways depending on climate, circumstances and culture.

To reset the future of agriculture, we have available the power and capabilities of technology to apply as we see fit. Our tendency has been to allow the technology to lead. Because we can build machines to work the land, agricultural practice is adjusted to be machine friendly. This includes gene modification techniques to design crops with special characteristics which make them more machine-harvestable and pesticide resistant. The march of 'progress' makes it possible for the whole agriculture process to be managed by only a few people, with more technical managers than farmers. Instead of letting technology dictate how this vital part of human existence is managed, the future of agriculture should be guided by good sustainable agricultural practice. This should dictate how to find synergies between agriculture, society and the planet, with appropriate technology applied in support. The alternative vision of future agriculture presented here shows the way forward in broad outline. It is far from complete and full of uncertainty. It gives a flavour of what is possible when the resilient economic approach is followed.

For this discussion of advanced agriculture, I make the assumption that the three objectives set out above are adopted.

First, agricultural practice should be sustainable indefinitely. It cannot be right that current agricultural practices degrade the ecosystem to the lasting detriment of future fertility and future agricultural output. The idea that reaping short-term benefit is acceptable needs to be resisted strongly in this vital sector. Second, agriculture should no longer be imposed upon nature, pushing aside biodiversity and encroaching ever further into natural habitats. Agriculture should work with nature rather than oppose it; after all, this is the only way to be sustainable into the long future. Third, the diversity and rich variety required for sustainable agriculture should also support diverse and rich rural communities: rich in lifestyle; rich in benefits; rich in engagement with nature; and rich in social interaction between people. I suggest that this is a reasonable set of aspirations; particularly when you consider the future models of agriculture which become possible when these objectives are accepted. Rather than driving people off the land, the migration of the last two centuries could be reversed, drawing people back into a new and stimulating version of rural life.

SUSTAINABLE INDEFINITELY

The first requirement of agriculture is that it should be sustainable indefinitely.

Sustainable agriculture is the production of food and other plant or animal products using farming techniques that protect the environment, public health, and communities without compromising future generations' ability to do the same.

Sustainability in agriculture is not something to fear. Jules Pretty provides a useful insight into how sustainability can influence the future direction of agriculture:

As a more sustainable agriculture seeks to make the best use of nature's goods and services, technologies and practices must be locally adapted and fitted to place. These are most likely to emerge from new configurations of social capital, comprising relations of trust embodied in new social organizations, new horizontal and vertical partnerships between institutions, and human capital comprising leadership, ingenuity, management skills and capacity to innovate. Agricultural systems with high levels of social and human assets are more able to innovate in the face of uncertainty.

Jules Pretty 2008: 451

The words above indicate that sustainable agriculture is far more complex than the current industrialized approach, and includes strong social components. This complexity should be embraced for the advantages it brings. Thinking in terms of machine efficiency leads to large fields of single crops tended by tractors and fed with fertilizer. If the starting point is to aim to be cost effective and maximize yield, this is where you end up. If the starting point of the analysis is to aim for sustainability and high yield, this generates different solutions. Such sustainable agriculture will have multiple different solutions depending on place and climate. When properly established, it can match and even exceed the yields of industrialized agriculture, though it is likely to be less cost-effective when considering short-term economic parameters.

There are many different ways of making agriculture sustainable. This is one of the strengths of this way of thinking; instead of standard solutions imposed upon a locality, the concept is to build up complex reinforcing and self-supporting systems. Permaculture is a term applied to systems of agricultural and social design simulating the patterns and features observed in natural ecosystems. Instead of flat fields with single crops, permaculture encourages growing crops in three dimensions. The top level is trees for fruits and nuts; below this is bushes growing berries and fruit; and on the ground vegetables; thus mimicking a forest ecosystem. Agroecology is another term which is used to describe ways of working which suit natural, social and human assets (Soil Association 2020). There are also advanced methods, which can be extremely high yield, using integrated aquaculture termed microponics or aquaponics. Such systems can integrate fish farming and growing plant crops in very efficient use of available space, which might only be a small backyard. Within this variety of sustainable agricultural systems long-term resilience can be achieved through applying waste from animals (or fish) to provide feed for plants, and growing crops to preserve (and increase) the fertility of the soil.

Currently, it is hard to make sustainable agriculture commercially viable because of the lack of an appropriate economic model. The measures I outline below improve the situation. This is how resilient economics can be used to implement solutions arrived at through logical analysis of desirable outcomes. Instead of ending up with an agricultural system dictated by the economic model, we end up with an economic model dictated by the desired agricultural system.

In addition to changing the economic model, there is also the challenge of consumer acceptance. In my household our vegetables arrive in a bag once a week from our local organic farm. They are seasonal, nutritious, healthy, and local. I am surprised and disappointed that so few of my neighbours take advantage of this service. The local supermarket has vegetables which look more uniform, come packaged in plastic, and when on a promotional offer are cheaper. People are so used to using the supermarket, or clicking online, that these are the default ways to shop. When our children were small there were complaints at the number of bugs amongst our fruit and vegetables. It is inevitable in farming which uses no chemicals and pesticides, and actively encourages good bugs to keep the bad bugs at bay, for little friends to arrive in the vegetable bag. To counter my children's resistance and demand for 'proper' packets of vegetables from the supermarket, I carried out a taste test. I bought a bag of supermarket carrots to compare with local organic carrots. I peeled both so they looked much the same and the family carried out a blind tasting. The local carrots won easily. This was the turning point; so now we eat great food without complaint and enjoy the surprise of opening the bag to see what the season has to offer (as well as check carefully for bugs hitching a free ride). Getting people to embrace seasonality and appreciate the freshness and quality of local produce is not something economics can do much about. Preparing good food may be slightly more time consuming and require more thought but it is healthy and interesting to be engaged with the people and processes of local agriculture. With the right policy nudges, it should be possible to turn back the tide of bland supermarket packaged food.

CONSERVE NATURE

The second requirement of agriculture is that it should work with nature, not against it.

There is growing pressure to increase agricultural output, which means growing pressure to take land away from nature to bring it into productive capacity. Natural vegetation is cleared and natural habitats destroyed. In the developed world, we are already well advanced in taking land away from nature thus reducing biodiversity. From a global perspective, there are still vast tracts of land in their natural state which tends to be in the poorer less developed countries. That I refer to these countries as poor and lacking development is perhaps a sad reflection on attitudes which need to change. Countries with large areas of virgin forest and other natural landscapes are rich in ecosystems and biodiversity. We desperately need an economic model which can preserve such wealth, supporting agriculture working alongside nature. In this section, I focus on the world's rainforests because this is where the greatest natural wealth is concentrated and where the current macroeconomic model is so damaging.

Let us consider an area of rainforest in Africa, South America or South East Asia. Some areas might be designated as national parks or nature reserves with legislation to keep them outside the reach of the economy. Such protection is important but does not dissipate the pressure to draw such land into productive use. If the country faces food shortages, the economy is weak, or politicians are corrupt (or all three), the legislation might be changed. This is a one-way process where natural habitats are always at risk. It is rare for agricultural land to be reclaimed for nature. So, there is a slow (or not so slow) expansion of the area of agricultural land at the expense of natural habitats.

Other ways are needed to conserve the planet's rainforests. Tourism is one way, employing local people and providing governments and communities with an economic reason to keep the forest in prime condition. This can help to retain protection for national parks and the best examples of natural habitats, but we need to go further. The way to do this is to work out how to harvest produce from the rainforest without chopping it down. Instead of cutting, burning, clearing, and planting soybeans or oil palms, we need much more advanced and clever thinking about how to exploit the land. Brazil nuts are a particular example as they are harvested from a tree which does not do well when planted alone in a sterile agriculture landscape but needs the complex forest ecosystem to thrive. Ramping up Brazil nut consumption means preserving rainforest and provides employment to local people entering the forest to harvest them (Guariguata et al. 2017). This is the sort of positive win-win dynamics of advanced sustainable agriculture.

In addition to protecting areas of forest, a good way to reduce pressure is to draw surrounding areas into productive use applying sustainable methods. Instead of a sharp delineation between nature reserve and commercial industrial agriculture, these are areas which blend the stewardship of nature with harvesting its bounty. Where permaculture seeks to build a forest-type ecosystem with cropping plants; we can take an existing forest and increase the proportion of cropping plants. Mature timber can be selectively felled; and cropping plants like nut and fruit trees and oil palms can be planted in and amongst the forest. The transition from virgin forest to managed forest can retain much of the ecosystem value and become a resource of value to the country and the local community. Instead of fencing off habitats to keep people out, people can be invited in to exploit and harvest using the compass of stewardship of nature to guide their actions.

Such managed biodiverse forests are not amenable to automation. Cutting down forests and taking the timber is easy for machinery operating at large scale, whilst selective felling which keeps the forest intact requires more skill and human involvement. Harvesting the seeds of the oil palm from long uniform rows of identical trees can be done with machine support, whilst harvesting from within a biodiverse forest requires human dexterity. If we make the strategic decision to exploit forest without clearing it, we can imagine using advanced technology in support. We might develop improved systems for felling individual trees, or make specialist small-scale machinery that can help people as they do the picking. These are choices to be made as to how to deploy technology to work with the needs of local people within the parameters of the local economy.

The rainforests are vast and generate their own microclimate. A few small-scale initiatives would do little to slow their clearance. As they contract, the microclimate could collapse and with it the forest, together with the agricultural capacity of the cleared land in the vicinity as the rains fail. This is not doom-mongering but a cool, hard appraisal of the consequences of the incentives provided by the current economic model. For the ideas presented here to make a real difference, there would have to be a large-scale shift in favour of sustainable agriculture. As attitudes change it would become feasible to start replanting permaculture pseudo forests with high yield, high value specialist foods such as nuts and fruits. This could reclaim previously cleared land designed to maximize their harvestable potential and protect the microclimate with an unapologetically profit motive, not perhaps for the big corporations or big landowners but certainly for local communities.

Utilizing natural landscapes in the ways outlined here can both support the community and produce agricultural outputs. This approach provides work, supports livelihoods, protects biodiversity, and could be sustainable indefinitely. Local communities can be employed to manage a working forest and harvest the fruits of the forest. It is this synergy with local communities where I turn next.

REBUILD RURAL COMMUNITIES

The third requirement of agriculture is that it should support rural communities.

Within the current economic system, rural communities tend to be regarded as poor and disadvantaged compared with city dwellers. I do not predict the income disparity changing, but I do foresee lifestyle benefits attracting people back to the countryside for an improved quality of life. The greater complexity of advanced agriculture will provide work, and quality seasonal food as a perk of employment. These will not be communities perched within vast landscapes of open ploughed fields ravaged by the wind and with little of interest for children (and adults). Sustainable agriculture, consisting of rich landscapes with diverse trees and a wide variety of crops, can provide delightful spaces to live and work. In addition to attracting an agricultural workforce, knowledge workers might be attracted out of cities to live in such communities because of the quality of life. The technologies of the Internet and videoconferencing mean that location is no longer important for many jobs (as work during the COVID-19 pandemic showed). Rural communities could be a diverse mix of people and activities. This is not an idealist's romantic vision but the result of a logical appraisal of how to maintain biodiversity and natural habitats in a world seeking more agricultural output.

Sustainable agriculture includes society as an integral component. Technology can be used of course to replace hard physical labour, but considerable human involvement is needed to manage such agriculture at the micro level. Currently, people who attempt to establish permaculture tend to be enthusiasts on a shoestring budget. They may need to keep costs down by employing workers like students on a gap year to balance the books – or too often not to balance the books. It is financially difficult to manage such complex agriculture within the current economic model. This does not mean that permaculture and other sustainable agricultural methods are wrong; it means that the current economic model is wrong. Again, the policy of a universal basic income comes to the rescue.

The universal basic income is a game changer for agriculture, showing the importance of this lever of resilient economics. This will be set at a rate which suits a particular country. In poor countries it will be set low and not go far, particularly in cities, but it should be sufficient to underpin rural communities based around agriculture. The workforce in a sustainable agrarian community could have lifestyle advantages and benefits-in-kind underpinned by a basic income. I anticipate such vibrant communities to proliferate and grow if we plant the seeds of such an economic model.

This discussion of advanced forms of agriculture illustrates the new thought processes, in particular the importance of seeing the economic model as the tool of agricultural policy, rather than its driver. It will play out in different ways in places ranging from Western Europe and North America to South America, Africa and Asia. In the developed world, we will have to rediscover sustainable practices to reverse out of excessive industrialization. In the developing world, there is the possibility of bouncing past the missteps of excessive industrialization to focus on enhancing long-standing local agricultural customs, thus avoiding the industrialization phase altogether.

Trade in Agricultural Products

The crops which can be grown in any particular region depend on the local climate and conditions. Few communities can be self-sufficient, unless located in equatorial regions where crops can be harvested throughout the year. Communities in places further north or south have traditionally needed to be well organized, using the summer growing season to conserve stores of food to tide them over the winter. This would lead to periods of bountiful fresh produce in summer months and a monotonous diet through the winter and early spring. Modern food supply logistics make this unnecessary with people in rich developed countries enjoying any food they desire at any time of year.

Trade in agricultural products is needed to satisfy needs

which cannot be fulfilled by local supply. Some current trade is hard to justify, especially through long supply chains provided by transportation reliant on fossil fuel costing money and producing carbon dioxide emissions. A prime example is flying fresh produce to European markets, such as mange-tout peas from Peru or roses from Kenya. This is so wasteful of carbon emissions in current generation aircraft that it would make common sense to consider a ban on such trade. This is not the current view of many policymakers. A superficial economic analysis can conclude that because consumers in rich countries are willing to pay the price such trade makes economic sense. In addition, benefits to the producing farmer are often cited in defence of such trade. A deeper analysis may find that it is not the poor farmer who reaps the financial benefit but the wholesaler facilitating the trade. There is also the fundamental problem that the environmental impact is not factored into the end price to the consumer. Resilient economic analysis should expose such inadequacies and align more closely with common sense.

There are circumstances where long supply chains can make sense. For example, the UK has close cultural affinity with a country on the other side of the planet, New Zealand. This country has substantial agricultural capacity on its two large islands and a small population; whereas the UK has a larger population on much smaller islands. Provided transportation is in a new generation of refrigerated ships running on solar and wind, such trade could be sensible and sustainable.

Free trade in agricultural products, particularly food, makes little sense. In Chapter 8, the obsolescence of free-trade policy was discussed and explained. Food is a good example to illustrate the necessity of moving forward with better, more nuanced trade policy. The fact that one place may have an absolute or relative advantage over another in agricultural products does not necessarily mean there should be trade. In one place, society may have adopted a particular agriculture model which suits their culture and circumstances. Such arrangements should not be sacrificed on the altar of free trade. Countries should be free to manage trade in agricultural products, setting tariffs as required. A country which chooses to drive down the price of agricultural products through machine efficiency should not be free to undermine another country with a sustainable agriculture system which respects nature and empowers rural communities.

In summary, trade in agricultural products should be used to provide society with what it needs in a sustainable manner based on self-sufficiency as the default choice, with countries in control of supplementing local supply with imports. There will be net importers and exporters, and particular trade corridors between countries where it suits both parties. As governments take back control, agricultural business will have to adapt to a resilient trading system where the economic model has been adjusted to protect the long-term viability and sustainability of this important sector. Agriculture is too important to allow the current casino culture of trading agricultural products to dictate outcomes.

Conclusions

Agriculture is integral to life on Earth. In pre-history humans were hunter-gatherers, wandering through nature harvesting its bounty. Obtaining food was the main activity taking up much of the conscious effort of human endeavour. Farming revolutionized society, meaning greater security of food supply and allowing many of the population to focus their efforts elsewhere. People became free to build the complex civilization we now enjoy. Advances in farming included: horses to replace human physical labour; tractors to replace horses; and now robots to replace tractor drivers. The next green revolution will focus on moving forward beyond industrial efficiency to grasp the rich complexity of advanced sustainable farming.

The resilient economic model of agriculture marks the transition from exploiting mechanization to a model of stewardship which delivers commercially-viable sustainable agriculture. Hunter-gatherers were travelling nomads, living at the mercy of nature, seeking food where it was to be found. Farmers put down roots on the land in order to exploit it. Stewards will work with nature to secure long-term food supplies in parallel with community building. Hunter-gathering was an enforced lifestyle; farming became a business; stewardship is a lifestyle choice with all the benefits that advanced sustainable farming has to offer. Instead of raw economic efficiency driving the design of agriculture, resilient economics can support a secure and stable agricultural sector. Self-sufficiency should be the default first choice; trade should be to satisfy real needs (rather than arbitrage between economies); and agrarian communities can thrive on the foundations of the introduction of the universal basic income.

My final observation on agriculture is with regard to the business of agriculture at all levels from single farmer to global conglomerate. Many advocates for sustainable agriculture, in their enthusiasm for better agriculture, blame business for the industrial approach which is so destructive. It is wrong to blame the corporate agricultural giants, although they can seem to be culpable for the short-term industrial model. The fault lies with all of us for allowing an economic model where the incentives are so negative to the long-term health of people, society and the planet. If we instruct our politicians to adopt a resilient economic model, agribusiness will become more fragmented and local. When *we* insist on changing the economic model, the agricultural sector is well able to rise to the challenge of delivering on the aspirations presented in this chapter.

CHAPTER 15

HOUSING

Can't see the community for the houses.

A house without community is simply a building. To become a home there needs to be a community within and around it. Housing and community should be inseparable issues. When treated separately it is possible to end up with great houses but no community life. Interestingly, it can go the other way, ending up with vibrant communities despite lousy housing, as some informal settlements demonstrate in the *favelas* of South America or shantytowns in South Africa. To make sense of the economics of housing, you have to look past the houses to the community.

Shelter is one of the basic needs of humanity together with food and water. Housing is therefore important to society; house building, ownership, and maintenance are important issues. The flip-side is the negative environmental impact of most current housing solutions. Buildings consume 32% of global final energy use (Cambridge Institute for Sustainability Leadership 2014). This comes predominantly from fossil fuel, used for heating, air-conditioning and appliances. Another negative aspect is endemic inefficient use of resources within the building industry, particularly in the developed world. Modern buildings include all sorts of monstrous hybrid materials in their construction.[31] This means that when they are refurbished they generate multiple skips of waste that is hard to recycle. The significant negative environmental impact of housing means that improving its

---

31 'Monstrous hybrid' is the term coined by McDonough & Braungart (2002) for materials which are an amalgam of bio and technical materials and are therefore very hard to recycle.

sustainability should be a key attribute of a resilient economic model for housing.

To jump straight to the essence of what we require of housing, we need shelter that is part of a community, designed for sustainability, such that it provides a happy home that does not impact negatively on its environment. The economic model has to support this aspiration.

Historically, there is a strong heritage of sustainable buildings dating from before the time when fossil fuel became ubiquitous. For example, in the tropics communities might live in clusters of attap roof buildings consisting of wooden frames covered with palm fronds to keep out the rain. Such buildings are totally recyclable, have zero carbon emissions and suit the locality. They do not have a modern look and feel, but I have lived in such buildings and they work just fine in a tropical climate. In desert regions, where day-time temperatures are high but it is cold at night, traditional buildings have thick stone walls and small shuttered windows. Such design keeps the building cool in the heat of the day but the stone retains the heat to remain warm at night. In the far north, or far south, buildings are made with thick insulated walls and double- or triple-glazed windows. We have not lost the capability to build houses to suit the environment, but fossil fuel has made us lazy. We have come to expect to be able to have any type of building we want, trusting it can be heated or cooled as required. We need to be much more inventive in the way buildings are designed, and communities planned to ensure we are resilient against the challenges of the 21st century. Part of this is relearning lessons from the past, so that buildings match the circumstances of the local environment.

Housing is evidently the provision of shelter, but of course people expect housing to be more than simply shelter. We want comfortable homes, status symbols, places of entertainment, and an investment. This last role is particularly problematic. For those families who can afford to step onto the housing ladder, their house is likely to be their single most valuable possession. Houses become a store of wealth and this is a quite different purpose to providing shelter. The confusion between wealth and shelter is a challenge when attempting to improve the economic model for housing.

The short discussion of housing which follows consists of selected insights to show how the framing of economics can generate resilient solutions. Sustainability and the needs of community are explored leading to adjustments to the economic model. First, let us consider ownership.

Ownership

The ownership of housing has significant consequences for its quality and sustainability. Houses can be owned by owner-occupiers, private landlords, commercial landlords, and the state. Each type of ownership has particular characteristics depending on the motives of the owner.

OWNER-OCCUPIERS

Owners who occupy property have a direct personal interest in how it is managed, the size of the energy bills, and how well it is maintained. A traditional financial model of such ownership starts with saving for a deposit on a first home. Typically, a young couple get themselves on the first rung of the housing ladder with a mortgage from a bank. As their family grows, they move up to larger properties and take on larger mortgages. Later in life, when they do not need so much space, they might downsize to a smaller retirement property paying off any outstanding mortgage. In reality it is seldom so simple. The idea of a house suitable for the needs of a family through the stages of life becomes confused with status, wealth and fashion. A house in Knightsbridge, an affluent area of London, might have multiple bedrooms, public rooms, an underground car park, and a home cinema. This goes well beyond what might be regarded as suitable shelter. This may be the extreme end of the scale, but everyone in the developed world regards their house as much more than a shelter in which to stay warm and safe.

LANDLORDS

Property is a pure investment from the perspective of a landlord. Landlords range from individuals with one investment property to commercial landlords with a large portfolio of properties as part of a dedicated business. The basis of the economic analysis for a private landlord is that the rent pays for their buy-to-let mortgage. In the early years there might be a rough balance between income and interest payments; over time the rent goes up and the value of the property increases making a good long-term investment. The more people regard property as primarily an investment, the higher prices rise, skewing the market away from homes being simply a place to live.

A key weakness of the rental sector is that energy efficiency improvements are a cost to the landlord with the benefit of reduced bills a saving to the tenant. Commercial landlords understand the need for regular maintenance to maintain the value of their property portfolio but often energy efficiency is not a priority for them. Tenants who appreciate paying a higher rent for a more efficient building are rare, so the raw economics steers landlords to do only the minimum to comply with regulations. Although energy efficiency measures make sense within a complete economic analysis, many landlords avoid such expenditure because of their narrow focus on maximizing the short-term return on their investment.

THE STATE

The other main category of owner is the state. The public sector has a reputation for building low-cost houses which are therefore often poor quality. This is short-sighted, driven by short-term economics. There is a sound case for state-owned, compact, affordable houses, built to high sustainability standards. The state can control what is built and ensure it is well-maintained, without being deflected by issues of status and other irrational desires.

In the UK, Margaret Thatcher introduced a policy to sell off state-owned houses to increase the proportion of privately-owned dwellings. Within the current economic model, this political decision transferred low-quality buildings into the private sector. If sustainability is brought to the fore, the situation changes. A resilient economic analysis would indicate that the state should build sustainable houses to be rented to the less well-off; and if eventually sold add highly sustainable buildings to the country's housing stock.

These different ownership models can facilitate or hinder progress depending on the circumstances.

Sustainability of Housing Stock

Governments tend not to put a high priority on the sustainability of the housing stock. Political pressures tend to focus on availability and affordability. Short-term political wins are possible through encouraging building low-quality housing which is available quickly and affordable to all. If politicians could find the courage to think long-term, high-quality sustainable homes are by far the better solution for all stakeholders. It is better for owners and landlords because of improvements to the quality of housing stock and better for tenants because running costs are lower. Despite the clear benefits, sustainability is slow to be embraced by the UK house-building industry (see Box 15.1 overleaf).

Box 15.1 Snapshot of a blinkered building industry

I attended a seminar on sustainable building practices held at the Beddington Zero Energy Development (BedZED) in London. BedZED was designed by the architect Bill Dunster in 2002 for the Peabody Trust. It is a showcase of advanced sustainable building design. The seminar covered sustainable materials, high performance insulation, advanced windows, improved ventilation systems, renewable energy harvesting, and design for sustainable living. It provided a compendium of best practice.

These are issues with which I am familiar, and I was keen to attend to gauge the extent to which sustainability was shaping the construction industry. I was pleased to meet at the seminar the technical director of the company which had built our house in 1998. We had bought the house new, described in the sales brochure as an 'executive home'. I commented to him at the coffee break that it was good to see him leading his company to embrace sustainability. I explained that we had recently upgraded the house with top-quality insulation, triple glazing, Solar PV, and solar thermal. I told him it was good that he was considering incorporating such high standards from the outset. I received a blank stare in response. No, he was not going to recommend that the company embrace sustainability. He found the seminar to be an interesting day out of the office, but the company would stick rigidly to satisfying minimum building control requirements. I tried to persuade him that it would be a good fit for his upmarket sales pitch to build to a higher and more sustainable standard, but he was not convinced. He explained that it would increase costs so he was adamant that it would reduce profits. The complete unwillingness to even engage in thinking through an alternative business model for sustainable housing exposed the blinkered thinking in which the industry is currently trapped.

This was an example of astounding complacency. If an upmarket builder is not going to consider building quality sustainable homes, there is little hope for the rest of the industry. The incident I report is from some years back and the situation is improving but at a pace which is well behind what is needed.

The principles of building sustainable houses are well established. The materials used should be recycled or biodegradable. High standards of insulation reduce the need for heating or cooling. The building layout should maximize (or minimize) solar gain depending on the season. The roof areas should be designed for harvesting renewable energy. Heat-recovery ventilation systems further reduce energy demand. Design parameters differ depending on local capabilities and local climate. The technical knowledge and know-how are well documented but what is lacking is correct framing of the economic case. We owned a house in Helsinki, Finland, in 2004–8 which showed us first-hand how housing could be so much better (see Box 15.2).

Box 15.2 Lessons for the UK from a Finnish house

In 2004 we bought a house in Espoo, west of Helsinki. It had been built in the 1980s to Finnish building standards. Standards of insulation are high, as you would expect in a country where the temperature is likely to be -30°C for extended periods during the winter. It had triple glazing and a well-insulated roof and walls. The insulation was so good that the heating did not come on unless the outside temperature was sub-zero. When it did come on the radiators were warm rather than hot (low-grade heat from a combined heat and power (CHP) plant) but the house was always toasty warm. It became obvious to me, living in such a house, that if you were to build such insulation into a house in the UK it would not need a heating system – except perhaps for short periods in the winter.

To build a house in the UK which uses close to zero energy for heating does not need advanced new technology – all it needs is the application of building practices which are standard in Nordic countries. It is economically viable there because of the harsh climate. Although it would be a fairly straightforward technical challenge to produce carbon-neutral buildings in the temperate climate of the UK, this is not considered to be economically viable. This is despite the main expense being a one-off cost when the house is built, leading to decades of minimal heating bills.

The UK climate does not make it an economic imperative to build to such high standards, but the UK could choose to think long-term and adopt sustainable standards. When we left Finland in 2008 and returned to our house in the UK, we decided to improve the insulation (in so far as we could in a house built to UK standards) and fitted triple glazing. Recently we added an extension built to the high standards I discovered in Finland. My intention was to have the confidence of my convictions and not to extend the central heating into the extension, but I was overruled by a higher authority (my wife). Over the years, the radiators in the extension seldom come on. The way the extension is built requires no additional heating in the temperate UK climate.

It is an economic imperative to build high-quality well-insulated houses in Finland because the climate is so cold. If you failed to invest in better buildings, the heating bills would be unaffordable. It seems strange that in the UK the blinkered economic analysis works against building to such high quality. Over the life of the building, sustainable design makes economic sense, but the builder is worried about making their margin on the initial sale, and purchasers have no easy way to appreciate the value of decades of low energy bills. It is the short-termism and insular nature of the industry, together with indifference from customers, which leads to such poor economic choices.

For the building industry to escape the straightjacket of conventional economic constraints, the analysis has to be switched around. First, the best course of action should be determined; second, the economic analysis focuses on making this viable. For our house in the UK, we set the objective of being as sustainable as possible. We rejected the option of demolishing it and starting again, as that would not have been a sustainable way to proceed with a relatively new house. I was careful to manage the project closely and keep costs under control, but I did not work out the pay-back period based on reduced fuel bills. The increase in the value of the house over the years since the work more than covers the cost of the project. To my mind, it made no sense to accept low standard buildings based on detailed economic analysis which compares build costs versus fuel bills over relatively short pay-back periods. In the UK it is technically easy to build zero-carbon houses, so we should build zero-carbon homes. This should be the default option for all new houses. It would soon become integral to the economic model for housing. This is another example of framing the decision on the most important criteria and then designing the economic model to fit.

The economics of sustainable housing can be quite straightforward. In ballpark figures, a sustainable house in the UK will cost 20% more to build than a standard house. If we decide that sustainability is the default, houses will either cost 20% more to build or, for the same money, we get a 20% smaller house. A large part of the value of the house is the site so the extra expense is proportionally less.

From the purchaser's perspective, to purchase a better house which costs more will require a larger mortgage. Over the life of the mortgage, interest payments will be more and the occupier will have smaller energy bills. It would be possible to go through the mathematics to work out a pay-back period relying on estimates of future energy prices which may be little better than guesswork over such a time frame. There seems little point. Over a period of twenty years, the change in the value of the house will make the initial higher building costs look like small change. We would have a much higher-quality house and be much more resilient against fluctuating energy prices. I suggest that the high-level economic analysis can focus on getting it right in principle knowing that the fine detail of the economic numbers is not particularly relevant to the decision. Some economists might chide me for being so cavalier with the numbers, but when you realize that burying your head in a spreadsheet is stopping you from seeing reality, it is time to turn away from the spreadsheet and focus on the core logic.

The barrier to clear thinking about sustainable homes is that too many stakeholders have got their heads buried in spreadsheets leading to the following oddities. First, energy efficiency measures which require significant expenditure are regarded as not financially viable. This is based on an analysis which assumes that energy prices remain affordable, so the financial savings from energy efficiency are not sufficient to justify the expenditure when taking a short-term view. Second, expenditure by one stakeholder does not offset directly with savings for another. So, landlords do not see a direct financial benefit from energy efficiency improvements because the tenant pays the energy bill. Third, new house builders resist building better buildings fearing losing margin on the sale. Where their profit margin is 10%, they baulk at a 20% increase in build costs without embracing the bigger economic picture. Each stakeholder is examining the cells in the spreadsheet which apply directly to them. This spreadsheet navel-gazing obscures the simple logic that sustainable homes are better long-term investments, cheaper to run, and future proof.

A way to overcome the barriers to sustainable homes is through regulations requiring minimum standards for houses. We would have to acknowledge that forcing standards on a reluctant industry will be difficult until the mindset of the industry changes.

When I invited local builders to bid for refurbishing our house, I received one particularly interesting response. This builder had spotted 'errors' in our specification. We met on site at our house. He proudly explained that he could save us money because he had noticed we were planning insulation levels far higher than required by UK legislation. By reducing the insulation, he could give us a lower quote. It was clear in his mind that this was the right way to build. He was equally certain that as the potential customer I would be delighted. He was surprised when I explained the error of his ways, and as there was no meeting of minds, showed him the door. I suspect he might also tell a story about meeting a householder who did not understand building regulations. I understand building regulations to be the minimum standard to be exceeded, not as a target to be met.

Basic building standards are there to stop the cowboy builders. Professional builders should be capable of doing much better. It seems to be ingrained in the UK industry that building specifications should be honed down to scrape through the minimum requirement at the least cost. On one hand this is rational economic behaviour; on the other it lacks simple common sense. Common sense says that long-term valuable assets like houses should be built to high-quality future-proof standards.

Sustainability is an important theme of 21st-century living which cuts across all sectors and is particularly important in housing. We have the technology for sustainable housing and it is simple common sense that it should be used. Sustainable housing is desirable and feasible, so the resilient economic case should be framed around delivering such houses, pushing past short-term conventional economic analysis.

Community Living

A man's house is his castle.[32]

Houses are significant financial assets which people take pride in owning and defend against intruders. The castle approach is typified by sprawling suburbs of individual properties each fenced off creating a checkerboard of private domains. The economic model of property defined by a fixed perimeter perpetuates the idea that houses are for the exclusive use of the owner or tenant. Building the cohesive communities needed to face the challenges of the future requires a better approach.

BALANCING PRIVATE AND PUBLIC SPACES

There is a fundamental trade-off between the amount of space individual households have for their exclusive use, and the way the community operates. Large individual building plots mean less dense development and less opportunity to construct communities. If everyone lived in a large house with extensive gardens, there would not be the density for viable public transport nor local clusters of shops and facilities within walking distance. Everything would have to be a car drive away, with shops and other services clustered in shopping malls surrounded by car parks. These shopping malls are a poor substitute for real local high streets of diverse shops and services operating as integral

---

32   The phrase 'For a man's house is his castle' is included in *The Institutes of the Laws of England*, 1628 (Ratcliffe 2018).

components of the community. Retaining and rebuilding such communities requires sufficient density for walking, cycling and cost-effective public transport connections. To achieve this requires relatively small private space for each household balanced with good quality public spaces. This spatial logic should frame the economic analysis.

Designing an appropriate economic model for balancing private and public spaces hinges on how value is ascribed to land and property. There are three components of a property's value: the land, the permission to build, and the building. Considering these three components of value allows us to think through resilient economic models of community living. Instead of building houses, we should build communities with a balance between public, private and shared space. The allocation of land between public and private space is something to decide when planning permission is granted. The uplift in value which comes with granting permission should pay for the development of facilities in the public space for the benefit of the community such as parks, schools, roads, walkways and cycleways. Where the local authority owns or has acquired the land, it has the power to draw up plans for the community. The economic model could be to sell plots of land with planning permission for individual houses and use this income to build the community infrastructure. Where private developers seeks planning permission, they should be required to pay the local authority an appropriate sum for the public infrastructure to be built, or required to build such infrastructure integral to the construction project.

In the end, the balance between public and private space is a political decision. It is for the politicians to ensure that there is a high proportion of public space, acknowledging that this is good for the community. Without such policy, the building industry will build a checkerboard of private properties with only enough public land for access roads. This is how a developer can maximize the financial return from the site – leading to the bland suburbs which are all too common.

At the community level, we need to strike a balance between private and public space. At the building level, the balance to be struck is between private and shared space.

BALANCING PRIVATE AND SHARED SPACES

The concept of balancing private space and shared space is also important but less well understood. This requires challenging the mindset of houses as single-family-unit castles. In houses there are intensely private spaces such as bedrooms and spaces we share with members of the close family such as a bathroom and kitchen. We also like to have space to entertain friends and hold parties. A modern house will have more space than required for day-to-day living. This is expensive in resources, heating and purchase costs. Improving economic and resources efficiency leads to utilizing shared space with other households. The logic is compelling.

For an example of living space shared between households, I turn to the Nordic countries. Here, a block of apartments might have a sauna shared on a rota allocated between the flats. The same concept could extend to shared entertainment areas which residents could book, or a residents' lounge where residents could mingle with other residents. When areas of private space for exclusive use are squeezed smaller it releases space and resources for high quality shared space. Frugal living becomes possible, without sacrificing quality of life, even for people living on a basic income. Their private exclusive space might only be a bedroom (perhaps en suite) with access to a shared kitchen, washing facilities and lounge area. How well such shared arrangements work depends on the behaviour of residents. Well-behaved residents (even if poor) would migrate towards well-run housing communities; whereas badly behaved residents would end up sharing with like-minded people and having to live with the consequences. Removing the castle mentality forces people to confront the reality of their behaviour and allows people to build strong communities where selfless and reasonable social behaviour pays, but selfish or anti-social behaviour does not.

DESIGNING FOR COMMUNITY LIVING

The resilient economic model for community living has a number of elements. First, the greater site has to be designed as a community rather than simply carved up into individual plots. At the initial stage, the local authority should leverage the value of granting building permission to ensure that sufficient funds are earmarked for public infrastructure built to a high standard. Second, to improve community living at the micro level, local authorities should use their power over planning permission to look favourably on developments which provide good quality shared space. This is particularly important to deliver affordable housing in places where property prices are high. The way to ensure sound management of shared buildings is to adopt the ownership model of a company owning the whole building with residents holding shares in the company rather than individual leases.

Designing for community living will allow us to advance beyond conurbations of sprawling suburbs to vibrant communities with high-quality public facilities at the community level and shared facilities at the building level. Breaking the mindset of houses as castles may not be easy, particularly for more affluent areas. It will take time for the benefits of community living to be appreciated by both rich and poor. Rich people in grand castles can be just as lonely as poor people in isolated cramped flats. Community living allows people to thrive.

Adjusting the economic model

Let us consider whether there are ways to tweak the economics of housing to make improvements, starting with supporting improved energy efficiency.

THE ECONOMICS OF ENERGY EFFICIENCY

The energy efficiency of buildings can be improved by application of the lever of taxation to drive up the cost of energy. This action underpins the economic case to build better buildings and refurbish old buildings to a high standard. People who live in improved energy-efficient buildings will have similar overall energy bills to what they might have had in the past, because although price per unit of energy will have gone up, the amount of energy used will have gone down. People who live in old inefficient buildings will be hit with higher energy charges, providing a strong incentive to make improvements. A short-term political problem is that higher energy costs are likely to have most impact on some of the poorest people in society. The convenient political response is to subsidize energy bills for the poor; this should be resisted. The sensible economic approach would be to use the additional tax income (supplemented by additional borrowing) for a massive programme of insulation for houses of the poorest and the most vulnerable families.

Whilst there is delay in adjusting the economic model in favour of energy-efficient buildings, there are ways to make progress. I have found that it is possible to break out of spreadsheet-navel-gazing with common-sense analysis. For example, companies with portfolios of buildings need to decide whether to refurbish to high energy-efficiency standards. Focusing on the financial numbers leads to decisions to spend the minimum which complies with legislation. This is because it can be hard to recoup the costs through higher rents whilst tenants do not appreciate the value of lower energy bills when making their decision of which property to rent. The resilient economic case is buried by the ignorance that arises from dealing with the issue using the raw financial numbers and a short-term view. The argument I have used successfully with commercial landlords is that although a higher rent may not be forthcoming, if there is a downturn in the rental market, more energy-efficient properties will remain fully occupied. Even a landlord who does not appreciate the sustainable investment view, can understand that their income is more secure when the risk of void periods is reduced.

Adjusting the economic model to improve the energy efficiency of buildings is relatively straightforward. It is more difficult to counter the distortion which arises from property being used as investment assets.

BUILDINGS AS INVESTMENTS

The primary role of buildings as places to live and work can be obscured when they are bought and sold as investments. When financial speculation takes over from sensible urban planning, it is time to think about adjusting the economic model.

A notorious example of property speculation is one of London's first skyscrapers. Centre Point was built for property tycoon Harry Hyams and completed in 1966. It then stood empty until 1975 making Harry Hyams a good return on his investment, despite the building standing empty. The building made him money, as property prices continued to rise, without the bother of bringing it into use.

During the period that Centre Point was vacant, London faced a housing crisis and the building became a lightning rod for housing protesters. It remained largely empty until 1980, when it was finally let as the headquarters of the Confederation of British Industry (CBI). Over the years, Centre Point has had a number of investor owners, each focused on its value as an investment. In 2015, it was converted into eighty-two luxury flats at prices ranging from £3-million to £55-million penthouses. Centre Point continues to be a valuable investment much more than it was ever a place to work or live. It is estimated that half the apartments in Centre Point have been sold to people who do not live in the UK. It makes sense, within the current economic model, to market London properties to Arab princes and Russian oligarchs as safe havens for their money. The property developer makes a profit; the government welcomes the inflow of foreign capital; and the new owners have what they believe to be a good investment. Everyone involved is happy, but no one involved is in real need of accommodation.

To steer the market to serve householders rather than investors requires action to limit speculation. One of the main determinants of house prices is the availability of mortgages. It is therefore important to have rules which limit the size and availability of mortgages. A measure commonly used is to limit borrowing based on multiples of income. Another significant factor in some places is demand from overseas investors looking for investment properties. Limits on foreign ownership can make sense. In the UK, there has been a huge expansion in what is called the buy-to-let property market with people investing in second, third or fourth properties. It should be no surprise that property suffers from speculative bubbles. The government should remove tax advantages for buy-to-let (such as allowing mortgage interest to be offset against rent) and consider other disincentives.

Rural areas have the challenge of property which is too expensive for local workers. There are small villages in Southern England which decades ago were home to rural communities and are now occupied by commuters who work in the cities. These are well-maintained, chocolate-box-pretty places which are completely dead from Monday to Friday during the working day. For these communities to thrive, housing should be considered in terms of who needs to live in the community and how much space they require. Such thoughts are sidelined when property is offered for sale on the open market, where the person with the deepest pockets wins. There are ways around this. For example, the planning process can be used to ensure that some properties are reserved for people who live and work locally. However, once built and sold, the owners will always be tempted to circumvent such restrictions, if they can, and sell on the open market to make a profit.

ALTERNATIVE OWNERSHIP MODELS

There are other ideas to reinforce communities which might seem old-fashioned but on examination have merit. A village might have a house for the local schoolteacher, and flats above shops for the shopkeepers. A house for the village police officer is not perhaps how modern policing would be arranged, but an example which still exists is school properties including a small house for the caretaker. This allows the school to recruit and retain someone on a low wage who is always on site and available. This can be extended to a house (or houses) owned by the school for teachers. Private boarding schools have used this for many years to attract staff who integrate into the community life of the school. The tenancy of houses linked to jobs is an idea worth reviving through appropriate models of house ownership by employers.

Reconsidering ownership models is one way to steer the housing market towards sustainable, affordable homes embedded in the community. If the government, directly or through housing organizations, builds houses, they can be designed to be first and foremost sustainable affordable homes. The potential uplift in value from granting planning commission can be curtailed by holding them in public ownership or through a not-for-profit holding company. Provided there are robust limitations to prevent such properties coming on the open market, the economic analysis can be neatly framed.

Let us assume that the site is either public land or a site without planning permission. Remember the three components of value: the site, the permission to build, and the building. First, such a site is cheap; second, the permission to build is something the local authority can grant; third, in such circumstances the only significant value component is the building itself. Framing the resilient economic argument in this way makes it affordable to build sustainable, compact, robust and energy-efficient houses. The rent for such homes can be set mainly to cover the construction costs. Although these will be higher for sustainable homes, where this is the only cost to recoup, rents can be affordable. As the government is in control, tenants have to accept that compact and sustainable is what the government provides. The temptation which exists in the private sector to build more spacious homes to lower sustainability standards can be resisted.

Houses in public ownership, established as affordable homes, are always at risk of being switched to become investment assets. Politicians can change legislation to be able to place such properties on the open market and reap a profit. This can be seen as an abuse of the system, but this might be appropriate. For example, this could be a route to market for compact quality sustainable houses which private developers are reluctant to build. It could also generate income to plough back into more public housing. A problem with the current economic model of public housing is the tendency to build at low-cost, complying with minimum standards. This is deeply ingrained in local government and completely self-defeating.

Applying the resilient economic approach will mean local authorities building quality sustainable homes, better than many in the private sector. There might be criticism for renting them to the poorest people in society, but whatever your politics this is correct. A left-leaning view might welcome poorer people living in quality affordable housing with low running costs. A right-leaning view might welcome that the housing is compact with the option to be sold at a profit as part of long-term plans to improve the country's housing stock.

I cannot in these few paragraphs fix the economic model of housing; but what I hope I have done is to show that there is much more to housing policy than simple economic analysis. We should have confidence to consider what we want from property and skew the economic model to deliver what communities need from the housing stock. Once again, rather than letting raw economics drive policy, policy should drive the economic analysis.

Conclusions

People need shelter which they can call home. The best way to provide this is sustainable housing developments, designed to work as communities. It is to be expected that such important infrastructure has financial value; but when houses are traded primarily as financial assets the economic model can diverge from the needs of society. Houses are both homes and investments. Too much emphasis on their value as investments can distort the housing market leading to sub-optimal solutions for people and the community. It is important that economic policy follows rather than leads in this important area. The priorities should be decided before setting the economic parameters. The economics of housing should be framed by strategic long-term priorities and care taken not to get caught in the trap of short-term payback calculations.

One requirement is to reduce the environmental impact of housing. The key insight in this regard is that significant changes to housing only come about when houses are built or refurbished. It is at these decision points when the economic case for sustainability has to be grasped. It will then take decades to ripple through the housing stock to deliver real reductions in CO_2 emissions. Sustainability in housing is straightforward in a technical sense; and straightforward in an economic sense if we have the gumption to drive energy prices high through taxation. Unfortunately, the politics is problematic because it requires politicians to justify higher energy prices to householders. Householders have to accept their responsibility to keep overall energy bills controlled through efficiency measures. It makes sense, but that does not mean it will be easy to establish this better economic approach. To deliver the energy efficiency which is vital to sustainability, government should aim to win the argument for energy taxes with the receipts steered to energy efficiency measures for less-affluent households.

Affordable housing is a more difficult issue because the dynamics of house prices do not fit the normal logic of supply and demand. If the property market dealt in supply and demand for places to live, the market might work for householders. Where the market deals in houses as investment assets, then it works for investors. To steer the market to serve householders rather than investors requires action to limit speculation. One of the main determinants of house prices is the availability of mortgages, so rules to limit the availability of mortgages make sense. Alternative ownership models which prevent affordable housing from being sold on the open market also have merit.

Finally, where housing is in public ownership, it has a bad reputation for being low-cost and inferior. It makes sense, from a resilient economic perspective, to build compact and sustainable public housing.

The insights provided in this chapter focus on the fundamentals of housing economics. This process of reframing economics continues in the next chapter, which is on transport.

CHAPTER 16

TRANSPORT

We have to escape the trap of believing that alleviating gridlock requires building more roads.

Transport infrastructure is vital to allow people to travel and enable the trade of goods and commodities. People have a practical need to commute to work, and also want to travel for leisure, meet other people, see places, and experience other cultures. Transport infrastructure influences people's choices of where to live and where to go on holiday. It is also a determining factor in deciding whether trade is commercially viable. Applying economic analysis to inform decisions about transport infrastructure appears to be straightforward, until you understand the distortions which can result by focusing on the economic analysis. Transport decisions can become disconnected from the real needs of society when the economic argument is allowed to dominate decision making. Transport policy has to be framed by objectives and priorities which sit above the pure economic analysis.

An example of straightforward economic analysis of transport infrastructure, might be a bridge over an estuary. People and freight wanting to move up or down the coast have to travel a long way inland before they find a place to cross the river. A bridge over the estuary would shorten the journey considerably. There is clearly a real need. The bridge can be justified by simple economic analysis based on reduced journey times. The cost of the bridge will depend on the width of the estuary and the potential savings will depend on the quantity of road miles saved. The economic analysis compares the savings over the life of the bridge compared with the cost. Provided the former exceeds the latter, it makes economic sense.

A different way to approach transport infrastructure is to build capacity to generate demand. This is certainly odd, but through economic goggles can appear to make perfect sense. An example is the way low-cost airlines justify establishing new routes. Two cities are selected which do not currently have a direct flight connection. There is no particular identified need, nor any history or heritage of direct transport links. Low-cost airlines have found that setting up the route is usually sufficient to generate demand to fill the seats. When the route exists, people consider new commuting profiles and different holiday options. The cities concerned welcome such new routes because they help their economies to grow by drawing in additional tourists and facilitating new business connections. Such transport infrastructure is not a priority and may be unnecessary, but the economic analysis adds up; the low-cost airline generates additional income and the city involved generates increased tourist footfall. Building transport capacity to generate demand makes conventional economic sense but does not comply with the common sense of resilient economics.

In this chapter I will show that infrastructure based on need is the way to ensure transport serves society. Although this seems obvious, I will go back to basics to work out how resilient economics should deal with transport.

To consider a new direction for transport policy, I need to first expose three shortcomings of the current approach, which I present as the three fallacies of transport. I will then examine how a new approach to the economic analysis can play out at different levels of transport provision from transport within cities to intercontinental travel. To set the scene, I will consider how to frame the economic analysis of transportation.

Reframing the Economics of Transportation

Considering the need for transportation, it makes sense to think about the needs of people, and the needs of society. Ideally the two would overlap, such that the needs of the individual and those of society are aligned. This might not be the case where society needs transport infrastructure but people living in close proximity are negatively impacted. It is common that the needs of society take precedence with appropriate compensation paid to local residents. For this to be accepted without protest, it should be clear that there is real net benefit to society overall.

Transport projects are an easy target for protesters where the need is not justified in terms of serving society. A trap to avoid is justifying transport infrastructure for the sake of the economy. It is not surprising that such arguments attract protest causing delay and additional cost. If we pause and reflect, the concept of an economy having transport needs is peculiar. It might provide jobs whilst it is being built, give the country an asset to hold on the national balance sheet, or provide improved connections on the assumption that this will support economic growth. These are familiar arguments but it is important to dig beneath these economic justifications to prise out the real need. In fact, the consideration of any transport infrastructure project should start with a real need, well before embarking on the economic analysis.

It is worth dwelling a little more on the thought that the needs of the economy might require enhancement to the transport infrastructure. If this is at odds with the needs of people and society, we should be very critical in our examination. If the deep analysis shows only an economic benefit, this would indicate there is a fault in the application of economics. Economic analysis for the benefit of the economy is always a bad idea. Economic analysis should be about facilitating real stuff in the real world, which serves people's needs. A justification arising in the virtual world of economics, to rationalize building infrastructure in the real world, that only serves the virtual economic world, is dysfunctional. When you become attuned to thinking about economics in terms of real-world impact, you start to notice such limitations of conventional economics.

The current perspective on economics has become ensnared by assumptions about growth and trade. This mindset sees transport infrastructure as inherently good. It appears as economic activity contributing to economic growth as it is being constructed, and once built it facilitates increasing trade. Economic analysis needs to escape such superficial thinking to think about real-world outcomes. This means positioning society uppermost in the analysis to decide priorities and outcomes. Applying such deeper thinking to transportation leads to the unexpected conclusion that the best solutions to transport bottlenecks can be changes to policy which reduce the need to travel. This can apply to both people and freight. Transport infrastructure should be built where there is real need, but resources can be saved and funds released to use elsewhere by adopting a policy of reducing the need for transportation. Making alterations to the way society operates, or business manufacturing is organized, may be the better option.

Economic policy designed to reduce the need for transportation uses fewer resources, causes fewer emissions, and can deliver better overall solutions for society. Transport infrastructure which is not built does not contribute to the growth numbers, so conventional economic thinking sees this approach as a wasted opportunity. The real opportunity is to save the countryside, save resources, reduce emissions, and improve quality of life. The real analysis of transport policy requires working out whom and what needs to travel, and either making changes which reduce the requirement to travel or designing appropriate infrastructure. When taking an elemental view to consider a gridlocked motorway it would appear you need more lanes and capacity. When you take a systemic view there may be other better solutions. It is such deep systemic thinking which is needed, focused on the needs of society, not the needs of the economy. I keep driving home the point that it is only society which has real needs. Imagining that the economy has needs, leads to bizarre outcomes and should be avoided.

The Three Fallacies of Transport

There is potential for significant improvements in transportation provided we can break the lock of outdated ideas. There are three fallacies which dominate current thinking and hold back progress:

1. To reduce congestion increase capacity;

2. High-capacity transportation is required to facilitate trade;

3. Transportation without fossil fuel is not possible any time soon.

I will examine each of these in turn because until these ideas are taken out of play it is impossible to open the analysis to better solutions.

FALLACY 1

To reduce congestion, increase capacity.

As roads get congested, transport planners increase capacity with new roads, additional lanes on existing roads, and improved traffic-control systems. For a time, the congestion is relieved, but it does not take long for the higher capacity roads to again be full of traffic. People respond to the increased capacity by taking jobs further away as longer commuter journeys become possible. Business is able to reap economies of scale by centralizing to fewer depots. Such responses to increasing road capacity ratchet up traffic to fill the new capacity. Unless expansion in capacity is a step ahead of the traffic growth, roads remain congested. We are forever chasing our transport tail without breaking the cycle to move forward to a lasting solution.

An interesting alternative view on the relationship between traffic and capacity is provided by the city of Copenhagen. Here the congestion fallacy is turned to advantage. The city embarked on a massive programme of building cycleways – and discovered that they became full of bikes. People were responding to the opportunity to make more journeys safely by bicycle. So, build more road capacity, you get more cars; build more cycleways, you get more bicycles.

Maybe we have been looking at congestion without understanding what is going on. There has been a tendency to examine the balance between capacity and traffic, and use traffic predictions to justify building more capacity. To my mind, the balance is not between traffic and capacity but between traffic and congestion. For a fixed transport infrastructure, more congestion provides pressure to reduce traffic; less congestion encourages an increase in traffic. There is a dynamic balance where equilibrium is a tolerable level of congestion.

There is a way to break out of the congestion trap. If capacity is hugely greater than the traffic demand there will be no congestion. This can be seen in the early days of motorway building by central planners in China before many people owned cars. These were empty multi-lane roads which flowed freely until car ownership increased substantially leading to the clogged roads and smog-filled cities of modern-day China. I do not recommend huge increases in road building; this would not be sensible or desirable. The same outcome can be achieved by drastically reducing demand.

A town or city might have a road transport skeleton consisting of main roads leading into town, inner and outer ring roads, and a myriad of connecting streets. This would be a typical layout, and subject to the normal parameters of traffic increasing to the point of tolerable congestion. Let us suppose that the city decides to pedestrianize the town centre, impose heavy taxes on private cars, low taxes on taxis, and invest in quality public transport including clean buses, trams and light rail. Let us suppose also that there is a push to expand the cycle infrastructure. These measures taken together can kill the demand for private car transportation. You can still choose to have a car, but it would be expensive to own and expensive to drive on the city streets. There is already amongst younger city dwellers an increasing tendency not to want a car. Those of us brought up in the age of the car might be slower to accept living without a car reserved for our personal use, but such a change of attitude is entirely feasible. Such demand reduction means the car infrastructure becomes vastly greater than the need. Land which used to be car parks and roads can be reclaimed for other purposes including cycleways and areas where people meet and walk.

Systems thinking applied to city transport policy can break out of the congestion trap, so that instead of dealing with congestion by building roads we focus on holistic transport solutions.

Let us consider the national road infrastructure and freight transportation to explore whether similar logic applies. Currently, goods and components are made in large factories serving large geographic markets. This has economies of scale for the corporation, provided the transport infrastructure has the capacity to cope. The same congestion logic that applies to cars also applies to freight. Freight expands to fill the capacity, supporting larger depots and larger factories. Where there is less transport capacity, corporations choose smaller and more numerous depots and factories. From a corporate perspective, business will lobby for high-capacity transport because it is more efficient for them. Governments do not have to comply with such demands in deciding what is important for society. We can choose to spend less on road infrastructure if that makes sense for society (perhaps spending more on other transport options), nudging corporations towards operating closer to the customer. The big picture analysis of the best and most economical solution might be quite different from the narrow perspective of a corporation. Such systemic thinking is part of the drive to shift manufacturing to operate within a circular economy. Goods will be assembled close to where they will be used, using parts from suppliers located close to the assembly plant. Freight and transportation costs will be low and the environmental impact of transportation reduced. Instead of building yet more freeways and motorways, the alternative is the transformation of manufacturing and supply.

I suggest that the preferred approach to congestion is to focus on demand reduction. This replaces the outdated approach of building transport capacity to match projected demand. The business case is built on measures which reduce demand, relieve congestion and make increased capacity unnecessary, facilitated by changes to economic policy. This requires more complex analysis but deals more directly with the key issues of transport infrastructure planning compared with the simple approach of continual expansion for temporary relief of gridlock.

FALLACY 2

High-capacity transportation is required to facilitate trade.

It is deeply ingrained in the mindset of many policymakers that high-capacity transportation is vital to the economy. In developed countries, failure to invest in increasing the capacity of ports, roads and airports is seen as a brake on trade and therefore a brake on the economy. For developing countries, the advice is to invest in transport infrastructure to facilitate trade as a prerequisite for economic success.

The argument that increasing the capacity of transport is always good is used, for example, by multinational corporations seeking access to a country's resources. Transport infrastructure might be offered as a benefit in exchange for permission to open a new mine. This is a standard tactic of the Chinese government to gain access to resources on the African continent. This is supported by advice from world institutions, such as the IMF and World Bank, that improving transport infrastructure is inherently good for the economy. The real need in this case of course is to transport the resource or commodity to a port for export. There is no inherent value to the country unless it also serves the needs of its society. Transport infrastructure is a scar on the natural landscape, which is justified when it serves a real need, but on its own has no intrinsic value. A road to a mine clearly has value to the mine's owners. The idea that a country is better off because it has another road to add to its asset base does not necessarily follow.

The mindset that transportation infrastructure is intrinsically good arises from the concept that trade is inherently good. When trade is seen through the lens of 'more is better', it follows that the same should apply to transport infrastructure, the more the better. In Chapter 8 it was shown that expansion of trade is no longer appropriate as a basis for economic policy. It is therefore not true that more trade is necessarily better; the same applies to transport infrastructure, more is not necessarily better.

As the resilient economic approach is better understood, it becomes clear that modern 21st century economies will be less trade-dependent, and less transport-dependent. To deliver the aspiration of the transition to a circular economy will involve much less trade in physical commodities and goods, as products are made according to the principles of full lifecycle design. The long commute to work will be replaced by more working from home, or within work facilities embedded in the community. A greater proportion of food will be sourced locally, particularly when the season is favourable. Exactly how the new economy evolves will depend on the decisions taken, but it can be foreseen that putting quality of life to the fore will lead to less need of transportation. Looking at future transport policy, it could make sense to deliberately restrict the capacity of transportation to facilitate the transition to a circular economy. This might be seen as a step too far at this early stage in enlightened thinking, but it is important to turn away from the fallacy that the economy necessarily requires high-capacity transportation to facilitate trade.

FALLACY 3

Transportation without fossil fuel is not possible any time soon.

Before the advent of fossil fuel, transport relied on horses for ground transportation and power from the wind to propel ships on the ocean. Transport was slow and limited in its capacity. The invention of the steam engine changed everything. Using railways, it became possible to travel further, faster, carrying greater quantities. The internal combustion engine was the next leap forward making transportation on land and sea convenient, fast and reliable. The introduction of the jet engine launched the modern era of high-capacity transportation by air, including venturing beyond the atmosphere into space. Currently, most transport relies on fossil fuel. We regard transportation as essential, so regard burning fossil fuel as unavoidable.

Transport in the 20th century took a particular direction because of easy access to plentiful fossil fuel. We are now living with the consequences. Air pollution and its implications for the global climate make it abundantly clear that fossil fuels should be phased out. The technology to make the transition exists, but it is a struggle to disentangle a transport system built up over many decades. It is particularly challenging because it requires a total transformation.

Policymakers tend to be conservative, thinking about minimizing the degree of change and disruption. For example, it would be simple for policymakers if there were drop-in alternative fuels to replace petrol, diesel and aviation fuel. All that would be required would be minor tweaks to engines to be able to burn the alternative fuel. Such simple analysis leads to the hope that the transport system can remain much the same, just running on different fuels. The folly of this approach is quite astounding. Progress is held up for as long as we insist that transport looks like it does now. We have a 20th-century transport system. We need the confidence and ambition to build a 21st-century transport system – and it will be different.

Take away fossil fuel, and the current transport system no longer works. That is the reality we face. Systemic change is required which will only come about with a total commitment to embracing the elimination of fossil fuel. We regard shovelling coal into railway locomotives as ancient technology. We should regard liquid fossil fuels with the same disdain and consign them to history.

Understanding the three fallacies of transport allows us to escape the closed thinking which holds back progress. It becomes possible to envisage much better transport provision.

Transport for Cities

The world is becoming increasingly urbanized. In 2008, the proportion of the world's population living in cities surpassed 50% and continues to rise. These people need to live, work, and get around. Transport is the lifeblood of the city, moving people and providing the means to deliver goods and supplies.

The great cities of the world were not built by economists. In 1666 the city of London was largely destroyed by a great fire and was rebuilt according to the design of Christopher Wren. In 1791 President George Washington employed Pierre Charles L'Enfant to design the federal capital on the Potomac River. In 1815 after Napoleon was beaten at Waterloo, Georges-Eugène Haussmann provided the vision to rebuild Paris as it is today. These acts of city renewal followed crisis. None of these visionaries were beholden to modern-day economists. If they had been forced to comply with what we regard now as sound economic analysis, our cities would be less grand, more utilitarian and rather dull places.

We need visionary leaders willing to employ architects who really understand sustainable design parameters. The optimism of emerging from the pandemic can be used to rebuild our cities for the 21st century. As we restore the economy, we can launch a new greener economy, part of which will be a surge of investment to make our cities sustainable, generate employment and cut carbon emissions. As we reap the twin benefits of economic renewal and reduced environmental load, the bean-counters should not be allowed to direct operations. If they do, the focus will be on short-term financial parameters with the result being 'sufficient', and 'fit-for-purpose'. These are not terms which summon up visions of vibrant successful cities. The accountants have valuable roles at the project level to ensure efficient delivery but great cities evolve because of vison and strategy. This is what is needed to deliver transport infrastructure to take us through the 21st century and into the 22nd century long after the current generation of policymakers have retired, and well beyond the periods normally used in economic analysis.

Allowing conventional economics to dictate the transport infrastructure of cities would mean a slow transition with short-term benefits taking priority. Future benefits tend to be discounted on the argument that long-term benefits are less certain and are therefore worth less than benefits which arise in the near future. Such thinking means that benefits which accrue into the long future, perhaps fifty years or more, are often effectively ignored. This can be interpreted in simple terms as 'there will be no benefit in my lifetime so why bother?' This leads to muddling along with a new road or a new bridge, but wholesale transformation is out of the question because the short-term costs are too high, and the benefits too far into the future. Effective strategic transport planning needs better application of economics than this. At the strategic level the focus should be on tackling the most important long-term challenges and setting clear priorities. This should take place before dropping down into the economic analysis.

FUTURE CITIES – TRANSPORT DESIGN

The problem of using economic blinkers in city transport design was brought into stark relief for me over a decade ago. As an expert in sustainability, I was invited to present a paper at a UN-sponsored conference on policy for city design in the developing world.[33] I planned to present my analysis that the developed world had made a policy misstep by designing cities around cars, and the infrastructure for cars. My advice was that developing countries should not follow the rich world's lead but bounce forward to 21st-century city design based around the needs of people, not the needs of cars. I arrived at the conference worried that I would be seen as someone from the rich world denying poorer countries the benefits of car ownership.

I presented my paper titled 'Cities for People: Removing Cars from Urban Life', with some trepidation but I was pleasantly surprised with the broad support I received from delegates from developing countries. Opposition came from the World Bank whose delegation was adamant that investment in road infrastructure was the foremost requirement for a developing city, arguing that the return on investment from building roads is better than investment in public transport. I was regarded as an economic heretic to question such 'wisdom'. One delegate, a senior bank official, privately supported my view, whispering in my ear how brave I was to present such an argument, but not wanting to break ranks by speaking out. It was deeply troubling to see first-hand the blinkered use of economic analysis to override sensible policy. It was clear to me then, and remains the bedrock of my concept of resilient economics, that important decisions with long-term consequences, such as the design of city transportation, are too important to be dictated by short-term economics.

My generation grew up in the age of the car. To pass the driving test was a rite of passage to adulthood. The freedom to travel, gave the freedom to live life to the full. We have come to see a

---

33 UNU-WIDER conference 'Beyond the Tipping Point: Development in an Urban World', London School of Economics (LSE), October 2007.

car as a necessary possession, not only to get around but to show who we are. What car you drive is used to judge your character and your worth. A car can be like the tail feathers on a male peacock used to show off and attract a mate – and just as useful on gridlocked city streets. It is heartening to see that many younger generation city dwellers are bucking old ideas about cars and do not want to own one – or in some cases don't even want to learn to drive. People are starting to demand clean, liveable cities with great public spaces, good public transport and safe routes for bicycles. This is the start of building the rational foundations of future cities. Cities do not change overnight (unless they have the misfortune of a hurricane or a tsunami) so a vision is needed to guide investment in infrastructure, so that bit by bit, as repair and refurbishment becomes necessary, cities can be renewed to be fit for the future.

It would be relatively straightforward to build sustainable cities, if the starting point was not the established cities we already have. Building new cities provides the opportunity to get it right from the start. Masdar in the Middle East is a new city being built from scratch incorporating the latest thinking in sustainable living. It is an interesting showcase of sustainable methods and technologies but this new city in the desert is only feasible because of money from oil. As the transition away from fossil fuel gathers pace, I fear for the future of Masdar when oil revenues are no longer able to subsidize such extravagance. Building new cities is not generally a luxury we can afford; the bigger challenge is the transformation of existing cities.

I propose three guiding principles for transport infrastructure to support resilient and sustainable cities:

1. Transport infrastructure built to conform to sustainability according to long-term strategic plans;

2. The value of open-to-sky space recognised for use by people or for solar energy collection;

3. Roads and public transport to be underground and separated from walking and cycling.

LONG-TERM STRATEGIC PLAN

Each city authority should draft a long-term strategic plan for sustainable transport based on the guiding principles shown above. The transformation required is huge, so the plans should be bold. Major infrastructure decisions made today will have consequences far into the future. Road, rail and other transport infrastructure is repaired and components renewed over a cycle of decades but major change takes place over a cycle of centuries. Unless a city is destroyed by war or wiped out by a natural disaster, the opportunity to change the structure arises on an incremental basis so it is vital to have a long-term strategic plan.

Cities are complex three-dimensional puzzles which can grow up, down or sideways to achieve optimal configuration. Simple economic analysis tends towards high-rise living in city centres where land is expensive, opening out to sprawling suburbs where land is cheap. Rather than succumbing to such economic simplicity, deliberate design policy should be applied before crafting the economic model.

RECOGNIZE THE VALUE OF OPEN-TO-SKY SPACE

Open-to-sky space is a valuable and limited resource which should be used well. Open space should be allocated for people to meet, exercise, walk and cycle. All roof areas should be covered in solar panels to harvest renewable energy, or used for urban agriculture. Once the current pollution challenges have been solved, such food will be grown close to where it is consumed, making it fresh and sustainable.

Too often in today's cities, open-to-sky space is either a road, car park or blank roof. Cities of the future should have none of this.

TRANSPORT TO BE UNDERGROUND

The third guiding principle is a logical extension of recognizing the value of open-to-sky space. Transport should be designed to be underground for all central city districts. This can be facilitated by the transition to all-electric transport eliminating the problem of fumes when transport is forced underground. Having made the strategic decision, the economic model then needs to be considered. A complete network of tunnels is likely to be prohibitively expensive. A different, more affordable, approach could be to shift the level at which people congregate and move around to a higher level. In effect building a platform at second floor level for walking, cycling, street cafes, parks and squares. All transport can travel on the space below.

The strategic decision to put transport beneath the level at which people live would apply mainly to central districts. This should guide each development over the decades ahead to build the new infrastructure piece-by-piece as renewal becomes due. Economic analysis can focus on ensuring this is carried out efficiently, as and when improvements become due, in a coordinated and affordable manner. Such a solution may be particularly relevant to the future transport for coastal cities.

Future of Coastal Cities

The challenge for the world's great coastal cities is particularly acute. Failure to address climate change means that a rise in sea levels is now certain; city planners have to think about the long-term consequences of this and how to respond. One strategic choice is to plan to abandon the coast and ensure all new investment goes to cities further inland, leaving the old coastal cities to slowly decline over the centuries ahead. An example of alternative innovative thinking which might allow such cities to survive is explored in Box 16.1.

Box 16.1 A future for coastal cities

Sea level rise due to climate change is an incremental threat to coastal cities. Eventually the world will take action to cure fossil fuel dependency, but the legacy of increased levels of carbon dioxide in the atmosphere mean the consequences cannot now be stopped. The IPCC predict that global mean sea level (GMSL) could rise 0.28–1.01 m by 2100 with a rise of 2 m not ruled out. The IPCC also predict that 'over the next 2000 years, global mean sea level will rise by about 2 to 3 m if warming is limited to 1.5°C, 2 to 6 m if limited to 2°C and 19 to 22 m with 5°C of warming.' (IPCC 2021: 28).

Many significant global cities could be inundated by rising sea levels, requiring hard strategic choices. An incremental approach would be to invest increasing sums in building ever higher sea defences. There will come a time when the defences are no longer affordable. It is important to think strategically and long-term so, for example, where London is at risk, the UK government could designate the inland city of Birmingham as its future capital city. Capital investment could be steered away from the old coastal cities towards inland cities on higher ground many decades in advance.

An alternative idea worth considering is whether it would be possible to increase the height of the city infrastructure by some metres. Perhaps it would it be possible to manage a transformation in which Manhattan became the Venice of North America.

There are many aspects of this tentative proposal to be examined before it could be accepted as a sensible and feasible plan for some coastal cities. It is presented here as an example of lateral thinking to bring bold plans into the discussion about the future of coastal cities.

I speculate whether a coastal city could be reconfigured over the decades ahead working with the principle of putting transport infrastructure beneath the level at which people live. Perhaps over the next two centuries, on an incremental basis, we can set a new 'ground level' for people, parks and cycle routes to allow transport to flow beneath. As sea levels rise, transport would have to be in waterproof tunnels and buildings refurbished or rebuilt with foundations designed to be secure against the new normal sea level, e.g. by using solid concrete walls up to the elevation of expected future sea level. Each new building, or each major refurbishment of an existing building would, over time, deliver a coastal city ready for higher sea levels, not by holding the sea back behind defences but by changing the reference ground level.

This discussion of transport for cities is a snapshot of what is possible, rather than a precise blueprint. Transport policy should be all about allowing people and goods to move about whilst protecting the quality of the city environment. Decisions should be taken on a strategic basis of what is good for society. The economics of city transport slots beneath the strategic level to help deliver policy on a project-by-project basis through making desirable policy feasible.

Intercity Transport

The following thoughts on the future of intercity transport illustrate the application of an adjusted mindset to give a flavour of possible developments. I will consider three categories: fast, standard, and slow. Fast transportation would be a premium service requiring additional investment to deliver shorter journey times and be expected to cost more. Standard speed transportation would be the default option designed to be efficient and affordable. Slow transportation would also be a viable choice when the total travel package is considered.

FAST INTERCITY TRANSPORT

Fast transportation is needed by time-poor people such as business leaders and senior officials. It is also needed for time-critical goods like urgent medical supplies. Such customers can afford high prices supporting greater investment.

Current thinking favours high-speed trains as the future for intercity transport. This is based on a relatively short-term analysis acknowledging that the environmental impact of current generation aircraft will have to be curtailed. It costs considerably more to construct a high-speed railway line (over 300 km/hr) in comparison with conventional trains at (up to 200 km/hr). The technology of high-speed rail may not be affordable for many countries as it requires a lot of investment to push the technology beyond its natural affordability sweet spot.

Conventional short-haul flights will come under close scrutiny until clean and quiet electric planes are developed and deployed. In addition to environmental concerns, such flights might be short and quick but the airport transit, security checks and waiting around mean the speed may not be significantly better than other options. For the rapid transportation of time-critical goods, transport could be by unmanned air vehicles or drones using advanced control technology to ensure safety.

Looking to the long-term, an appropriate intercity ground transportation system may be the Hyperloop. The Hyperloop concept consists of pods travelling within sealed tubes carrying people or freight. The tube is partially evacuated of air so the pods can travel with little air resistance meaning high energy efficiency and speeds as fast as aircraft, even hypersonic (Opgenoord and Caplan 2018). The Hyperloop is hard to justify on a conventional short- or medium-term economic analysis. Even so, it is being championed by the entrepreneur Elon Musk. It is proceeding quickly through proof-of-concept to the construction of prototypes because of his willingness to ignore conventional economic wisdom. It seems clear that he is betting on the right technology for the late 21st century, but whether the first businesses in this new sector can make the economic numbers add up is open to doubt. If, instead of investing in high-speed rail, governments were to join with such radical strategic thinking, they could be planning the routes and securing the permissions to build the Hyperloop network. Governments are dealing with public money so can be expected to be risk averse and not commit until the technology is proven. Strategic thinking by both business and government working together could push this forward at pace. Business would be expected to shoulder the financial risk and government reduce the regulatory hurdles to clear the way. This is an example where the combined effort of government and business can be hugely beneficial to society, overriding short-term economic factors to deliver the long-term prize.

It is interesting to further unpick the need for fast intercity transportation. The primary need is a service for time-poor people. One solution is the provision of speed in exchange for a more expensive ticket. There is however another valid solution. Instead of investing in speed, invest in making the time spent on the journey pleasant and productive. This means that time is not wasted but is well spent. If the time in transit can be used as effectively as time in the office, this approach becomes an alternate solution. For example, standard speed rail could include a proportion of exceptional quality rolling stock where people can work (or sleep) in seclusion and comfort.

STANDARD INTERCITY TRANSPORT

Standard intercity transport should be affordable to all, reliable and provided by standard robust technology within the capabilities of the country to build and repair. Roads require least upfront investment by government but cars are not efficient in resources and energy, and there is also the problem that when everyone goes by car, the journey is slowed by congestion. Trains are therefore a better option for the backbone of intercity transport supported for the local leg of the journey by a reliable bus network or taxis (perhaps self-driving). Extending the analysis, leads to considering policy to ensure that there are pleasant places to live in relatively close proximity to places of work thus reducing the need to travel at all.

The challenge remains of what to do about freight. A lot of freight goes by road with the convenience of pickup and delivery as one contiguous journey. Lateral thinking leads to policy to encourage smaller and more numerous factories and storage depots to reduce the need for intercity freight capacity. Where freight needs to move, the backbone of intercity freight could be rail with an efficient transition of containers from road to rail, and rail to road. There is another less obvious intercity freight solution: by taking advantage of the opportunities of slow travel.

SLOW INTERCITY TRANSPORT

Slow travel tends to be regarded as old-fashioned because in the past that was all that was available. There are good reasons to embrace again the advantages of slow travel. I foresee a resurgence in slow travel between cities. Applying technology to improve slow travel could deliver some intriguing solutions.

Let us consider the challenge of intercity freight. Currently, huge trucks charge along main roads and onto smaller roads as they near their destination. The tachographs in the drivers' cabs limit the hours that can be driven, so the economic solution is to drive as close to the speed limit as the law allows, maximizing the distance travelled in a working shift. The concept of automating these huge fast juggernauts is a fearful prospect. Using a combination of automation and slow speed may be more attractive and much less threatening.

Slow freight travel could take place in the dead of night using the slow lanes on motorways and freeways. Long convoys of autonomous vehicles in tight formation could crawl along relatively slowly with a human operator in the cab of the lead vehicle (in case of unforeseen problems). All the following vehicles would be under automatic control. Slow speed would be safer, need less energy, and make the journey cheap and simple. The close coupling, which automation could facilitate, would save yet more energy by keeping vehicles in the slipstream of the one in front. The speed may be slow but the journey time less so, as the convoy would not need to stop every couple of hours as computers do not need to take a rest break. When the convoy arrives at its destination city, it can park up in a designated convoy park. In the morning, human drivers can take over each of the vehicles to navigate the final few miles safely on local roads.

Slow train services can also be made attractive for travel overnight. The rolling stock would need to be fitted with quality sleeping berths for passengers at a range of price points from basic to luxury. It makes sense to give passengers enough time for a decent night's sleep. So, by slowing the train, relatively shorter journeys become viable sleeper routes. Instead of getting up early and dashing to catch a high-speed train, an alternative would be a slow snooze arriving in time for a leisurely breakfast.

Intercontinental Transport

Intercontinental transportation has never been better, nor its economic model so distorted, as it is now. Flying is the default option for people traveling internationally. People who have tried to follow their conscience and travel without the environmental impact of flying find that the alternative options are limited.

When I was a small boy in the 1960s, my family travelled from Australia to the UK by the cheapest means available. This meant five weeks on board a ship, the P&O *Orcades*. For me, it felt like a marvellous holiday. For my mother, with four small children, it was less relaxing, as she worried that one of us would find a way to fall overboard. My father, an academic, enjoyed the freedom to focus on writing his next book. This was when flying was too expensive for a family of modest means. Now the economics has changed considerably, with flying by far the cheapest option. The current distorted economic model means that passenger ships designed for efficient travel from A to B are almost non-existent. People go on cruise ships to relax, drink cocktails and lounge by the pool, but not to travel from A to B. Travelling in style, slowly by ship, could become again a standard way for intercontinental travel, if flying were not so ridiculously cheap.

Transport choices for intercontinental freight depend on the nature of the goods, its value, and the urgency with which it is needed. The economics of long-distance freight, using current parameters, throws up some very odd outcomes. Fresh fruit, vegetables and flowers are flown out of Africa to markets in Europe. Prawns are caught in the north Atlantic, shipped to China to be shelled and shipped back to be sold in the UK. Common sense should be enough to understand that this is madness. Slavish adherence to an economic model which leads to such outcomes has to be wrong. The sensible way forward is to work out ways to reduce the need for international freight. This does not mean closing down trade of course, it means adopting the principles of trade presented in Chapter 8. Trade should satisfy real needs; self-sufficiency; reciprocity; and coordinated regulations between trading parties. Trade framed in this way will be more sustainable, more useful and much reduced in volume.

The current international transportation system is impressive, high capacity, fast, and obsolescent. It evolved through the 20th century, and suits the 20th century, but it is not fit for the 21st century. The outdated economic model of international transportation locks transport into the past, preventing the leap forward required. We have the technology and the know-how for sustainable travel but we do not have the economic incentive. When the economics are negative, progress is stymied. A brief examination of aviation followed by shipping illustrates the self-inflicted bind we are in.

Special Case – Aviation

There is a hugely polarized debate about aviation. At one extreme, there are environmentalists who are vehemently anti-aviation, and urge us not to fly. At the other, the aviation industry is defending its position and some passengers are determined to fly regardless of the environmental impact. In between, there is a middle group who want to travel but would rather not be responsible for negative environmental impact, and are ashamed that there are not better options.[34] I am in this middle group and

---

34 The term 'flygskam', arose in Sweden and translates as 'flight shame'. This is where people feel ashamed, or are shamed by others, to take a flight.

believe that we are the silent majority who need to find the courage to speak out and demand action.

It has to be accepted that for aviation to advance there will be disruption in the short- to medium-term. Environmentalists are wrong to oppose aviation; they should oppose its environmental impact. The industry is defending the current model of aviation knowing that real change will require aircraft manufacturers to develop much cleaner air vehicles and current fleets to be retired early. There will be commercial disruption and bankruptcies of a number of industry players ranging from leasing companies to aircraft manufacturers. Industry players without robust forward-looking development plans will be culled. This is the cost of moving forward, and from society's perspective should not block progress.

Looking to the immediate future, it is interesting that the COVID-19 pandemic of 2020–21 has already begun the process of culling the old aviation industry, and has provided a chance to rebuild according to a different economic model. For example, in July 2020 British Airways took the strategic decision to retire early all of its Boeing 747 jumbo jets, with the last flight taking place on 8 October 2020. This leaves the airline with a slimmed down fleet of more modern fuel-efficient planes. At the time of writing, a willingness by governments to grasp the opportunity to accelerate this transformation is not yet evident.

Looking backwards, it is worth explaining how aviation became trapped in a policy cul-de-sac. The flaw in aviation economics is encapsulated in the Convention on International Civil Aviation which was brokered at a conference convened in Chicago in 1944. Article 24 of the Chicago convention ensures that aviation fuel remains tax-free. It made sense in 1944 when the focus was on using aviation to cement world peace. It should come as no surprise that seven decades later this is now out-of-date. The economics of the aviation industry is predicated on the continuation of tax-free fuel. It has been clear to me for some time that this holds back the industry (McManners 2012 and 2017). The stumbling block is the United States which is resolutely opposed to any change and no country seems willing to expend political capital to change the status quo. The economic response of the UK government has been to increase taxes on flights through applying Air Passenger Duty but that simply makes flying more expensive without changing the underlying model.

A resilient economic analysis concludes that significant taxation should be applied to aviation fuel. This would be hugely disruptive because of the huge quantities burnt by the aviation industry. I argue, bring it on. Let us begin a determined drive to transform the aviation industry to force it to be much more efficient with the fuel it burns. If you are interested in a possible better future for aviation, you can read my book *Fly and Be Damned* (McManners 2012).

Special Case – Shipping

Shipping suffers from a similar problem to aviation. There are no agreed international rules to tax fuel for ships. As with aviation, no country can take a lead because shipping companies would simply fuel up somewhere else. There is therefore very little incentive to construct ships which exploit renewable clean propulsion. Strong winds blow across much of the world's oceans, and where winds are light propulsion can come from large fold-out solar panels. Clean shipping is relatively straightforward technology but without an economic case, shipping continues to burn millions of tonnes of fossil fuel. The fuel used is low-grade high-sulphur fuel, because it is cheaper. Such dirty fuel would not be allowed in ground transportation but out on the open ocean there are few restrictions. The case for international agreement to tax fuel for shipping is cast iron in principle but seems to be politically toxic.

It is very odd that we allow transportation to remain trapped in a 20th-century model. Current ships are better than the early coal-fired steam ships, but not greatly so. Ships still burn dirty fossil fuel (sulphur-laden bunker fuel) for propulsion long after better technology has been available. We could have a new generation of ships powered from renewable sources with advanced automated sails doubling up as solar panels. The precise blueprints for such ships have yet to emerge, because the economic case to design them is weak. We need such ships, so we need a resilient economic model which will support their construction. This will need international agreement for significant taxation on fuel for shipping in order to drive the transformation.

Conclusions

Transportation is an expensive and important part of infrastructure requiring long-term strategic thinking; which is not well served by short-term economic analysis. Long-term strategic plans are needed, such that when renewal or replacement becomes due, the next step can be taken towards long-term improvement. Such piecemeal alteration is the affordable option in developed countries. In developing countries, where extensive transport infrastructure may not yet have been built, there is the possibility of bouncing forward to avoid the rich world's mistakes.

To bring the economic analysis into line with a sensible strategic transport plan requires correct framing within a mindset of uncompromising commitment to long-term goals. We should push back against the assumption that increasing capacity reduces congestion, recognize the limitations of increasing transport capacity to facilitate trade, and understand that the economic model can be changed to embrace transportation not reliant on fossil fuel. This enlightened approach to transport planning should focus on real needs, recognizing that the cheapest solution to a lack of transport capacity is always to adjust related policy to reduce demand. How world leaders respond to the special cases of aviation and shipping will gauge when the world is ready to push forward with sustainable transport solutions. Until policy is rejuvenated with more realism and common sense, I fear transportation will remain trapped in grubby fossil-fuel dependency.

CHAPTER 17

ENERGY

We need to divorce energy
supply from fossil fuel and
accept the economic consequences.

Energy is a fundamental need of modern society. In the developed world, secure energy supply is taken for granted. In poorer countries, reliable energy supply is seen as a prerequisite for development. The main challenge which holds back progress in this important sector is that energy supply has become shackled to fossil fuel. In this outdated economic model, more energy means more harmful emissions. The linkage must be broken to get the energy we need without the harmful emissions.

The solution is obvious and deceptively simple; to stop using fossil fuel to generate energy. Although technically feasible, economically it seems to be impossibly difficult. This is because the current energy economy is heavily invested in the technology of fossil fuel. The economic model is based on huge sunk capital costs of a complex energy infrastructure designed to use cheap fossil fuel. The current economic model collapses if fossil fuel is removed from energy generation. Again, the solution is obvious; it is to change the economic model. This simple logic reframes the energy challenge, which becomes how to design and implement an economic model for energy which is not reliant on fossil fuel. In the context of resilient economic thinking, this is obvious, but it is fundamentally different to what has been tried so far. The world's half-hearted attempts to cure fossil fuel addiction have focused on replacing fossil fuel with other energy sources whilst attempting to keep the current economy intact.

Current Energy Markets

Energy markets respond to both supply and demand, but current energy markets are primarily demand driven. Fossil fuel has been easily and widely available, and easily transported, so energy demand has been relatively easy to satisfy. Investment has flowed into fossil fuel extraction and power stations burning fossil fuel. As demand increases, more coal mines are opened, oil and gas wells drilled, and power stations built. There is a lead time involved, so planners need to make predictions of future demand, but there is a clear and simple logic to increase capacity in line with projected demand. There was a slight wobble in the world's commitment to fossil fuel in the 1970s when the Organization of the Petroleum Exporting Countries (OPEC) restricted oil supplies, driving the oil price higher and initiating a dialogue about reducing reliance on oil. The oil producers saw the danger of their cash machine being unplugged, so have been careful to keep oil affordable and not to threaten supplies again. Through the 20th century there seemed little need to invest in renewable sources, although investment did flow into large-scale hydro.[35]

Wind and solar are now contributing a greater share to supply but their intermittency makes them troublesome. The reliability, certainty, scalability, and affordability of fossil fuel means it is still the preferred choice. The world remains locked into an economic model dependent on fossil fuel.

The Peculiar Economics of Fossil Fuel

I like to describe the economics of fossil fuel as 'rational

---

35 The only significant renewable energy harvested in the 20th century was large-scale hydro where the advantages were obvious. For a single capital outlay, a facility could be built which would deliver energy for decades, effectively for free once the initial investment had been recouped.

incompetence'. To fully understand the evolution of the fossil-fuel economic model it is useful to go back to the 19th century when the roots of the current economic model were put down. Oil was discovered in Texas close to the surface where it was easy to extract. Entrepreneurs rushed to setup simple wooden rigs to look for oil. Each time a new strike was made, the supply of oil increased and the price went down. The emergent oil barons therefore had a problem with maintaining profitability. They started to look for ways to encourage the consumption of oil. The introduction of gas-guzzling large cars, for which America became infamous, can be seen as a consequence of this economically rational response. In a market suffering from oversupply, it makes economic sense to drive up demand.

Economic sense is not always the same as common sense. It could be argued that in the early days of consuming fossil fuel, the long-term negative consequences for the climate were not understood. Pausing to reflect, even in the context of the 19th century this was a wasteful use of resources. So, from the earliest days of the application of economic theory, rational incompetence has been allowed the space to propagate. Notions of husbanding resources for the long future have tended not to enter the economic analysis.

Through the 20th century and into the opening decades of the 21st century it became normal to allow the price mechanism to balance supply and demand of fossil fuel. Now that the negative environmental consequences are understood, there are strategic choices to be made about fossil fuel. This will mean changing the dynamics of the market. Instead of allowing rational incompetence to surface again by insisting that renewable energy competes within the same market as fossil fuel, we need to change the economic model. One of the commonest economic statements about renewable energy is that it has to be cheaper than coal.

Such economic rationality is environmentally and strategically incompetent. The current economic model is so familiar and so entrenched, that whilst society is addicted to fossil fuel, people do not notice how disconnected from reality energy economics has become. Curing the addiction means not getting caught up in rational incompetence. Like a junkie high on heroin, we fail to see the plain logic that quitting is the cure.

New Economic Model for Energy

The necessary starting point for considering a new economic model for energy is to accept that the current economic model cannot survive. To argue that the economic model is fine, and all that is needed are alternative energy supplies to replace fossil fuel, is to get caught in the contradictions of an untenable position. This is an example of the mindset of putting the economy first, and illustrates the need for a different mindset. Assuming there is willingness to break out to a new economic model, I propose that it should have the following three attributes:

+ facilitates closing down fossil fuel;

+ assumes the energy market is dominated by renewable energy;

+ operates to deliver stable energy prices.

First, the energy market should conform to the strategic decision to close down fossil fuel. This will be tough for a number of stakeholders including oil-producing nations and the corporations which extract and sell fossil fuel. Investors are already steering clear of coal assets as they realize that infrastructure such as coal-fired power stations will become obsolete before they reach the end of their design life. Bankruptcies will follow.

How soon depends on how strong the determination to transform the energy market is. Some stakeholders, such as those employed in the fossil fuel industry and those who own shares in fossil fuel corporations, will suffer. This should be recognized as little more than a normal realignment of capital as the energy market changes – and is to be expected. Accepting the normality of clearing away the old fossil fuel legacy will allow the transition to be quicker and the consequences to have less lasting damage.

Second, the energy market will be dominated by renewable energy, tending towards a supply-driven market. Instead of building energy supply capacity to match demand, the availability of renewable energy is accepted as the prime constraint. Investment will need to flow into both energy harvesting and efficiency measures to balance demand with supply. Places where renewable energy supplies are limited will become the leading innovators in efficiency measures, not just on an elemental basis but systematic efficiency from the way society is organized. Energy prices will be high and customers will need to be frugal to keep their overall costs affordable. Where there is ample renewable energy, such as sunny or windy locations, energy could be cheap making it attractive to energy-intensive industries such as aluminium smelting.

Third, stabilizing energy prices will be important to provide a dependable investment environment. In the current energy market, reliant on fossil fuel, energy prices depend on fossil fuel prices. A significant proportion of the cost of fossil fuel are the extraction and processing costs which are predictable and ongoing. Although fossil fuel prices fluctuate with changes in demand the market is relatively stable. The energy market reliant on harvesting renewable energy such as wind and solar behaves differently. Exploiting these renewable energy sources requires large upfront capital investment but completed projects have exceedingly low operating costs. As the switch to renewable energy gathers pace there could be wild gyrations as waves of investment push prices down followed by a dearth of investment until prices rise again. It would be sensible for government to act to stabilize energy prices to maintain a consistent environment which supports investment in both renewable energy capacity and efficiency measures.

During the transition to the new economic model, tax should be ratcheted up on fossil fuel to make legacy fossil fuel infrastructure less and less affordable. Current efforts focus on getting the renewable industry up and running through subsidies paid for by levies on energy bills. These subsidies should be withdrawn concurrently with increasing tax on fossil fuel. Other fiscal measures to stabilize energy prices might be required in the short-term until renewables reach scale. As the new economic model for energy matures it could become stable by default. An example of the innovation which could ensure such stability is the use of hydrogen. As this enters the energy mix, as an option for transport and other uses, facilities to make hydrogen by electrolysis will be required. If there is significant such capacity, only tripping in to take electricity when the price is cheap, this could provide a secure floor to electricity prices without the need for regulatory action.

Understanding the desirable attributes of a new economic model for energy will help the new energy market to evolve quickly. It should facilitate closing down fossil fuel; be designed for the vagaries of renewable energy supplies; and ensure price stability. Such a different economic model should be welcomed for the advantages it brings accepting that much of the legacy energy generation capacity will no longer be economically viable.

Fossil Fuel – Curing the Addiction

A key attribute of the future economic model for energy is that it should underpin closing down fossil fuel consumption. This is undoubtably correct but is likely to meet considerable resistance from people worried about the economic consequences. It is therefore worth reminding ourselves exactly why this is necessary. The evidence is provided by the Intergovernmental Panel on Climate Change (IPCC). This international body was set up in 1988 under the auspices of the United Nations to provide policymakers with regular assessments of the scientific basis of climate change. Huge amounts of evidence have been considered from the world's top scientists generating a multitude of reports. The evidence that we must stop relying on fossil fuel is well documented and now incontrovertible.

The UN-brokered discussion about what to do about fossil fuel has been running for over three decades, which should have been ample time to negotiate and implement a solution. If the world had moved quickly from talk to action, the last thirty years could have been used to allow fossil fuel assets to reach the end of their design life and be replaced with other energy sources. Such clarity of thinking has been resisted by people peddling the false hope that the economy does not need to change. This is all the addict needs as an excuse to carry on regardless, accepting blindly the spurious argument that it is not economically viable to shift quickly away from fossil-fuel dependency. Those who oppose action because of risks to the 'economy' are misguided. The risk to the stability of the global climate has much greater long-term significance than any short-term economic considerations.

It is mad to pretend that defending the economy is more important than dealing with climate change. It is even madder to lean on the possibility that it might not be as bad as predicted to justify inaction. It is like driving fast along a motorway in thick fog listening to traffic reports on the radio that there is congestion ahead and maintaining full speed on the chance that the road ahead may be clear. Of course, the right action is to lift your foot off the accelerator and be prepared to brake if necessary. The strategic decision with regard to fossil fuel is clear; we need to listen and accept the evidence of the IPCC and transition away from relying on fossil fuel.

The core logic of curing fossil-fuel addiction is clear and has three elements: the economy can run without fossil fuel; carbon trading does not justify inaction; and energy should be treated as a valuable commodity to be used sparingly.

First, we do not *need* fossil fuel. Its use is a choice which has been made and the direction along which society has travelled. That does not mean we have to stick with it; we can change direction by making a different choice. People who claim that the economic consequences of eliminating fossil fuel are too great to tolerate, are misusing economics. The correct economic decision frame is to make the strategic choice to eliminate fossil fuel and accept consequential changes to the economy. The politics is difficult but the economics is straightforward.

Second, the promises of a global carbon market should not be allowed to delay progress. Pussyfooting around pretending that carbon trading can provide an easy and smooth transition is wasting time. Where carbon markets can have a useful role is in directing investment within national economies to where it can have most impact; but the concept of a world carbon market is little more than a distraction and a smoke screen for inaction (see Markets for Pollution section in Chapter 7). The existence of carbon markets can be helpful but do not expect them to solve the climate challenge.

Third, in the early stages of the energy market beyond fossil fuel, energy may be in short supply until renewable capacity comes on stream. It would make sense to accept this and change the market dynamics during the transition. A prime focus becomes efficiency measures to drive down demand to connect with constrained supply. If efficiency measures increase rapidly, concurrently with increasing renewable energy supply, it should be possible to constrain demand for fossil fuel to hold fossil fuel prices down through the transition.

A conventional economic analysis would await predictions of high fossil fuel prices before ramping up investment in efficiency measures. This might make economic sense on a project-by-project basis but at the macro level the overall effect is that cash is sucked out of the economy and transferred to the coffers of oil-producing nations. Governments can fix such economic illiteracy by driving up taxes on fossil fuel according to a long-term escalator to ensure a stable environment for investment in efficiency. This can help ensure that the underlying price of fossil fuel (before tax) remains cheap, with the tax revenue remaining within the national economy. Paying for oil imports is a drain on the economy so the economically literate strategy is to act early to drive up the end-user price through taxation whilst the base oil price is low.

Curing fossil fuel dependency appears incredibly difficult through the lens of a conventional economic analysis but the elements of the solution are straightforward when it is accepted that the economic model will be different. The measures discussed above are sufficient to ensure that the future energy market escapes fossil fuel dependency. It is simple forthright logic which can be compared with persuading an addict to come off heroin. Of course, it is the only way; but the addict, befuddled by too many fixes, will come up with all sorts of reasons why it may not be possible.

Challenging Conventional Economic Barriers

In this chapter, I keep returning to the entrenched defence of the current fossil fuel energy economy. I do this because such resistance is a high barrier to overcome. Two incidents help to drive home the point that a conventional economic perspective is blocking progress.

In June 2017 I attended a lecture hosted by the Martin School, Oxford University, delivered by Amory Lovins, founder of the Rocky Mountains Institute (RMI). I had gone to the lecture to hear the output of RMI research into the future beyond fossil fuel. The Martin School and the RMI are well-respected organizations which carry out research at the cutting edge of thinking. The former is a pioneering research organization with 'research programmes that cut across disciplines to find solutions to the world's most urgent challenges' (Martin School 2020). The latter carries out world-leading research into 'solutions that cost-effectively shift from fossil fuels to efficiency and renewables' (RMI 2020).

In the lecture, titled 'Disruptive oil and electricity futures', Amory Lovins explained research showing that it would be possible for there to be a relatively rapid evolution to low-carbon world energy systems (Lovins 2011). He related an interesting account of a discussion with senior staff at one of the major oil companies. The engineers and technical people understood the analysis and were agreed that such a transition is feasible. However, the oil company's economists did not believe it was possible. Why an economist should oppose the idea of a rapid transition to low-carbon is an intriguing question. There is something about the way conventional economics is taught which leads economists to think economy first, instead of thinking about how to alter the economy to support the transition. This is backwards thinking presented thus: here is the economy, and it must not be put at risk as we plan for the end of oil. Forward thinking looks like this: we need a plan for the end of oil, and what sort of economy would facilitate this?

In a world ruled by conventional economic analysis, I suspect that the oil company economists were giving their bosses sound, but depressing, advice. Whilst important decisions are based on conventional economic analysis there is no chance of a rapid transition to a low-carbon energy economy. It cannot be done because we insist on defending the economy we have – instead of deciding to make the transition and accept that the economy changes. A low-carbon economy has different parameters to a fossil fuel economy. The main change is that energy has greater value, driving greater efficiency. What could be wrong with that? Close examination of a low-carbon economy shows it works well, but it works differently, and that seems to be enough for some people to resist the transition.

A further insight into how economists can misread the challenge of fossil fuel was provided by the editor of an economics journal where I published a paper. I will not embarrass the editor by naming the journal. The paper went successfully through the process of peer review and was about to go to print. In the final version the editor had spotted a 'mistake'. I had written about the transition to low-carbon energy as a period of 'low oil price'. The editor, who was perhaps understandably too busy to read and digest the full argument in the paper, had amended this to 'high oil price'. Fortunately, I was informed and I was able to get the change reversed back to the original wording before it went to print. To this economist, it was second nature that it would require high oil prices to justify investment in low carbon. The argument I made in the paper was that through the right policy choices we can manage a transition in which oil prices are kept low. This was completely at odds with the mainstream economist view at the time, so required detailed and careful argument.

The economists working for oil corporations and editors of economic journals are examples of systemic denial of the limitations of conventional economics. I find it astounding that this is allowed to continue. The scientists on the IPCC remain stoical, the general public indifferent, and politicians inactive.[36] Scientists should be angry, the general public should demand action, and politicians should be spurred into action. We should all push back against the defenders of conventional economic analysis and insist energy economics is brought back into line to serve society.

The Role of Energy Efficiency

The most effective energy solution is often to invest in energy efficiency. It can be cheaper than building new energy generation capacity. Such efficiency could be element-by-element, process-by-process, and house-by-house. It could also be systemic efficiency through how cities and associated infrastructure are designed and built. Focusing effort on energy efficiency has always made sense, but the switch to renewable energy makes this increasingly worthwhile.

Energy efficiency and economic efficiency should go together hand in glove, with a balance between them. Whilst energy comes from fossil fuel, with its associated environmental impact, it makes sense that energy efficiency comes first. After the

---

36 Interest in and concern about climate change are growing but a general apathy towards measures which could affect lifestyles remains dominant.

transition to renewable energy, in places where there is an abundance of energy, economic efficiency may come before energy efficiency. Even so, the principle of energy efficiency should be part of the future energy market. Let us take as an example the point when the UK shifts to 100% renewable energy. We have the technology and know-how to do this and complete it within a decade – provided change to the economic model is accepted. The UK has some of the world's best sites for wind power so we would expect that wind would be a major energy source. Wind is intermittent and so on very windy days there could be a huge excess of energy. An economically efficient method could be to pay turbine owners to shut down or other players to dump energy to stop the grid overloading. Thinking about energy efficiency takes us down a different route. In this way of thinking, we would seek energy-intensive industries, such as hydrogen production by electrolysis, to be set up to be able to start up and shutdown at short notice, to make efficient use of the spare energy. Entrepreneurs are likely to spot such opportunities in any case, but policymakers can get ahead by facilitating such energy efficient solutions.

In any particular locality, there will be a balance between investment in harvesting renewable energy and investment in energy efficiency measures. The total level of investment will depend on the energy price. When energy prices rise (indicating more demand than supply) investment will increase; when energy prices are weak (indicating more supply than demand) investment will tail off. Whether the investment is channelled into efficiency or renewable energy harvesting depends on the relative cost of each unit of energy saved or harvested. When energy harvesting is relatively cheaper, investment will go there; when energy efficiency is relatively cheaper, investment will go in that direction. In a sunny location with consistently clear skies, it would be expected that investment would flow into solar energy collection. In Northern Europe, with relatively less renewable energy potential, it would be expected that investment would tend to flow into efficiency measures.

Energy efficiency will become an increasingly important parameter in future energy markets. Energy production and energy efficiency can be considered as equivalent for investment purposes and should proceed in parallel.

Fixing the Energy System

Reforming current energy systems will be difficult. We are locked into a model of energy infrastructure consisting of customers plugged into a power grid supplied by power stations. The engrained view is that this is the right model and will remain the same model into the future. Such thinking looks forward to anticipate cleaner power stations, wind farms and solar farms; but the expectation is that the overall system would be much the same. This lack of ambition for transforming energy infrastructure arises from reluctance to consider changing the current economic model.

ACCEPTING NATURAL MONOPOLIES

The market for electricity established in the UK is an example of bringing market forces into energy supply. The market separates generation, distribution and selling energy to customers. This has been designed to prevent one corporation having a monopoly. The problem is that efficient energy services are natural monopolies and the quasi market does not change this. Although in the early years the market squeezes generators to trim costs and put downward pressure on prices for consumers, a grand game then ensues between commercial companies and the regulator. The former group seek to maximize their profits; the latter seeks to ensure the customer gets a good deal on price. It is bureaucratic, costly to administer and there is little interest in delivering systemic energy efficiency.

The aspiration which should frame economic modelling going forward is for 100% renewable energy. This will require efficient energy systems operating within the budget of renewable energy which can be harvested. When considering such renewable-based energy systems, it soon becomes clear that we are often dealing with a natural monopoly. Setting economic policy to break the monopoly (which might be an objective through the lens of conventional economic policy) can undermine the sustainability of supply. A different approach is required.

Let us consider, for example, a region with a thriving forest industry with a ready supply of forestry off-cuts and waste. An efficient renewable solution for this region could include combined heat and power plants. The wood is burnt to both generate electricity and to heat buildings. It is not efficient to have one CHP plant for every house and not efficient to build large CHP power stations. The optimum size is somewhere between. Modest CHP systems have the best engineering efficiency, for a group of buildings or scaled up to serve a small community. Energy is saved by the combination of appropriate scale to generate electricity and short pipe runs to minimize heat loss. CHP is clearly a natural monopoly. The appropriate economic model would be community ownership or perhaps a local entrepreneur who lives within the community and is held to account by the community. National companies might serve local CHP companies with equipment, services and expertise but an efficient CHP business is inherently local and it is hard to see how it can be anything other than a monopoly.

ON OR OFF GRID?

To be on the grid, or not on the grid, is a choice to be made when energy comes from renewable sources. When I fitted our house with solar PV panels, I toyed with the idea of going off-grid. Batteries would be needed to have electricity at night and, in a Northern European winter, there would not have been enough overall energy. Analysis generally shows that where a grid exists, it is better to make use of it rather than set up multiple local storage solutions. Where grids do not yet exist, such as parts of Africa, India and other less developed countries, avoiding investment in a grid and focusing on local renewable energy solutions makes sense. This is particularly true if there is strong and reliable solar radiation.

In Northern Europe there is sufficient solar potential for good supply in the summer months but isolated local systems are unlikely to be viable without other sources of supply. The grid could be vital to maintaining energy supplies. It might be possible to connect Europe's grid with huge solar farms in the deserts of North Africa. Whether such a project comes to fruition will depend on how well Europe manages to balance efficiency measures with localized renewable energy harvesting. If there remains considerable unmet demand, hence high energy prices, investment in a high-capacity cable to North Africa could be justified. In the UK, the grid will continue to be needed because of the huge potential of offshore wind on the remote islands off Scotland. The UK's main population and industrial centres are further south so the grid is required to transport the energy from where it is harvested to where it is consumed.

HANDLING IRREGULAR SUPPLY

The future energy market will be reliant on renewable energy so will require being able to handle irregular supply. Fossil fuel was easy. Power stations could be built as required wherever they were needed. Fossil fuel has been available in quantity, easily transported, and simple to store until needed. Renewable energy is usually harvested as electricity at times and places dictated by the vagaries of the weather. Dealing with intermittency requires a solution. Batteries are one option. Although expensive in capital and resources, these work for small isolated systems and can provide resilience to grids.[37] Pumped hydro is another, where water is pumped up to a reservoir when there is excess energy in the grid and released through turbines when the energy is needed.[38] Another potential energy storage system for grid resilience consists of huge weights suspended in disused mineshafts which are winched up when energy is abundant and lowered down at times of need with the winches becoming generators (IET 2019).

There will be efforts to smooth supply through storage systems but with 100% renewable energy there are bound to be supply fluctuations. The challenge can be framed as making such fluctuations predictable to give customers the information to respond accordingly.

A DIFFERENT ENERGY SYSTEM

The current economic model for electricity supply in the UK has cheap night rates on domestic supply to encourage vehicle charging and electric storage heating at night when demand is less so there is spare capacity on the fossil-fuel-powered grid. There are multiple alternative technical fixes to deliver a different energy system.

---

37 The battery farm (Hornsdale Power Reserve) built in South Australia by Elon Musk has a capacity of 100 MWh and can power 36,000 homes for one hour (Delbert 2020).

38 The UK has four operational pumped hydro plants, with plenty more sites which could be used such as old mountain quarries. A fifth is planned in Snowdonia with a storage capacity of 700 MWh. The largest facility in the world is being constructed north of Beijing, the Fengning Pumped Storage Power Station, with an installed capacity of 3,600 MWh (Wade 2017).

This section shows the thought process required to break out into new and different thinking without presenting *the* solution.

This proposal for a different electricity supply system is based on two supply options; one at 240 v and another at 400 v. The detail is shown in Box 17.1. The 240 v supply is the premium service and guaranteed to be always available 24/7. This would be for all the equipment for which we require consistent and reliable supply ranging from computers and lighting to refrigeration and cooking facilities. The 400 v supply is the value service, the availability of which depends on supply and demand. The prime use for the 400 v service would be heavy industry, domestic heat pumps and electric vehicle charging. With appropriate control and management systems a stable and predictable electricity system could be built to suit the intermittent characteristics of renewable energy. Having settled on the desired engineering solution and the basis of the supporting economic model, the detail of how electricity is bought and sold can be allowed to evolve.

Box 17.1 Future reactive energy supply

The future energy system will need to be reactive to supply fluctuations. This is primarily a technical challenge that requires an engineering solution. Strategic thinking considers first the solution and then designs the economic model to deliver it.

The solution proposed is simple, robust and resilient, based on two supplies: one at 240 v and one at 400 v. The higher voltage is more efficient so worthwhile for heavy load applications but not safe for appliances and equipment handled by people (240 v provides a nasty jolt but a 400 v electric shock will kill). The 240 v supply is designed to be a guaranteed always-on supply for homes, offices, schools and hospitals. This will power computers, lighting, cooking, refrigeration and people-facing appliances. Meanwhile the 400 v supply will be used for industrial processes, heat pumps and-charging electric vehicles. These will be the primary heavy electric load applications of the future. The 400 v supply would have multiple circuits for each locality with big industrial customers each on their own circuit. Grid management can turn these circuits on and off. The availability of the 440 v supply can be predicted some hours ahead, as sources such as wind energy and solar energy are predictable over such timescales.

The economic model to fit this engineering solution would then need designing, together with appropriate information and control systems. The information could be supplied continuously online on the availability of the 400 v supply. Guidance could be provided twenty-four hours ahead, with accurate predictions for three or four hours ahead.

Industrial users with particular needs could negotiate price and power availability terms to suit their business needs. Electric cars could be plugged in and automatically access the grid availability data and charge accordingly. This could be completely passive by plugging in the car and it charging when the circuit is live. The same could apply to domestic heat pumps keeping the system simple and robust. I would expect industrial customers to have commercial agreements to operate when there is ample energy and minimize energy demand when the market is tight. Times of abundant energy will be windy days in the summer; times when energy might be tight are windless winter nights. The availability of the 400 v supply will be where the response takes place ensuring the 240 v supply is always on.

This examination of energy supply is a simple straightforward analysis using economics as it should be used to deliver the required outcome. Whether the particular idea presented above survives will depend on whether better ideas emerge. The future reactive grid may look nothing like my proposal in Box 17.1 but it serves to demonstrate a mindset to frame economics in support of analysis, rather than driving it. The danger of focusing on economics first is that you could end up with a complex market solution to adjust the current economic model rather than a complete rethink and new economic model. In this case, I suggest the solution proposed is simple and easily explained but you arrive at it by considering the engineering realities, not by undertaking an economic analysis. That comes later to work out how to deliver the desired solution.

Conclusions

Energy is an essential need of modern society; fossil fuel is not. Maintaining the connection between the essential need for energy with the consumption of fossil fuel means fossil fuel has a higher status than it deserves. It is imperative that we disconnect energy from fossil fuel and switch mindset quickly as it will take at least a decade to orchestrate change in the energy infrastructure. The technology exists, and it is getting better, but it is already good enough. We have to challenge rational incompetence and be willing to redesign the economic model. As I repeat again and again throughout this book, economic models are virtual constructs which can be changed at will. Changing the economic model would be relatively easy – if we have the courage to do so. What would then follow would be a disruptive reconfiguration of the system of energy generation and use.

Turning our back on fossil fuel means turning our back on the fossil fuel economy. Embracing renewable energy means embracing the new economy in which energy has much greater value. The new energy economy is a much better economy because it works in close alignment with the needs of society and helps to lift us out of the era of fossil fuel. This short chapter is not *the* blueprint for the new energy economy but it outlines a different mindset which opens out the analysis to break the current stalemate. Instead of defending the current economy, thus maintaining reliance on fossil fuel, we should take the strategic decision to no longer rely on fossil fuel – and force the transition to a different energy economy.

PART 4

IMPLEMENTATION

You never want a serious crisis to go to waste. And what I mean by that it's an opportunity to do things that you think you could not before.[39]

Rahm Emanuel, President Obama's Chief of Staff,
November 2008

The fourth and final part of this book is about how to get the concept of economic resilience embedded into the fabric of policy. Continuing with conventional economic policy focused on growth will keep the world on its current trajectory towards economic, social and environmental collapse. This need not be so. The future holds great promise, but it requires a different approach to economics. There have already been two global crises this century, both of which have hit the economy and society hard. There will be further crises and we will need all the resilience we can muster to get through them and thrive.

Economic policy has significant influence over decisions which impact the real world. As economic policy is crafted, it should be borne in mind that economics is an abstract concept, rather than a precise science. We can select economic concepts, and apply them, as we see fit. Unlike problems in the real world, fixing economics is totally under our control. All that is required is successful persuasion to change the mindset employed.

Change in the real world can be slow and difficult. The real world consists of people and the infrastructure we need, all operating within the biosphere of planet Earth. Cities, factories, farms, forests and oceans are real and tangible and need to be managed with care. Economics provides mental models to help, and the economic model has to be appropriate to time, place and

---

39   Rahm Emanuel, President Obama's Chief of Staff, advising the president to make use of the chaos of the Financial Crisis of 2008. Interview with the *Wall Street Journal*, 19 November, 2008.

circumstances. Whilst the prevailing mindset of policymakers is the drive for economic growth, the real world will continue along the downward spiral we have initiated. Clipping the wings of economics will bring it back to roost as the servant of society. Switching to the resilient model of economics should give economics a less dominant role to allow a stronger focus on social and environmental outcomes.

At this key juncture in world affairs, a deliberate choice is required in the way economics is framed. We need to reconnect the economy with the needs of society; to build a safe, secure and better future, full of promise and potential.

CHAPTER 18

LAUNCH A REVOLUTION

The greatest danger in times of turbulence is not the turbulence — it is to act with yesterday's logic.

Peter Drucker, *Managing in Turbulent Times*, 1980

We should be building on the opportunities of the first two crises of the 21st century to launch a revolution in the conduct of economic policy. If we respond to the turbulence of the last two decades by using yesterday's economic logic, we will be in great danger.

Economics has huge influence over our lives. It has grown from a specialist subject with a narrow focus to become the dominant lens through which policymakers see the world. When economic objectives start to dictate what happens in society, caution is required. The concepts of economics may be sound, but they do not exist in isolation. Economics only has real purpose when it serves society.

We use economic policy to manage affairs efficiently, provide a framework to fund investment, and facilitate exchange of goods and services. These are all important to support the smooth operation of society. However, economic policy starts to drift off course when it is focused on the economy. This is like the skipper of a yacht focusing on trimming the sails and maintaining boat speed rather than navigating to the journey's end. When the success of economic policy is measured by growth it is like recording the distance sailed rather than progress towards the destination port. Economics should be a supporting function to serve society, with success measured by positive outcomes for society. We expect the skipper to keep the boat in good shape and sailing efficiently but above all it should be heading towards our desired destination.

I suspect that most people who pick up this book will have started with a mindset which accepts as normal that economic policy should focus on the economy. You may also have been familiar with the common perspective that the health of the economy is assessed by the extent to which it is growing. After assimilating the analysis of the preceding chapters, I expect most readers to join me in at least questioning such 'wisdom'.

Abandon the Growth Objective

To initiate revolutionary change in economic policy, the first step is to abandon the growth objective. This is where I expect entrenched opposition because my questioning goes right to the foundations of current economic thought. It is natural for people with long experience of a particular way of working to resist change. Economists act in good faith applying what they were taught at university. What is taught at university is based on research which digs ever deeper into economic theory. Such digging, focused on the application of economics to grow the economy, is like digging a hole focusing on its breadth and depth without pausing to reflect on what purpose the hole might have. As the hole gets deeper and wider, and the view beyond the confines of the hole more obscured, we can find that we are in a deep dark hole with no easy way out.

There is a well-known maxim that if you are in a hole stop digging. Instead of using economics to drive the extraction and use of scarce resources as efficiently as possible (making the hole ever deeper), economics should be used to support building sustainable societies which are in tune with the systems and processes of the planet. You don't need grand theories or complex analysis to see that this is correct. This is common sense. It is only a small further step to realize that we must abandon the growth objective (stop digging), followed by adopting economic policy which respects planetary limits (begin to climb out of the hole). This is how to commence laying new economic foundations for vibrant and resilient societies.

I am guilty of mixing my metaphors when I liken the conduct of economic policy to sailing a yacht or digging a hole, but the combination works rather well. When sailing it is important to know where you are heading; when digging you need to know the purpose of the hole. A world where the oceans are full of yachts going around in circles, and people on land are digging holes to no purpose, would be an appropriate metaphor for the world of today chasing economic growth without a clear idea of why or to what end. Economics needs to be framed by direction and purpose and this simple insight is at the heart of this book.

Challenging Economic Fundamentalism

Adjusting economic policy to serve society, and protect the environment, should be totally normal. Instead, such demands on economic policy can be regarded as heresy by economic fundamentalists who place the economy above all else. This odd situation has come about through accepting the assumptions that a strong economy is good for society, and a strong economy is a prerequisite for investing in environmental protection. There is an element of truth behind these assumptions, but when used to justify focusing on the economy and demoting society and the environment to secondary factors, something is wrong. There may be a correlation between the strength of an economy and social and environmental metrics, but we should be wary about claiming a causal relationship. A country which runs a sound economy is likely to be capable of enacting good social and environmental policy. However, sound social and environmental policy comes from putting effort into social and environmental policy not as a by-product of good economic policy.

Care is needed to keep economic fundamentalists in check. Fifty years ago in the UK there were a couple of dozen economists working in government, mainly in the Treasury. They were advisors with specific roles related to managing and monitoring the economy. Their work focused on the simplified virtual world of economics generating data to help decide policy. By 2015, this had expanded to more than 1,400 economists working in government spread across all departments.[40] Instead of being a few advisors among the many, economists have become omnipresent, and economic analysis has become the prime basis of decision making. Framing decisions with a simplified economic perspective has taken over, almost without being challenged. In this power grab opposing views tend not to be given weight, especially if they conflict with the economic analysis.

It takes time, and deep reflection, to understand the problem of economic fundamentalism. There is something very attractive about delegating to economic analysis and trusting market forces. An incident a decade ago brought home to me the core problem. This was an example of extreme economic fundamentalism which initially I took to be a joke. The incident took place at a major international conference which drew together senior people from

---

40 The UK Civil Service recruit economists into the Government Economic Service (GES) who are then allocated across government departments. When the GES was founded in 1964 it had twenty-two economists including eighteen who were already working in the Treasury's Economic Section. By 2015 the GES employed over 1,400 economists spread throughout government (Ramsden 2015).

business, government and academia. It occurred at the start of a brainstorming break-out session to explore possible responses to the challenge of climate change. The chairperson of the session was a senior and respected professor of economics from one of the leading universities. In the opening statement it was explained that the session was completely open to all ideas to draw out a full range of possible options, no matter how radical. The intention was to brainstorm without restriction or constraints and under 'Chatham House' rules, so people could speak without fear of being identified (I respect that by not being specific about who was involved). It is the statement which followed which took me by surprise. This senior economist and chairperson added one 'small proviso' that whatever is proposed should 'not interfere with free trade, nor cost more'. I started to smile, thinking perhaps the chairperson was being self-deprecating about the economics profession and would get a laugh from the audience before retracting it. But no, this was absolutely serious and the audience accepted it without question. If I had been thinking quicker, I might have challenged the statement, but the session quickly broke out into brainstorming subgroups. I probed within my group whether anyone else was unhappy that our thinking had been constrained not to interfere with free trade, nor consider options which would cost more. No one else thought it was odd, and the group were content to accept the constraints.

The lesson I learnt from this incident is that there exists a deep-seated attitude that to be feasible, a proposal must not challenge economic orthodoxy. The research I was carrying out at the time was exploring the unintended consequences of free trade and the dangers of putting price before all else. It had become clear to me that restricting analysis to accept, without question, free trade and the absolute role of price, ruled out any prospect of lasting solutions. From my research this had become crystal clear, but the people around me seemed to have been so brainwashed by economic fundamentalism that they had closed their minds. If you are dipping into this penultimate chapter without reading the previous chapters, you too may not appreciate how ridiculous this incident was. All of us have been hoodwinked by economic fundamentalists, over many years, such that breaking out into clear thinking about economics is hard.

As I reflect on the incident described above, I accept that to many economists it might seem completely normal to put the economy first as this, after all, is the nature of their profession. It is also not surprising that mainstream audiences would allow them to do so, as the idea that the economy trumps other issues has propagated widely. I do not blame the economists, but I do blame compliant audiences who are willing to follow such an erroneous lead. This self-censorship of thought processes seems to be a self-defence mechanism. If we were to accept that economic parameters are simply one source of information, and economic analysis just one input, decision making becomes much more complicated. It also opens up the possibility that there are situations where the economic analysis might be wrong. Advice which might be correct according to economic theory can be bad advice. That can be disconcerting to people who have come to rely on advice from economists. The true reality is that economics is one of a number of supporting functions and is not on its own a sound basis for strategic decision making. Economic fundamentalists would have us accept that environmental policy and social policy are externalities of the economic model. Quite so, which means economics is insufficient when setting direction and making key decisions. The economic analysis is only one input within the frame of higher order policy. Instead of the easy cop out of defining some issues as externalities in order to be able to ignore them, we need to integrate social and environmental priorities at the heart of policymaking. Economics should be positioned in its correct place within the hierarchy of policy as a mechanism for making the best and most sustainable solutions economically viable.

As a supporting function, economics is extremely useful, but when it becomes the dominant force it risks conflicting with society's values and undermining environmental security. Rescuing economics from the fundamentalists is vital to restoring confidence in economics and shifting economics back onto secure intellectual and practical foundations.

The Sustainable Revolution

The change required to shift mindset in favour of resilient economics is revolutionary but also common sense. We should not be afraid to launch the revolution knowing that, despite the uncertainty of exactly where it leads, the principles of resilient economics are correct for our times. Past industrial revolutions have come about primarily from advances in technology. The next revolution should have a different dynamic driven by environmental priorities and social objectives, directing technologic development to where it is needed and using sound economics to facilitate delivery. It is not another Industrial Revolution we need but a Sustainable Revolution.

Looking to the future, I am optimistic, because I have come across many people who have reservations about orthodox economics – even though they cannot pinpoint quite what is wrong. There is therefore an appetite to consider alternative approaches to economics. My optimism is tempered by caution because our future is not preordained. The future will be the future we create, either by design or by mistake. I prefer the former. Rather than sleepwalk into the future I would prefer to walk boldly forward in full knowledge of the likely consequences. Of one thing we can be sure, the changes required are revolutionary.

Further advances in technology will include artificial intelligence able to offer tremendous opportunities to improve our lives. The Founder and Executive Chairman of the World Economic Forum, Klaus Schwab describes the future as the Fourth Industrial Revolution (Schwab 2016). This will connect computers, artificial intelligence, biotechnology and society in complex and novel ways. These are early aspirations which do not yet have form and substance. Over the next decade the Fourth Industrial Revolution will take shape in ways we may not be able to predict.

An additional complication, which is not a substantive part of the current narrative, is the imperative to connect these capabilities to work in tune with the planet's natural systems. Currently, this difficulty is seen as a challenge too far. There are already ample challenges, so there is no bandwidth for yet another. In my view, we need an even more radical revolution that takes us beyond industrialization. This Sustainable Revolution will start the deliberate process of living within the safe limits of the planet, adopting sustainable processes and sustainable economic policy (McManners 2008).

Klaus Schwab describes our current times in the following way: 'There has never been a time of greater promise, or one of greater potential peril.' (Schwab 2016). If we navigate into the future focused on delivering the next *industrial* revolution it will indeed be a time of peril. If we set our direction with sustainability as our guide it will be a Sustainable Revolution with great promise. Correctly framing economics will be the key to ensuring human progress is on a safe trajectory.

Avoiding Catastrophe

Considering potential catastrophe is more likely to scare people than to mobilize support for action; but we need to be scared.

We need to be woken out of our stupor and become willing to engage with real change. The positive perspective on how to build the future comes in the next section. The pessimistic section below is needed to set the context, even though I am certain it can be avoided.

It looks as if the Fourth Industrial Revolution will be the last hurrah for industrialization – and could be the last hurrah for civilization if we fail to control it. This deeply pessimistic thought should make us wake up and take notice. We need to be careful as pessimism is a negative emotion more likely to lead to lethargy and inaction rather than fixing the situation. Despite this, I believe that a realistic assessment of possible outcomes is important to frame the search for a solution, to provide the impetus to set an ambitious and optimistic agenda for future progress. We need to think about our future, not in terms of yet more advanced forms of industrialization, but in terms of moving beyond industrialization.

Let us consider where we might be three decades into the future, half way through the 21st century. We are likely to have artificial intelligence which threatens to rival our own; robots capable of many tasks; the ability for routine space flight; and emerging capabilities to build and sustain human communities on other planets. I sketch out these tentative ideas assuming that planet Earth remains the cradle of human civilization. This will only be so by finding an accommodation between human needs and planetary stability. A possibility, which should not be discounted, is that the Fourth Industrial Revolution could take a dark and dangerous direction, turbocharging human progress without respecting planetary limits. It is hard to envisage civilization surviving such environmental calamity. We like to think of civilization as robust and permanent – as I am sure the Romans did at the height of their empire. Archaeologists dig up wonderful mosaics and relics of a civilization which had enormous power and reach. The Romans had the capability to build complex infrastructure, including sanitation and heating, but this knowledge was lost during the Dark Ages which followed.[41]

Global civilization at the start of the 21st century is neither robust nor permanent. I can envisage global society unravelling in an unseemly struggle over diminishing resources. The current globalized economy has enormous complexity and interdependencies. Advanced computers are not something you can construct from a textbook rescued from the rubble of civilization. The know-how and capabilities required are held in complex living networks of designers and machines including skilled workers on the factory floor passing their skills onto apprentices. Business executives understand that to close down a complex system, it may not be possible to get it running again without borrowing expertise from other plants which are still operating. If a wave of instability and conflict closed every factory, and every university, we would very soon lose the wherewithal to reboot. I do not predict Armageddon but it is worth reflecting that if we allow apocalypse to play out it could usher in a new Dark Age. Future generations of archaeologists might discover strange relics such as CDs and memory sticks, long after losing the capability to read them.

It would be stupid to allow an apocalypse. Although we can be incredibly stupid, now is not the time to allow stupidity to define our actions, otherwise the future could be dire. Fortunately, there are people of principle with courage who can ensure common sense flourishes. We can hope such people rise to the challenge. One such level-headed saviour was the little-known Stanislav Petrov.

---

41 The 'Dark Ages' refers to the period between the 5th and 15th centuries when there was cultural and economic deterioration in Western Europe following the decline of the Roman Empire.

Box 18.1 Unsung Hero – Stanislav Petrov

Stanislav Petrov was a Lieutenant Colonel in the Soviet Air Defence Forces who saved the world from nuclear Armageddon at the height of the Cold War. On 26 September 1983 he was the duty officer at Serpukhov-15, the secret command centre outside Moscow where the Soviet military monitored its early-warning satellites over the United States. The alarms went off indicating the launch of intercontinental ballistic missiles from the United States.

The siren howled, but I just sat there for a few seconds, staring at the big, back-lit red screen with the word 'launch' on it.[42]

His responsibility was to report this up the chain of command so that his superiors could authorize a counterstrike within the 20 minutes it would take the missiles to reach the Soviet Union. With hundreds of people in the command centre looking to him to do his duty he felt that something was wrong. He decided to report it as a system malfunction and wait to see what happened. It was only much later that it was discovered that sunlight reflecting off clouds had been mistaken for missile launches.

I categorically refused to be guilty of starting World War III.[43]

The incident remained secret until after the Soviet Union collapsed in 1991. This unsung hero retired to a small town outside Moscow and died in relative obscurity on 19 May 2017.

In this Cold-War incident in 1983, Stanislav Petrov was expected to comply with the Soviet early-warning system protocol to initiate the launch of intercontinental nuclear missiles against the United States. He was a middle-ranking person who had the courage and clear thinking to choose not to comply. The world

---

42 BBC Interview 2013.

43 *The Man Who Saved the World*, a documentary film directed by Danish filmmaker Peter Anthony, released in 2014.

needs a groundswell of such people to resist the simplistic economic analysis being offered that fails to fully take into account important consequences.

Decisions should not be bound by the straightjacket of their impact on the economic numbers but made on examination of what is right for a society living on a finite planet. This should not be a difficult concept for humans to grasp, as it is the application of common sense; but it would seem almost impossible for *Homo economicus* to understand. The brute stupidity of *Homo economicus* should be resisted to ensure that the human intellect can be applied according to human values to take us forward into a safe and vibrant future. *Homo sapiens* survived the competition with the Neanderthals; the competition with *Homo economicus* could be just as important.

I do not intend to be a doom-monger, but I think it important to open people's minds to the inherent fragility of the civilization we currently enjoy. That means we should treat what we value with care. The Fourth Industrial Revolution has the potential to give us even greater capability, even more tools, even more opportunities to progress; but the direction of advance is not fixed. We are not destined to explore the universe nor doomed to trash the planet; these are only possibilities. We could achieve both of course. The technology of sealed life support units needed to live on other planets could be the same technology we find that we need to survive on planet Earth, after we have transformed it into an industrial wasteland. This should not be the future, of course, and does not need to be the future, but is possible if we stay on our present course. As I write this manuscript, in the comfort of my study, in a stable country with all the resources I need, I can use logical analysis to understand that some futures are simply unacceptable. There are some trade-offs between advantages and negative consequences that simply should not be made. When the negative consequences have sufficient severity, the avoidance of such consequences becomes a limitation to available choices.

There are people who argue that we should only worry about the short- and medium-term and let future generations look after themselves. Such people need to be faced down, and forcefully faced down if that is what it takes. If we are on a ship in a storm and there are people who not only refuse to help batten down the hatches but get in the way of those who are making the ship secure, they should be resisted. If such people persist, they should be forcibly restrained and locked up below decks. This is the time for forward-looking people to take control of the bridge and steer civilization into calmer waters. Our destiny could be to advance to other planets in other solar systems; to go there because we want to explore and because we can, not because we have to leave a broken planet.

When we advance to the Moon, in an emergency it would take a few days to escape back to the safety of Earth. For settlements on planet Mars, the escape route back to Earth would be much more convoluted and difficult. These are scary thoughts. Even scarier is the possibility that living on Earth may only be possible in sealed life support units. The beautiful blue planet we enjoy now may only exist within virtual reality computer systems built by future generations to show what life used to be like. Beyond the Fourth Industrial Revolution, this might be our future. It is our generation's responsibility to make sure the future does not play out that way.

The pessimistic view outlined above, of a disastrous future, makes a strong logical argument to take action to change direction; but humans can react in ways which are not logical. Humans gripped by fear are prone to take a fatalistic view that it will happen anyway, so why bother to try to change the outcome. That is not a sensible approach. Instead, I will switch to an optimistic perspective, to ensure we shift from denial to clear thinking, from procrastination to action, and that economics is aligned with a successful future for humanity.

Avoiding catastrophe is important, of course, but the approach which could galvanize action is to focus on building a better future.

Taking Back Control

The future could be full of promise provided economic policy is aligned with a rational response to today's challenges. History has lessons to draw on, such as the pyramids of ancient Egypt which were a rational economic response to the challenges of the day. The River Nile flows through a desert region providing an incredibly fertile plain. The climate, soil and ample water meant that growing the food people needed could not have been easier. We cannot know the mindset of the Pharoahs – and I do not expect that they carried out what we would recognize as an economic analysis – but the challenge they faced can be framed in economic terms. The challenge was to maintain social cohesion when it required so little work to live well. The approaching era of automation and robots could mean modern civilization faces a similar challenge.

Building the pyramids was a rational response by the pharaohs to the challenge they faced. There was enormous disparity between rich and poor but there was work for all. From the evident success of ancient Egypt, we can assume that overall people were content and I assume had pride and a sense of belonging. The pyramids might be seen through a contemporary economic lens as a wasteful demonstration of power and riches. I suggest they served a real rational purpose in a society where work could have been in short supply. Many of the world's grand churches may have been built on similar logic where communities were short of work and leaders in society could cement social cohesion with such projects. As we enter the era of robotics, allowing raw economics to drive policy, there will be fewer jobs for humans. We will need deliberate policy to engage everyone in society to ensure social cohesion.

Taking back control, by challenging economic orthodoxy, and adopting the concept of resilient economics, can facilitate engaging people in building communities and infrastructure which suit our time and place in history. We will not accept being put to work building vast monuments in which to bury our political leaders, but all of us should expect to have a secure livelihood. The modern equivalent of the pyramids could be to build high-quality facilities built to last and operate as vibrant communities sustainable into the long future. We would build them because we want to live well, not because it would be good for the economy. We can be sure that if we construct such communities with great care, designed to work well for the human residents, they would fail a conventional economic analysis. That does not mean the aspiration is wrong; it means that conventional economics is inadequate to the task. We should decide on the future we want and force the economic analysis to conform to our wishes.

Conclusions

The world needs a revolution in the conduct of economic policy. Yesterday's logic of growth economics has become dangerous and needs to be resisted. Such resistance, coupled with a vision for how economic policy can put the world onto a safe and sustainable trajectory, could set off a process of real change. Revolutions do not come often, but when they do, the outcome is unpredictable. There will certainly be disruption, and there will be people and organizations which lose out, but dismissing the old economic order will provide new opportunities. A secure and thriving society can be built on the back of the Sustainable Revolution supported by resilient economics.

CHAPTER 19

CONCLUSIONS

Build back better.[44]

The economic consequences of two crises just over a decade apart have left the world economy in a perilous state. The financial crisis of 2008–9 exposed the shortcomings of interconnected global finance. Before the crisis, the close coupling of global finance gave the illusion of strength. The crisis exposed the reality of a system which, far from being resilient, was actually prone to occasional massive collapse. The COVID-19 pandemic of 2020–21 was a further warning that appropriate economic policy is a vital part of any crisis response. If the world is to be able to navigate safely through the next crisis, economic policy must be framed by resilience. Adopting the package of measures presented in this book will give society an improved capability to cope with crisis in a successful manner and bounce back when the immediate cause abates.

Learning from Crisis

The two global crises which rocked the world economy in the first decades of the 21st century have opened people's minds to the possibility that something might be amiss with current

---

44 'Build back better' was used widely as an aspiration for post-pandemic recovery. It is one of the guiding principles of the United Nations Office for Disaster Risk Reduction (UNDRR) Strategic Framework 2022–2025. In April 2021 President Joe Biden presented his 'Build Back Better Plan' for economic recovery. The UK government used the term to describe their post-pandemic economic recovery plan (UK government 2021).

macroeconomic policy. We can carry on regardless, and hope that for the next crisis we can again muddle through, but such huge imbalances have built up within the financial system that further options for extreme economic measures are now limited. Alternatively, we can learn from crisis to reboot economics in ways which would not have been countenanced at the start of the new millennium.

It would be unrealistic to hope to return the economy to where it was before the financial crisis. Back then, economic globalization was in its ascendancy with the resulting economic growth welcomed for the apparent wealth it generated. Although those who had most to gain were global corporations, powerful countries, and the richest investors, the prevailing attitude was that everyone would benefit. It was claimed that some of the new wealth would trickle down to people who were less well-off, although the evidence was limited, and whether such trickle down would continue during a downturn was doubtful.

The financial crisis of 2008–9 exposed the fragility of a pumped-up global economy focused on growth. Following the crisis, additional safeguards were introduced but the core problem remained. Many of us were convinced that economics had come adrift from its moorings, and no longer had a close relationship with real-world reality, but when times were good such concerns could be ignored. The COVID-19 pandemic of 2020–21 was a further warning that economies designed primarily as efficient and lean wealth-generating machines may not have the resilience to ride out an unexpected crisis.

The double whammy of two crises just over a decade apart provides us with the opportunity to go beyond issuing warnings to thinking through how to change economics to be less crisis prone. Before crisis hit, it was not perceived that the current approach to economics could be a problem, so there was no compelling reason to consider changing direction. Now that weaknesses with the current approach to economics have been exposed, the appetite for solutions should grow. Having struggled through two crises in relatively quick succession it should be clear that the framing of economics really has to be different.

The systemic problems with economics are solvable. It boils down to backing off from a blinkered focus on economic growth, to then be able to reconnect economics with society and its challenges. It is a statement of the obvious that the economy should be in harmony with society and constrained by the environmental limits of the planet. Economic fundamentalism has been allowed to undermine this truism, putting both the planet and society at great risk. Bringing economics back down to Earth may well blunt growth, constrain corporate profits, and reduce some people's monetary wealth, but there is no reason that the overall package should be negative for society. A resilient economy, with a stable business sector, and people's livelihoods secured, has every chance of facilitating the sort of vibrant cohesive society which makes people feel safe and content.

In developing the framework of resilient economics presented in this book, it became necessary to hold economics to account. It is not enough to ignore important social and environmental issues by calling them externalities of the economic model. The current conventional approach of making plans based on economic analysis, and subsequently carrying out social and environmental impact assessments, is flawed. Such an approach is not simply insufficient, but I argue is the reverse of what should be happening within the decision-making process. Important decisions should be framed by social and environmental priorities, and only then consideration given to crafting the economic model which can deliver the desired outcome. Such analysis is more complex but should reconnect the economy with the needs of society, drawing economic policy closer to real-world reality.

Rejuvenating Economics

Rejuvenating economics requires putting aside outdated economic ideas to introduce new concepts. Many established ideas will survive but framed differently. Some of the ideas at the core of resilient economics are not new but have been sitting at the fringes of economics waiting to be fully appreciated.

The difficult and painful first step is to accept that growth is not the economic panacea once thought. The pursuit of growth is deeply embedded in the current economic model. To remove it will be like having a rotten tooth extracted. We can expect the extraction to be painful, but you can be sure the outcome will be worth it. To expose the limitations of the growth objective, and decide that it is no longer fit for purpose, is not an argument easily accepted. It will be seen by many as a radical departure from what is considered to be sound economic policymaking. The logic for putting aside this economic rule of thumb is rock solid, but policymakers will then lose the compass they have been using for many years, leaving a gap in how to navigate economic policy. They will need something to replace it. This is provided by resilient economics, but navigation becomes harder. The economic analysis through this different lens is more complex, more nuanced, and requires a significant shift in mindset in order to be applied well.

If you have read the preceding chapters slowly, carefully, and digested the content, I hope that your mindset has been opened to at least consider advancing beyond the economics of growth.

Disregard the Growth Objective

To reinforce the argument for abandoning growth as the primary objective, let us consider a simple example.

For this example, I want to start with a reminder of what is meant by the economy. It is the sum of all economic activity ranging from huge projects to routine day-to-day activities. The economic numbers for each of these added together equals GDP. One of the myriad activities which comprise the UK economy is my drive to work. On an ordinary day, my contribution to GDP is tiny. My electric car will have been charged overnight using the cheap night-time tariff, costing just a few pounds. Let us suppose that on a particular day I crash my car on the way to work. Perhaps it's a minor bump, and I exchange insurance details with the other driver before continuing into work. Both cars need repairs, providing repair workshops with business and the insurance company pays out. On this day, my contribution to GDP has been increased. If the crash were to be serious, then my contribution to GDP would be much greater. There would be economic activity in treating me in hospital and the car might have been written-off requiring the purchase of a new car. The economic contribution to GDP of my drive to work would now be significant. It is obvious that crashing my car isn't positive for me, the other driver, nor society. According to the simple measure of GDP, my actions would have contributed to increasing growth in the UK economy. This simple example shows that GDP is not sufficient as a measure of progress and going forward may lose its relevance entirely. Within a resilient economic frame, it might be judged better to work from home more often, and when travelling to work use safe routes which encourage the use of a bicycle. Such desirable outcomes would reduce the contribution to GDP of my daily commute below what it is now.

Whether growth has ever been a sensible objective of economic policy, and GDP a sensible measure, is debatable. Perhaps when first introduced a century ago it gave a general indication of economic activity and was an approximate measure of the health of the economy. As we stopped regarding GDP as a simple economic statistic, and elevated it to the primary objective of economic policy, economics became trapped in an incestuous game of economic policy designed to boost the economy. Whether it is policy to boost airport capacity, build grand shopping malls to encourage us to buy and consume all sorts of stuff we don't really need, or design mobile phones with new features to encourage us to upgrade every year; it is so engrained in growth economics that these are logical decisions because they will boost GDP. In the growth model of the economy it would be wrong to discourage flying, or to design quality products which can be easily upgraded or repaired. Such improvements to the way we live would dent GDP and the economy would suffer, so according to growth economics, such changes would be negative. GDP needs taking down from the pedestal we have elevated it to and parked in its proper place. It should be regarded as no more than a simple statistic. Within a resilient economy we find that GDP has limited relevance, and certainly should not be an objective of policy, let alone *the* objective of policy.

So, the first step in renewing economics is to abandon the growth objective. This leaves a gap in how economic policy is decided. If GDP is not to be used as the measure of the state of the economy, then what measure should take its place? Posing this question forces us to think deeply about the future direction of economics. Until this leads to a change of mindset, policymakers will continue to search for ways to assess the health of the economy. The mental block that makes it difficult to comprehend this new approach to economics, is our continued focus on *the economy.* The concept of resilient economics shifts the focus of economic policy to higher order objectives for society.

Principles of Resilient Economics

To formulate the principles of resilient economics required reflecting on what we mean by the economy. It is a concept which arises from economic theory but it is hard to pin down in precise terms. The economy isn't real. People, places, factories, farms, schools, and communities are real. Economics provides mechanisms to facilitate the management of this reality. Consideration of whether the economy is strong or weak draws us back to old ways of thinking. To make sense of the new approach to economics, it might be better to drop the term 'economy' altogether. This summary of the principles of resilient economics is framed, not by its impact on the intangible economy, but on reality and the needs of society.

SUBSIDIARITY

The primary principle of resilient economics is 'subsidiarity' (Chapter 6). This ensures that economics engages and meshes with society at all levels:

> *The principle of economic subsidiarity is that economic decisions should be taken at the lowest most local level unless there are clear benefits to society for the decision to be taken at a higher level.*

Economic subsidiarity ensures that there is deliberate and careful examination of economic policy such that people, communities and, at world level, countries, are empowered to run their economic affairs. When decisions are taken at the lowest possible level in the hierarchy of society, buy-in from those involved is maximized leading to outcomes aligned with people's needs.

Although the principle of subsidiarity is firmly established in political and social policy, its inclusion in current economic policy is limited. Subsidiarity does not require that all decisions are delegated. Decisions can be taken at higher levels when there is a common benefit or advantage from doing so. Such decisions are an imposition on the lower levels so may not be welcome. An appropriate balance needs to be struck between the power of higher-level authority and the self-determination of lower levels.

MARKETS

The second principle of resilient economics is how to approach markets (Chapter 7). Markets need to be designed and implemented in support of society. The invisible hand of market forces has a useful role in the efficient implementation of policy, but markets do not automatically deliver desirable outcomes. Markets must be designed with care and regulated accordingly. Where a market is small, its procedures are transparent, and participants behave honestly, formal regulations can be minimal. At the other end of the spectrum, large markets with opaque procedures, where gaming is the normal behaviour, need tight regulation and should be treated with caution. In the middle, for markets of appropriate scale, with transparent procedures, where participants use the market for its intended purpose, sensible light-touch regulation should suffice.

Markets are capable of basic tasks, but they need clever well-crafted policy to provide a framework for how they operate. The pure economic efficiency of the market has to be constrained to deliver the overall outcome which society needs. Market fundamentalists get attracted to the simplicity of 'leaving it to the market'. This is an abrogation of responsibility. Such a blinkered approach may work in the short-term but ends up eventually failing unless proper control is exerted from the outset. By the time a market has failed, the damage has been done. The challenge for policymakers is to bring markets to account before they fail, before the problems become hard to fix, and perhaps even before the market is allowed to begin operating.

TRADE

The third principle of resilient economics defines trade as providing society with what it needs which cannot be produced or obtained locally (Chapter 8). Although the concept of free trade has strong theoretical foundations within the pantheon of economic ideas, we need to look beyond the narrow economic perspective to embrace the higher order policy of resilient trade. It is not about delivering maximum economic efficiency, nor arbitraging between national economies, but about the security of supply and long-term sustainability. An example of economic efficiency leading to ridiculous trade was explained in Chapter 8. I discovered that prawns were being caught off the coast of the UK and shipped to the Far East to be shelled, and then shipped back to the UK packed and sold in supermarkets. Conventional economics compared the differential cost of labour to do the shelling with the cost of shipping. As the former was greater than the latter, the prawns were shipped halfway around the planet and back. It is common sense that this makes no sense. Blinkered adherence to economic analysis can lead to such situations, and we accept it because we have allowed economic analysis primacy in decision making. Bringing trade back to focus on real needs requires a different economic model which puts friction into trade rather than promoting it.

Levers of Resilient Economics

There are three prime levers that can be used to implement the principles of resilient economics: money, tax, and universal basic income. The lever of money is the lifeblood of the economy (Chapter 9). Tax can be applied to both raise income for government and drive change (Chapter 10). Leveraging universal basic income can align the economy much closer to the needs of society. (Chapter 11).

MONEY

The management of money, and how it is allowed to flow, is crucial to economic health. Local currencies need to flow freely within a locality; national currencies need to flow freely within a national economy; inter-currency flows are needed to support trade between countries. The focus should be on currencies supporting real-world transactions. Restrictions on inter-currency flows make sense, enhancing stability and putting governments in control. Such restrictions may also reduce the potential for short-term economic growth, but we should look to the greater prize. The benefit of such constraints is stability. Instead of lurching from crisis to crisis, such an approach would support countries in maintaining control of their economies and ensure that local difficulties are isolated and do not infect other economies.

TAX

Taxation has a dual role, raising income for the government and driving change. There should be clarity of purpose, fairness in how tax is applied, and enforcement with the minimum of bureaucracy and the maximum of effectiveness. Appropriate taxation is a powerful economic lever when elevated from simple revenue generation to a lever to drive change. In this role, the government should not become over reliant on such revenue because as change is achieved, it is to be expected that tax receipts tail off.

The concepts of money and tax are familiar, even if the way they are applied needs to change. The third lever uses the novel concept of the universal basic income.

UNIVERSAL BASIC INCOME

Universal basic income (also referred to as citizen's income) has been discussed for many years at the fringes of economic debate. No country has fully implemented such arrangements, so there is a lack of empirical evidence for its efficacy. I admit to rejecting universal basic income as part of sensible economic policy when I first encountered it. It took time for me to be persuaded of its merits, and it will take time for governments and policymakers to understand its potential, and even longer to embrace it.

The way universal basic income can help to maintain social cohesion through the coming decades of increased automation and robotics is perhaps its biggest attraction. Citizen's income, in conjunction with withdrawal of minimum wage regulation, can be a prime economic tool to help navigate the transition ensuring that employing people remains affordable. Without it, the economic pressure to eliminate jobs will decimate communities leading to polarization between rich elites served by robots and a huge underclass of the unemployed. The universal basic income can be used to draw people into meaningful and fulfilling activity, engaged in society through new models of work which blur the distinction between paid work, voluntary work, and leisure activity.

The economic lever of universal basic income supports a society run by people for people; with robots relegated to menial, dirty or dangerous tasks. It would be possible to implement citizen's income in a cost-neutral manner without further delay; but the initial benefits would hardly seem to justify it. It is only when a variety of community models are developed, underpinned by the foundation of a basic income, that its value will become fully apparent.

Applying the Resilient Economics Toolbox

The full potential of adopting resilient economics was explored in Part 3. It became clear that the world faces complex interconnected challenges which need complex interconnected solutions. For example, early in my research into resilience and sustainability I examined transportation. Initially, I was enthusiastic about biofuel. This seemed to offer a drop-in replacement for liquid fuels across the transport sector. Here was the solution, so problem solved. Not so. My initial enthusiasm was soon tempered as I examined the detail. The quantity of biofuel required would require a huge proportion of the world's agricultural capacity, and cannot be justified. The solution for sustainable transport required something far more complex, including changes to city design parameters and alterations to patterns of trade. Chapters 12 to 17 provide further examples, outlining the consequences of adopting resilient economics on different sectors. These can be read individually, but it is not until you reflect on the sum of improvement across all sectors that the transformative value of the resilient approach becomes apparent.

As the argument in favour of a resilient approach to economics is accepted, and we move on to implementation, these are not minor changes. This is not tweaking conventional economics, but fundamentally changing it. It will not be possible to select the easy bits and sneak them into policy to bypass resistance. Resilient economics is a coherent framework which needs to be implemented in its entirety. Perhaps the key aspect is that it requires a different mindset, without which it will not be possible to deliver on its potential. When mindset change occurs, new economic policy could be rolled out surprisingly quickly. Economic policy is something which is in our control and which can be changed quite rapidly. It is about choices and priorities. When choices have been made and priorities set, it will then take time for consequences in the real world to start to play out. The sooner a resilient economic mindset is adopted, and economic policy altered, the sooner the transition to a safer, more resilient world.

Radical changes to economic concepts which have held sway for decades are not going to be easy. The way forward will meet resistance, but if resilient economics is not embraced, the next crisis could be terminal.

Looking to the Next Crisis

We should expect that another crisis with economic consequences is already on its way. Climate change is one obvious candidate, but it could be another pandemic, or war over diminishing resources, or a dangerous confrontation brought about by political instability in a country with nuclear weapons. The cause of the next major crisis could be any one of a number of things. Economic policy cannot prevent crisis, but adopting resilient economic policy in advance can put governments in the best position to get through the crisis and come out the other side and recover.

It is worth reflecting on what might have happened if world leaders had recognized earlier the risks of the economic policy of the 1990s. If they had foreseen the possible consequences of allowing economic policy to drift away from close alignment with the needs of society, perhaps the 21st century would not have been quite such an economic roller coaster. If the concept of resilient economics had been adopted at the turn of the century as a prudent response to the emerging problems of turbo-charged growth, we might wonder whether the financial crisis of 2008–9 or pandemic of 2020–21 could have been any less severe.

The situation the world faced in 2008–9 was a global financial system more interconnected than at any point in history and so complex that risks were hidden, buoyed up by ill-founded confidence that strong returns would continue. My analysis before the crisis was that the system we had created was inherently unstable making a financial crisis inevitable (McManners 2008). If resilient economics had been adopted in the years before, growth would have been subdued and opportunities to profit from trading within the financial system less, but it would have been resilient and resistant to financial contagion.

Not everyone agrees with my analysis of the inherent instability of massively interconnected global finance. The 2008–9 financial crisis has been blamed on particular circumstances. Let us assume for the sake of argument that the Financial Crisis Inquiry Commission were correct in blaming US sub-prime lending as the primary cause (The Financial Crisis Inquiry Commission 2011). Adopting resilient economics and applying the principle of subsidiarity would have meant national economies were more self-sufficient and global financial flows less open. We would have foregone the growth turbocharger of open global markets, but the financial system would have been less interdependent and more stable. The United States is such a large component of the global economy that its economic problems would still be expected to ripple out beyond its borders, but not to the extent seen in 2008–9. Resilient economics may not have prevented the financial crisis, but a crisis made in America would have stayed in America. In a resilient world economy, with a focus on stability and restricted flows of capital, I suggest that the global economic consequences of US sub-prime lending would have been limited.

For the crisis of 2020–21, the emergence of a virus such as SARS-COV-2, which causes the disease COVID-19, should have been expected. The world had already had to deal with SARS[45] in the early 2000s, which also started in China. Whether more resilient economic policy within China, with a greater focus on social and environmental issues, might have reduced the risk of the virus emerging, is debateable. What we can be sure of is that a more resilient world economy would have fared better. In a global economy consisting of a network of resilient national economies, less reliant on global supply chains, countries would have been more self-sufficient. The world would have been in a much stronger position to have weathered the economic consequences of the COVID-19 health crisis. Not only would a less connected global economy have had fewer virus transmission routes, but as governments closed down travel to prevent the spread of the virus, the economic consequences would have been less severe. The COVID-19 crisis is more likely to have remained a Chinese epidemic rather than expand quickly into a global pandemic.

A specific economic aspect of the COVID-19 crisis was the scramble to protect people's livelihoods as the economy closed down. In the UK, the government started paying companies to keep staff on their payroll, even though there was no work for them. Instead of such ad hoc measures, universal basic income, implemented in advance, would have kept society ticking over. With citizen's income deeply embedded in economic policy, people's basic livelihood is secured against almost any economic shock. Properly implemented, it becomes an integral part of the

---

45 Severe acute respiratory syndrome (SARS) caused by the Coronavirus SARS-CoV first appeared in Yunnan province, China, in 2002.

economy so, in times of crisis, does not require huge additional borrowing to put in place ad hoc measures. If the lever of universal basic income had been applied years before, fully and completely, the economic shock of the pandemic would have been less. We do not know the timing of the next pandemic, and hope it will not be any time soon, but we can be sure there will be another so we should be prepared.

So, the first two decades of the 21st century would not have been crisis-free through early adoption of resilient economics, but the impact would have been less, and recovery rather quicker. Adopting resilient economics without further delay, could put us in a strong position to face the next crisis.

Embedded Resilience

The general principle of putting outcomes for society ahead of the economy, provides a radically different frame to policy. Economic policy will no longer be designed to deliver economic outcomes measured by GDP, turnover or profit. The task becomes constructing resilient economic frameworks to deliver higher-order objectives for society. The precise detail will evolve as people understand the altered way of thinking and grasp the opportunities it offers. The sector-specific chapters of Part 3 are not precise blueprints but give the flavour of how such thinking can open up new doorways into the future. These alternative ways forward are off the agenda, or may not even be understood to be possible, because of the constraints of conventional economic analysis.

Writing this book, examining world society and speculating on how it could be different, has been an inspiring process. When viewing society and the planet in its glorious complexity, we can look forward to the possibility of a stable world community consisting of a huge variety of countries with a wide variety of economic models rubbing along reasonably well. It can be envisaged that such a structure could be sustainable into the long future. In some respects, the 20th century economic toolbox has delivered what was expected of it. We asked for growth and we got growth. An economic toolbox for the 21st century should be designed to provide resilience, to be able to deal with the challenges ahead. There will be failed initiatives, missteps in policy, and countries which make a mess of the freedom of the approach championed here. Despite such potential shortcomings, the consequence of mistaken economic policy decisions will be localized and contained. The overall global financial plumbing may have less capacity, but resilience is the greater prize. We can replace the false promise of expansion and growth with the security and stability of resilience. Instead of watching over our shoulder fearing the next economic collapse, we can move forward with confidence.

The mindset of the economic policy presented in this book could lead to a renaissance. At the very least, it will slow down humanity's charge into oblivion. It should give us the chance to reflect on what really matters in life, to examine priorities, and reset our aspirations.

Closing Comments

I have an optimistic and positive view of the future which underpins my thinking, but wishful thinking will not be enough to rescue the future. Attempting to predict what comes next, analysing trends and making logical deductions, produces worrying insights. Extrapolation using conventional logic predicts a society where some people will do exceedingly well and others will suffer badly, all taking place on a planet which is being trashed.

If we do not change direction, we can be sure that this is where we are heading. Such a destination is not preordained but it is certain if we stick doggedly to a conventional economic mindset. The risks of switching to resilient economic policy are small compared with the risks of carrying on regardless. The biggest risk of all is that inertia and denial take hold of economic policy to reinforce the current position, with additional safeguards and regulations, but without fundamental reform. This would be like a gambler doubling up on each losing bet, hoping to win eventually even though they know in their heart that quitting gambling and knuckling down to the hard graft of a real job is the only true way to a prosperous future.

Rather than work with predictions based on the logic of raw economic efficiency and short-term selfish behaviour, I prefer to work with a vision of the future based on aspirations to live well in vibrant societies that work for everyone (each in their own way) on a planet which we value above short-term economic gain. There are examples where visions of the future can change the course of history. No one in 1960 was predicting that we would land a man on the Moon, but in 1961 President John F. Kennedy offered the United States and the world a vision. Eight years later, in 1969, Neil Armstrong stepped onto the Moon. This would not have happened (or not have happened so soon) without such a compelling vision. We have the chance now to change the course of history by adopting a vision of a sustainable and resilient economy whilst there is still time to switch direction before it is too late.

The eight years from Kennedy's vision to humankind setting foot on the Moon, is long enough to take the concept of a sustainable and resilient economy out of the pages of this book and into full implementation. To take inspiration from Kennedy's words: We choose to adopt resilient economics not because it will be easy, but because it will be hard; because the new economic ethos will serve to organize and measure the best of our energies and skills, because the challenge is one that we are willing to accept, one we are unwilling to postpone, and one we intend to win.[46]

My vision must become *our* vision. Fortunately, mindset change can be almost instantaneous, requiring only the time to read and digest this book.

My final closing plea is that if you agree with my assessment, then do something to help put economics back in its proper place as the loyal servant of society. Conventional economics has been elevated to have far more influence than it deserves. Adopting the ideas of resilient economics brings economic policy back down to Earth, puts society first, and demotes economics to a facilitating function. Instead of being the basis for key decisions, economics becomes the servant of policy. After reading this book, if your mindset has shifted, and you can persuade two or three other people to follow, we can establish overwhelming demand for change to break the stranglehold of economic fundamentalists. Enough people thinking differently, with optimism and enthusiasm for a better future, can make it so.

---

46 Borrowing from a section of President John F. Kennedy's speech delivered at Rice Stadium, 12 September 1962.

Ali, Z. (2020), 'The world's 100 largest banks, 2020', S&P Global Market Intelligence, 7 April 2020 [https://www.spglobal.com/marketintelligence/en/news-insights/latest-news-headlines/the-world-s-100-largest-banks-2020-57854079; accessed 2 June 2020].

Bambrough, B. (2021), 'Bitcoin Price Prediction: How Far Could The Bitcoin Bull Run Go?' *Forbes*, 25 Feb 2021 [https://www.forbes.com/sites/billybambrough/2021/02/25/bitcoin-price-prediction-how-far-could-the-bitcoin-bull-run-could-go/?sh=5a8afb7817a3; accessed 25 May 2021].

Bank of England (2008), *Financial Stability Report*, October 2008, Issue No. 24.

Bank of England (2020), Banknote statistics, [https://www.bankofengland.co.uk/statistics/banknote; accessed 14 May 2020].

BanksDaily (2020), The World's 10 largest banks by total assets (2007) [https://banksdaily.com/topbanks/World/2007.html; accessed 2 June 2020].

British Antartic Survey (2020), The Ozone Hole, [https://www.bas.ac.uk/data/our-data/publication/the-ozone-layer; accessed 2 June 2020].

BBC News (2019), 'Timeline: Renewable Heat Incentive scandal', 23 Oct 2019, [https://www.bbc.co.uk/news/uk-northern-ireland-38301428; accessed 19 April 2020].

Booth A.L. (2008), 'Environment and Nature: The Natural Environment in Native American Thought', *in* Selin H. (ed.) *Encyclopaedia of the History of Science, Technology, and Medicine in Non-Western Cultures*, Dordrecht: Springer.

Bristol Pound (2020), Bristol Pound – the UK's largest local currency, [https://bristolpound.org/; accessed 14 May 2020].

Cambridge Institute for Sustainability Leadership (2014), 'Climate Change: Implications for Buildings', Key Findings from the Intergovernmental Panel on Climate Change, *Fifth Assessment Report*,

June 2014 [available from: www.cisl.cam.ac.uk/ipcc].

Cammett, M., I. Diwan, A. Richards and J. Waterbury, (2018), *A political Economy of the Middle East*, New York: Routledge.

Davies, G. and R. Davies (1998), A comparative chronology of money: Part 1: From the origins of agriculture to the Industrial Revolution, *Journal of Management History*, 4(3), 160–85.

Delbert, C. (2020), Elon Musk's Battery Farm Is an Undeniable Success, *Popular Mechanics*, 10 March 2020 [https://www.popularmechanics. com/science/a31350880/elon-musk-battery-farm/; accessed 27 May 2020].

Edmonds. T. (2013), The Independent Commission on Banking: The Vickers Report, Standard Note: SNBT 6171, 30 December 2013, House of Commons Library.

European Union (2007), Protocol (No 2) on the application of the principles of subsidiarity and proportionality, annexed to the Treaty on European Union and the Treaty on the Functioning of the European Union by the Treaty of Lisbon of 13 December 2007.

Folke, C., R. Biggs, A. V. Norström, B. Reyers and J. Rockström (2016), Social-ecological resilience and biosphere-based sustainability science, *Ecology and Society* 21(3):41.

Food Miles (2020), Food Miles Calculator, UK, [https://www.foodmiles. com/food/uk; accessed 16 May 2020].

FoodPrint (2020), Sustainable Agriculture vs. Industrial Agriculture, [http://www.sustainabletable.org/246/sustainable-agriculture-the-basics; accessed 17 May 2020].

Fountain, H. (2017), On Nuclear Waste, Finland Shows U.S. How It Can Be Done, *New York Times*, 9 June 2017 [https://www.nytimes. com/2017/06/09/science/nuclear-reactor-waste-finland.html; accessed 10 May 2020].

Graeber, D. (2014), *Debt-updated and expanded: the first 5,000 years*, Melville House.

Guariguata, M. R., P. Cronkleton, A. E. Duchelle et al. (2017), Revisiting the 'cornerstone of Amazonian conservation': a socioecological assessment of Brazil nut exploitation, *Biodiversity and Conservation* 26, 2007–2027.

Haq, M., I. Kaul and I. Grunberg (1996), *The Tobin Tax: Coping With Financial Volatility*, Oxford and New York: Oxford University Press.

Helliwell, J., R. Layard and J. Sachs (2017), *World Happiness Report 2017*, New York: Sustainable Development Solutions Network.

Heydon, K. (2019), *The Political Economy of International Trade*, Cambridge: Polity.

Hiilamo, H. (2019), Disappointing results from the Finnish basic income experiment, Press Release, University of Helsinki, [https://www.helsinki.fi/en/news/nordic-welfare-news/heikki-hiilamo-disappointing-results-from-the-finnish-basic-income-experiment; accessed 15 May 2020].

HM Treasury (2011), *The Government response to the Independent Commission on Banking*, Dec 2011, UK: The Stationery Office.

IET (2019), Storing renewable energy in mineshaft weights may be cheaper than using batteries, 21 October 2019 [https://eandt.theiet.org/content/articles/2019/10/storing-renewable-energy-in-mineshaft-weights-is-cheaper-than-batteries-report-finds/; accessed 27 May 2020].

IMF (2016), 'IMF Executive Board Concludes 2016 Article IV Consultation with Bhutan', Press Release No. 16/313 [https://www.imf.org/en/News/Articles/2016/07/06/17/05/PR16313-Bhutan-IMF-Executive-Board-Concludes-2016-Article-IV-Consultation; accessed 17 April 2020].

IMF (2020), About the IMF, [https://www.imf.org/en/About; accessed 2 June 2020).

IPCC (2021), *Summary for Policymakers. In: Climate Change 2021: The Physical Science Basis. Contribution of Working Group I to the Sixth Assessment Report of the Intergovernmental Panel on Climate Change*

[Masson-Delmotte, V., P. Zhai, A. Pirani, S. L. Connors, C. Péan, S. Berger, N. Caud, Y. Chen, L. Goldfarb, M. I. Gomis, M. Huang, K. Leitzell, E. Lonnoy, J. B. R. Matthews, T. K. Maycock, T. Waterfield, O. Yelekçi, R. Yu and B. Zhou (eds.)]. Cambridge University Press. In Press.

Jeffrey, K., H. Wheatley and S. Abdallah (2016), *The Happy Planet Index: 2016. A global index of sustainable well-being*, London: New Economics Foundation.

Keen, M. and J. Strand (2006), Indirect Taxes on International Aviation, IMF Working Paper, WP/06/124.

Kuznets, S. (1934), *National Income, 1929–1932*, 73rd US Congress, Senate document no. 124.

Lam, N., S. Pachauri, P. Purohit, Y. Nagai, N. Bates, C. Cameron and K. Smith (2016), 'Kerosene subsidies for household lighting in India: what are the impacts?', *Environmental Research Letters*, Vol. 11/4. [available from: https://iopscience.iop.org/article/10.1088/1748-9326/11/4/044014; accessed 26 March 2021].

Layard, R. (2005), *Happiness: Lessons from a New Science*, London: Allen Lane.

Lee, Simon (2009), *Boom and Bust: The Politics and Legacy of Gordon Brown*, London: Oneworld.

Le Quéré, C., R. B. Jackson, M. W. Jones et al. (2020), Temporary reduction in daily global CO2 emissions during the COVID-19 forced confinement, *Nature Climate Change*, online 19 May 2020, [https://doi.org/10.1038/s41558-020-0797-x].

Lovins, A. B. (2011), *Reinventing Fire: Bold Business Solutions for the New Energy Era*, Rocky Mountain Institute Report, US: Chelsea Green Publishing.

Mackay, C. (1841), *Memoirs of Extraordinary Popular Delusions and the Madness of Crowds*, London: Richard Bentley.

Martin School (2020), What is The Oxford Martin School?, [https://www.oxfordmartin.ox.ac.uk/about; accessed 28 June 2020].

References

Mason, M., R. McDowell, E. Htusan and M. Mendoza (2015), Shrimp sold by global supermarkets is peeled by slave labourers in Thailand, *The Guardian* [https://www.theguardian.com/global-development/2015/dec/14/shrimp-sold-by-global-supermarkets-is-peeled-by-slave-labourers-in-thailand; accessed 10 May 2020].

McDonough, W. and M. Braungart (2002), *Remaking the way we make things: Cradle to cradle*, New York: North Point Press.

McDonough, W. and M. Braungart (2013), *The upcycle: Beyond sustainability – designing for abundance*, London: Macmillan.

McKechnie, W. S. (1896), *The State & the Individual: An Introduction to Political Science, with Special Reference to Socialistic and Individualistic Theories*, Glasgow: James MacLehose & Sons.

McManners, P. J. (2008), *Adapt and Thrive: The Sustainable Revolution*, Reading: Susta.

McManners, P. J. (2010), *Green Outcomes in the Real World: Global forces, local circumstances and sustainable solutions*, Farnham: Gower.

McManners, P. J. (2009), *Victim of Success: Civilization at Risk*, Reading: Susta.

McManners, P. J. (2012), *Fly and Be Damned: What now for aviation and climate change?* London: Zed Books.

McManners, P. J. (2014), Reframing Economic Policy Towards Sustainability, *International Journal of Green Economics*, 8(3/4), 288–305.

McManners, P. J. (2016), Developing Policy Integrating Sustainability: A Case Study into Aviation, *Environmental Science & Policy*, 57, 86–92.

McManners, P. J. (2017), *Reframing Economic Policy towards Sustainability*, UK: Routledge.

McManners, P. J. (2020), *Face up to Climate Change: Demand change now*, Reading: Susta.

Mill, J. S. (1844), *Essays on Some Unsettled Questions of Political Economy* (First ed.), London: John W. Parker.

NASA (2020), Apollo Spinoff, [https://spinoff.nasa.gov/flyers/apollo.htm; accessed 15 May 2020].

Opgenoord, M. M. J. and P. C. Caplan (2018), Aerodynamic Design of the Hyperloop Concept, *AIAA Journal*, Vol. 56, Issue 11, pp. 4261–70.

Peel, M. E. Terazono and A. Schipani (2013), From Thailand to Ecuador: A tale of two shrimp farmers, *Financial Times*, 25 September 2013. [https://www.ft.com/content/8f230656-21e0-11e3-bb64-00144feab7de; accessed 10 May 2020].

Pretty J. (2008), Agricultural sustainability: concepts, principles and evidence, *Philosophical transactions of the Royal Society of London, Series B, Biological sciences*, 363(1491), 447–65.

Ramsden, D. (2015), 'The First 50 Years of the Government Economic Service', Lecture by Dave Ramsden at Kings College London, 27 April 2015.

Ratcliffe, S. (2018), *Oxford Essential Quotations* (6 ed.), published online, 2018 version, Oxford: Oxford University Press [accessed from: www.oxfordreference.com].

Ricardo, D. (1817), *On the Principles of Political Economy and Taxation*, London: John Murray.

RMI (2020), Get to know us, [https://rmi.org/about/; accessed 28 June 2020].

Rock, L. (2017), The American care model that benefits old and young alike – and could soon come to the UK, *The Observer*, 2 April 2017.

Ross, M. L. (2015), 'What Have We Learned about the Resource Curse?', *Annual Review of Political Science*, 18: 239–59.

Samuelson, Paul A. (1948), *Economics: An Introductory Analysis*, New York: McGraw-Hill Company.

Schmalensee, R. and Stavins, R.N. (2017), Lessons Learned from Three Decades of Experience with Cap and Trade, *Review of Environmental Economics and Policy*, 11/1: 59–79.

Schumpeter, Joseph A. (1942), *Capitalism, Socialism and Democracy*, New York: Harper and Row.

Schwab, K. (2016), 'The Fourth Industrial Revolution: what it means, how to respond', World Economic Forum. [https://www.weforum.org/agenda/2016/01/the-fourth-industrial-revolution-what-it-means-and-how-to-respond/; accessed 3 May 2020].

Sekeris, P. G. (2014), The tragedy of the commons in a violent world, *The RAND Journal of Economics*, 45: 521–32.

Sheppard, E. (2017), 'It's like being reborn': inside the care home opening its doors to toddlers, *The Guardian*, 6 September 2017.

Smith, A. (1759), *The Theory of the Moral Sentiments*, London: Millar.

Smith, A. (1776), *An Inquiry into the Nature and Causes of the Wealth of Nations*, London: Strahan and Cadell.

Soil Association (2020), An Introduction to Agroecology, [https://www.soilassociation.org/what-we-do/better-food-for-all/transforming-the-way-we-all-farm/an-introduction-to-agroecology/; accessed 17 May 2020].

Stevens, J. (2015), How Russia hurts UK dairy farmers: Sanctions banning import of EU products leads to slump in demand, *Mail Online*, 27 August 2015 [https://www.dailymail.co.uk/news/article-3212177/How-Russia-hurts-UK-dairy-farmers.html; accessed 2 June 2020].

Taylor, S. D. (2012), *Globalization and the Cultures of Business in Africa: From Patrimonialism to Profit*, Bloomington: Indiana University Press.

The Economist (2020), A grim calculus: The stark choices between life, death and the economy, 4–10 April 2020.

The Economist (2021), The digital currencies that matter, *The Economist*, 8–14 May 2021.

The Financial Crisis Inquiry Commission (2011), The Financial Crisis Inquiry Report: Final Report of the National Commission on the Causes of the Financial and Economic Crisis in the United States, US Government Printing Office, [https://www.govinfo.gov/content/pkg/GPO-FCIC/pdf/GPO-FCIC.pdf].

Thompson, E. A. (2007), The tulipmania: Fact or artifact?, *Public Choice*, 130(1), 99–114: 109.

Thornhill, J. (2016), A universal basic income is an old idea with modern appeal, *Financial Times*, 14 March 2016.

Tobin, J. (1978), A Proposal for International Monetary Reform, *Eastern Economic Journal*. 4 (3–4): 153–159.

UK Government (2021). 'Build Back Better: our plan for growth', Report presented to Parliament by the Chancellor of the Exchequer, March 2021.

UN (2014), 'Global governance and global rules for development in the post-2015 era', Policy Note, Committee for Development Policy, Department of Economic and Social Affairs (DESA) of the United Nations Secretariat, United Nations Publication.

UNEP (2015), Waste Crime – Waste Risks: Gaps in Meeting the Global Waste Challenge, A UNEP Rapid Response Assessment, Nairobi: United Nations Environment Programme.

Ungoed-Thomas, J. (2007), British prawns go to China to be shelled, *The Sunday Times*, 20 May 2007.

Vecsey, C. and R. W. Venables (eds) (1994), *American Indian Environments: Ecological Issues in Native American History*, Reissue edition, first published 1980, New York: Syracuse University Press.

Venables, A. J. (2016), 'Using Natural Resources for Development: Why Has It Proven So Difficult?', *Journal of Economic Perspectives*, 30 (1): 161–84.

Victor, P. (2010), Questioning Economic Growth, *Nature*: 468, 370–71.

Wade, A. (2017), How pumped hydro storage can help save the planet,

The Engineer, 13 November 2017 [https://www.theengineer.co.uk/pumped-hydro-storage/; accessed 27 May 2020].

WEF (2016), World Economic Forum Annual Meeting 2016: Mastering the Fourth Industrial Revolution, Geneva: WEF [http://www3.weforum.org/docs/WEF_AM16_Report.pdf; accessed 15 May 2020].

Weinstein, M. M. (2009), 'Paul A. Samuelson, Economist, Dies at 94', *The New York Times*, 13 December 2009.

West, S., A. C. Baker, S. Samra and E. Coltrera (2021), Preliminary Analysis: SEED's First Year, Stockton Economic Empowerment Demonstration (SEED) [available at: https://www.stocktondemonstration.org].

WTO (2019), World Trade Organization Annual Report 2019.

WTO (2020a), 'Principles of the trading system', Understanding The WTO: Basics, [https://www.wto.org/english/thewto_e/whatis_e/tif_e/fact2_e.htm; accessed 11 May 2020].

WTO (2020b), 'Top 10 Reasons to Oppose the World Trade Organization', [https://www.wto.org/english/thewto_e/minist_e/min99_e/english/misinf_e/00list_e.htm; accessed 11 May 2020].